OPEN TO CRITICISM

BEACON SERIES IN CONTEMPORARY COMMUNICATIONS

David Manning White, *General Editor*

Open to Criticism

Robert Lewis Shayon

Beacon Press   Boston

The author gratefully acknowledges permission to reprint the following
articles from *The Christian Science Monitor:* "Toynbee, TV, and Chicago,"
June 3, 1950; and "Senate Crime Hearings Furnish Real-Life Drama,"
March 20, 1951; © 1950 and 1951, The Christian Science Publishing
Society; and from the *Chicago Sun-Times Book Week,* the article "Just
Like the Man from Glad," October 5, 1969. Numerous articles from
Saturday Review, in whole and in part, are reprinted here by permission of
Saturday Review and are copyright 1951, 1952, 1953, The Saturday Review
Associates, Inc., and copyright 1955, 1957, 1958, 1959, 1960, 1961, 1962,
1963, 1964, 1965, 1966, 1967, 1968, 1969, 1970, Saturday Review, Inc.

For WIZ and NON

Contents

Preface

*A book should serve
as the ax for the
frozen sea within us.*

FRANZ KAFKA

I AGREE.

The "frozen sea" at which this book is aimed is the general public's misunderstanding of criticism, its low appreciation of criticism's true nature, significance, and power: what it really is, how it operates, and what are its ends. You might say that the subject of this book is criticism: its object is the making of critics—not only professional critics of the arts, of society, of the various departments of human affairs, but also and especially "people critics," alert, perspicacious individuals who know how to confront the assorted phenomena of their own lives, their own worlds, and their own relationships, how to analyze them, to manage them dialectically, and to discover in the dialectic creative new possibilities for human dignity and mutuality.

The critical spirit is the supreme manifestation of human intelligence which sets man off from the animals. It is the world's best hope. Political, social, and economic solutions for mankind's problems appear and vanish, leaving their negative and affirmative residues, arousing great expectations and decaying into disenchant-ment. Millennial states beckon us and ever recede, and so it should be: but it is possible for men to shape their destiny; there are better patterns for individual and social living; they are attainable— this I believe. The essential condition is criticism.

The nurture of the critical spirit is an ancient art. I seek through this book to make my contribution to it, to celebrate it, to exalt it in human consciousness, and to spread its contagion. I do so by writing about my own intensely personal view of criticism, as developed over a period of twenty years as a contributing editor and regular TV-radio critic for *Saturday Review*. My idiosyncratic view of criticism embraces a method and a theory—which I set forth in the opening chapters. Then, having explicated principles and techniques, I train my guns of both method and theory upon a selection from my own pieces of criticism. I criticize my own criti-cism because that is the best use to which I can put it. It would have been easy to turn this book into a critique of American broad-casting, but I have resisted the temptation: perhaps another time. This is a critique of criticism because criticism is what I wish to reveal to the reader.

Insofar as the pieces in this book were originally written about aspects of national and international life as reflected by television and radio—those most massive, giant-eyed historians of our times— the pieces themselves and my retrospective commentaries on them cannot help revealing something about our national mind and its values in an age of great crisis, but this is a secondary premium. The book comprehends a view of criticism of broad social and cul-tural rather than exclusively literary and esthetic perspectives. It is an amalgam of criticism, anthology, and biography, a record of one critic's intellectual development.

I am indebted to Coleridge's romantic poem *The Rime of the Ancient Mariner*, upon the essential architecture of which I have scaffolded a variety of personal interpretations and insights that I have drawn from Coleridge's powerful verses. Nor is that poet the only creditor of this work: others are Alfred North Whitehead, from whom I also draw major insights, Arnold Toynbee, Karl Jaspers, Plato, Nietzsche, Lewis Carroll, Karl Mannheim, Karl Popper, Arthur Koestler, and a miscellany of philosophers, scientists, critics, and poets. I have often wrestled with the feeling, while preparing the manuscript, that the book is too rich with quotations, but on such occasions I have resorted to further quotes to relieve my anxiety. It was John Ruskin who said:

> There are few thoughts likely to come across ordinary men, which have not already been expressed by greater men in the best possible way; and it is a wiser, more generous, more noble thing to remember and point out the perfect words, than to invent poorer ones, wherewith to encumber temporarily the world.

Emerson denied that

> valuable originality consists in unlikeness to other men . . . The greatest genius is the most indebted man . . . Great genial power, one would almost say, consists in not being original at all; in being altogether receptive; in letting the world do all, and suffering the spirit of the hour to pass unobstructed through the mind.

Accordingly, I have so suffered—not only the spirit of this hour but also, as the reader will find, of more ancient hours. Such gentle martyrdom, I hope, along with whatever originality there may be in the book, will be of interest to the general reader, and especially to students of criticism and of the mass media.

A number of omissions will strike the reader who may have welcomed a more comprehensive selection of pieces that cover a wider range of programs and of institutional categories in broadcasting. There are no pieces about television and radio drama, or about the other performing arts—of which I have written many. Educational (public) broadcasting is underrepresented, as are the problem of the fair representation of black Americans in broadcasting and the advancing technology of communications, including satellites, pay TV, and cablecasting. I would have preferred a broader treatment of the subject matter, but the book shaped itself and made its own demands.

I remember warmly and with gratitude William D. Patterson

and John Beaufort, who set me on the path of criticism. I owe a great deal to a number of graduate students at The Annenberg School of Communications, University of Pennsylvania, who shared my seminars in Mass Media Criticism, in which they compelled me to clarify my own standards and values of criticism. It is far more difficult to think, I have learned, than to do: and the students' insights and challenges helped me to understand criticism better.

An extra measure of thanks is due David Manning White, General Editor of the Beacon Series in Contemporary Communications, who not only instigated this book but also, at crucial points in its unfoldment, played Hermit to my Mariner. The book will justify itself if it makes one more Mariner: the ultimate would be the making of the Mass Mariner.

R. L. S.

Westport, Connecticut
September 1970

Part One

A Theory of Criticism—
Techniques and Principles

CHAPTER ONE

Criticism as an Act of Cell-Firing

It is an ancient Mariner,
And he stoppeth one of three. . . .

ALMOST ANYONE can remember ("By thy long gray beard and glittering eye,/ Now wherefore stopp'st thou me?") the first stanza of Coleridge's imaginative chaunt, *The Rime of the Ancient Mariner, in Seven Parts.* George A. Miller, in *The Psychology of Communication,* has some interesting observations on The Magical Number Seven, Plus or Minus Two: Some Limits on Our Capacity for Processing Information; his speculations might be focused on the question, "Why did Coleridge write the poem in seven parts?" Seven, of course, has long been used as a symbol of infinity—the seven wonders of the world, the seven churches in Asia, the seven deadly sins, the seven ages of man, and so on.

Miller suggests that seven may roughly represent the limits of man's channel capacity to process information and to make judgments. The limitation, he conjectures, may be "built into us either by learning or by the design of our nervous system." He writes:

> Perhaps there is something deep and profound behind all these events, something just calling out for us to discover it. But I suspect that it is only a pernicious, Pythagorean coincidence.

If seven really is the comprehensive symbol, the number that represents the total configuration, then Coleridge knew what he was doing, consciously or unconsciously, in formulating *The Rime of the Ancient Mariner* in seven parts. Kenneth Burke, among other literary critics (including John Livingston Lowes, who studied the poem in his scholarly work, *The Road to Xanadu*) has enlightened us by showing that the poem is a "symbolic action," a clue to the major problems of human relationships that Coleridge experienced—his unsuccessful marriage, his art, his curse of drug addiction, and his Christian convictions.

The English biologist J. Z. Young, in *Doubt and Certainty in Science* (the Reith Lectures, delivered over the BBC in 1950), concludes that:

> . . . the brain tends to compute by organizing all of its input into certain *general* patterns. It is natural for us, therefore, to try to make these grand abstractions, to seek for one formula, one model, one God, around which we can organize all our communication and the whole business of living.

This book is grounded in such a central organizing construct: it sees criticism as a way of life. The critical act, I maintain, is the creative act; and vice versa. It is a process that seems to be the very essence of life itself and of the action of the universe. Our scientific behavior, our esthetic behavior, the way the brain functions— all testify to a system in which one cell fires another, and another fires yet another, and circuits are closed and keep firing, with periods of rest, to begin firing once more, interacting with other circuits, etc. . . . Creation is perhaps the wrong word to describe this: continuity would be better. Professor Young asks:

> Do we need to consider that the universe started at all? . . .
> Perhaps we make our world picture with a beginning and
> an end because we have conceived too narrowly of our own
> beginnings and ends. If we could only look farther behind and
> ahead we might see a different picture.

Nuclear fission is another example. The nucleus is split; its elements are released; they fire into other nuclei, and the chain reaction builds until it reaches—odd, isn't it?—a *critical* mass. Closure, insight, patterning, inspiration, "aha!" "Eureka!"—these are all words that have been used to describe the same phenomenon. Cartoonists represent it visually when they show a man with a bubble over his head, leading from where his mind is supposed to be; and in that bubble a glowing light bulb has just been turned on. The point that I am stressing here is the "critical mass." A vital contemporary need is for more "critical" intelligences, as understood here, to be applied to the world's problems.

If we had more such authentic critics, televised politicians and advertisers would not be able to sell us their policies or their products. We could more readily see through prejudices in others and in ourselves. We would have "perspective"—an ordering, an arrangement of what confronts us in time, in space, and in thought. All people are critical, at different levels of intensity, insight, and awareness. All of us are truly critics-in-being, some more awakened than others. Some don't even know that they are critics; some critics who consider themselves critics of a higher order would benefit from a reevaluation of their competency. Most people think of criticism, if they think of it at all, as scratchy nay-saying, crusty, dour negativism. Or they take it to be a matter of taste, judgment, evaluation, expertise, as evidenced in their estimate that criticism is "reviewing." All these matters, of course, are subsumed in the critical act; but they are not, by far, the end of it.

This books aims at furthering the critical chain reaction that is already in being, that has been in being since man began to think at all. Critical cells that fire other critical cells in one global, cooperative collectivity of insights, opposing doubt to certainty and rigor to imagination in an endless dialectic, creating for old visions new visions which do not obliterate but rather incorporate the former into dynamic, new complexities and unities—this is the march of genuine criticism that I hope to augment. R. W. Gerard, in his essay "The Biological Basis of Imagination" (in *The Creative Process,* edited by Brewster Ghiselin), wrote:

> A few years back the only well-recognized (neural) pattern
> was the reflex arc. A message entered along a sensory nerve,
> continued through the nervous system along direct or relayed

connections, and finally emerged in a motor nerve. Except as messages were in transit, the nervous system was presumably quiet. Today we know, largely from the electrical pulses of the "brain waves," that nerve cells are continuously active in wake or sleep, and many beat on like the heart.

In our context, the critical faculty, though apparently inactive in many individuals, is actually quietly idling, like a motor. It needs to be revved up, to accelerate critically, and to fire other idling motors. There are motors idling, within critics-in-potential, at just the right rate of revolutions, give or take a tolerable variance. Once revved up, they can hopefully take off to make their own critical contacts. I have come to understand that I, myself, was once an idling critical motor. It was not until I was confronted with the job of writing criticism regularly, covering television and radio, that I began to receive the firings of other cells in my reading, talking, and thinking about criticism. In this sense, one might venture that the whole world is an idling critical dynamism, with circuits bending back upon themselves, and none able to say where, when, how, or in whom the first critical cell began firing.

In teaching and in public speaking, as well as in my twenty years of writing criticism, I have pursued the cell-firing path: now I hope to open the circuitry further to a wider ambience. If my chain-reaction, cell-firing analogy is valid, I have faith that there will be receptive contact at some other cell points. In this I take my cue again from *The Rime of the Ancient Mariner*, a cell-firing poem. The Ancient Mariner is the activating agent and the Wedding Guest is the idling motor. The essential nature of their collision is described in the poem's final verse:

He went like one that hath been stunned,
And is of sense forlorn;
A sadder and a wiser man
He rose the morrow morn.

The "stunning" I read as the impact that the Mariner's tale had on the Wedding Guest. The "sense" of which he has been robbed is the vision he had of things before he met the Mariner. "Sadder" I do not read in any somber mode, but rather as more thoughtful, sober, and perceptive. "Wiser," certainly, by virtue of the rearrangement of his universe that the Mariner had wrought. Can anyone doubt that, as he "Turned from the bridegroom's door," he pondered the Mariner's message?

> He prayeth best, who loveth best
> All things both great and small;
> For the dear God who loveth us,
> He made and loveth all.

One may assume, after Coleridge had done with him, that in our world of imagination, in which today he still lives and moves, the Wedding Guest has, himself, a tale to tell—of a graybeard loon that fixed him with a glittering eye, and made him sit, "like a three years' child," on a stone, while the Mariner unfolded to him a "ghastly tale," impelled by a "woeful agony."

This double tale now, most assuredly, within the Wedding Guest's heart burned; and he perforce must have been compelled to search for listeners, playing his small but necessary part in the widening circuitry. What fired the Ancient Mariner? His experience at sea with the Albatross and the slimy snakes and the ghostly, dead men crew that brought him home to the shrieking Pilot and the holy Hermit and the Pilot's boy "who now doth crazy go." And, moving from them to a prime mover, what fired these creatures of the mind that lived only in Coleridge's imagination—itself a firing of cells from his wife and drugs and church and guilt and Wordsworth's companionship, reaching vertically into every corner of his experience since childhood, and horizontally to the infinity of constituents that comprised his gestalt?

One cell, firing another in a critical chain reaction, need not necessarily make literal contact as the Ancient Mariner made with the Wedding Guest. The key to the relationship is in the poem's second line: "He stoppeth one of three." Why *this* particular one? Random choice? Hardly. Coleridge himself provides the answer when, near the end of the poem, the Mariner, explaining his communication obsession, says:

I pass, like night, from land to land;
I have strange power of speech;
That moment that his face I see,
I know the man that must hear me:
To him my tale I teach.

How did the Mariner know that the Wedding Guest was *the* one of three? Coleridge offers no hint. One speculates that a man like the Mariner, who had known life, and life-in-death, was now possessed of more than "at-sight." He must have had "insight." There is an intuitive affinity between artist and audience, between critic and reader. The sound of idling motors can be an orchestration of sympathetic frequencies. Our gestalts make our choices for us in the mystery of communication, dictating, below conscious levels, those "facts" to which we give our selective attention. The critic, in absentia, and the reader, at a distance, choose to pair off. The scene of *The Rime of the Ancient Mariner* is, after all, a wedding; and the Wedding Guest could easily have brushed off the graybeard loon, magnetic eye or not, if he had really wanted to do so. His staying was the moment of contact—and the motor started revving.

CHAPTER TWO

The Dialectical, Three-Beat Method

"THE CREATIVE ADVANCE into novelty" is Alfred North Whitehead's "ultimate metaphysical ground," as set forth in *Process and Reality*. I take the felicitous phrase to be not only the end but also the method of criticism. It is novelty that triggers the critical mass. J. Z. Young (in *Doubt and Certainty*), replying to the question, "Why must anyone seek for new ways of acting?" answers:

> In the long run the continuity of life itself depends on the making of new experiments . . . the continuous invention of new ways of observing is man's special secret of living. . . . A really useful and interesting brain is always starting off on new ways.

To stress the interconnectedness, the networking of learning and living, the patterning and modifying of patterns, he asserts that:

> Biology has shown us to what an extraordinary extent our ways of observing and speaking are not our own, but, like our whole organization, are inherited and learned.

It is a population of consciousness with which we are dealing, he argues, not an individual consciousness; it is a system, and we improve that system if we "pass on ways of observing and describing that are a little more powerful than the ones we received." The concepts of novelty and of critical mass cannot be stressed too strongly. Pierre Teilhard de Chardin elaborates this dual concept throughout *The Phenomenon of Man;* he speaks of "the spring and secret of hominisation":

> A gigantic psycho-biological operation, a sort of *mega-synthesis,* the "super-arrangement" to which all thinking elements of the earth find themselves today individually and collectively subject . . . The outcome of the world, the gates of the future, the entry into the super-human—these are not thrown open to a few of the privileged nor to one chosen people to the exclusion of others. They will open to an advance of *all together,* in a direction in which all *together* can join and find completion in a spiritual renovation of the earth . . .

In his foreword, "Seeing," Teilhard writes:

> Fuller being is closer union; such is the kernel and conclusion of this book. But let us emphasize the point; union can only increase through an increase in consciousness, that is to say in vision. And that, doubtless, is why the history of the living world can be summarised as the elaboration of ever more perfect eyes within a cosmos in which there is always *something more to be seen* (italics RLS). To try to see more and better is not a matter of whim or curiosity or self-indulgence. *To see or to perish* is the very condition laid upon everything that makes up the universe, by reason of the mysterious gift of existence. And this, in superior measure, is man's condition.

This is criticism, I maintain; and to elucidate it here requires some elementary contact with the ancient doctrine of "the one and the many," which Plato, Socrates, and the Eleatic philosophers Parmenides and Zeno toyed with in the dawn of Western thought, and of its inevitable corollary, dialectical thinking. "Opposed elements stand to each other in mutual requirement," wrote Whitehead:

> In their unity, they inhibit or contrast. God and the World stand to each other in this opposed requirement. God is the

infinite ground of all mentality, the unity of vision seeking physical multiplicity. The World is the multiplicity of finites, actualities seeking a perfected unity. Neither God, nor the World, reaches static completion. Both are in the grip of the ultimate metaphysical ground, the creative advance into novelty. Either of them, God and the world, is the instrument of novelty for each other.

Earlier in *Process and Reality* Whitehead speaks of "the production of novel togetherness":

The ultimate metaphysical principle is the advance from disjunction to conjunction, creating a novel entity other than the entities given in disjunction. The novel entity is at once the togetherness of the "many" which it leaves; it is a novel entity, disjunctively among the many entities which it synthesizes. The many become one, and are increased by one. In their natures, entities are disjunctively "many" in process of passage into conjunctive unity.

The Rime of the Ancient Mariner, as a poem, a work of art, represents "a creative advance into novelty," "a novel entity," "a production of novel togetherness"; it is a synthesis of disjunctions into "a conjunctive unity." In this case, subject and object were employed by Coleridge as "instruments of novelty for each other." Coleridge, as a gifted, intuitive creator, undoubtedly knew intimately and comprehensively the nature of the creative process as a collision of the one and the many. An archetypal expression of the fundamental relationship between the one and the many, diversity and unity, singularity and multiplicity, disjunction and conjunction is Coleridge's hooking of the concepts of "one" and "three."

"One," philosophically, is not a number but a transcendental individuality. Thus, Whitehead:

The consequent nature of God is composed of a multiplicity of elements with individual self-realization. It is just as much one immediate fact as it is an unresting advance beyond itself. Thus the actuality of God must be understood as a multiplicity of actual components in process of creation. This is God in his function of the kingdom of heaven.

The reader will note the phrase, "unresting advance beyond itself." It may be translated, in terms of a theory of criticism, into the notion, "something more, something beyond . . ." Thus, in the process of criticism, there must be what Whitehead, in another context, describes as "the insistent craving that zest for existence be refreshed by the ever-present, unfading importance of our immediate actions, which perish and yet live for evermore."

What is intimated here is an ascending order of complex unities which are broken up, dissolved, and reformulated into new and higher unities that retain in themselves the unobliterated former particularities, yet provide merely new platforms, new unities, from which the process may be carried still higher. The concept "three" is essentially the same as "one," except that it is the ultimate phenomenon seen from the perspective of multiplicity passing into unity. The two concepts cannot be torn apart; each strives toward the other, along a gradient of polarity; each, in Whitehead's term, is "all in all." The symbolic shorthand of "one" and "three" for unity and multiplicity is to be found in all historical cultures, eastern as well as western.

If Christians have their "Father, Son, and Holy Ghost," the divine Trinity; if the Greeks had the three-fold doctrine that man is composed of soul, body, and spirit—why, then the Hindu trinity is *Trimurti* (Sanskrit, "having three shapes") interpreted religiously as the three gods Brahma, Vishnu, and Shiva, or metaphysically as the three principles of creation-maintenance-destruction operative in cosmo-psychology. *Tripitaka*, the Buddhist canon of the "Three Baskets," consists of "the basket of discipline," "the basket of Buddha's sermons," and "the basket of metaphysics." The concept of three is ubiquitous in mankind's symbolic activity: the reader can surely summon up by memory any number of examples from almost every field of human thought, including but not limited to literature, mythology, theology, and the natural and social sciences.

Literary critics, of course, have made extensive use of the triad. Stanley Edgar Hyman, in *The Armed Vision*, notes how the American critic R. P. Blackmur converts "all his duos into trios":

Poetry is a double agent (content and form, the raw material of life and the shaping imagination), criticism is a double agent (analysis and appreciation, intimacy with particulars and evaluation of achievement), and poetry and criticism together are a double agent (. . . craft and elucidation). The double agent is in fact any pair of critical terms—form and content . . . writer and reader . . . tradition and revolt, expression and communication—and out of their interaction arises a third thing, the point, the essay, or, in this case, Blackmur's book . . .

Hyman describes Blackmur's "new mysticism of the triple." He speaks of the critic's use of "three levels of meaning," "three impacts," and "triple significance." To show how Blackmur's "new preoccupation" is made explicit, he quotes from the latter's review of a work by Wallace Stevens:

A triad makes a trinity, and a trinity, to a certain kind of poetic imagination, is the only tolerable form of unity. I think the deep skills of imagination, by which insights, ideas, and acts get into poetry, thrive best when some single, pressing theme or notion is triplicated. . . . The doublet is never enough, unless it breeds. War and peace need a third phase, as liquid and ice need vapor to fill out and judge the concept of water. . . . The doublet needs what it makes. This is the habit of the creative mind.

Coleridge's archetypal expression, probably unconscious, of the one and three relationship is found in the second line of his poem: "It is an Ancient Mariner,/ And he stoppeth one of three . . ." The number three reappears almost at once in the poem's fourth verse: "The Wedding-Guest stood still,/ And listens like a three years' child." Coincidence? Possibly. But why "one of *three*"? Why not a dyad of Wedding Guests or a group of four, five, six? The numbers two, four, five, as well as seven, as we noted earlier, have demonstrated their appeal to various symbolic systems in the evolution of disparate cultures; but none, I believe, can rival the rhythmic dominance of the numbers one and three. There is something primordial as well as ultimate in this particular combination, which evokes the ghost of multiplicity on the other side of one, and the spectrum of individuality, unarticulated but waiting, beyond three.

The poem is replete with cadences that beat the triple rhythm:

The fair breeze blew, the white foam flew,
The furrow followed free:
We were the *first* that ever burst
Into that silent sea. (italics RLS)

If three signifies closure, it also implies a new start. The phrase "three's a crowd" is an intuitive popular recognition of this fact. Animal psychologists experimenting with rhesus monkeys have observed that in play, two monkeys will pair off and continue their play until approached by a third, at which approach the two cease their play and separate. Three is the end of a unified one, and the beginning of fragmentary new "ones."

A good critic, at this point, should say: "What is all this nonsense about the mystical three-in-one and one-in-three? What has it to do with the business of looking at a piece of art, or any symbolic communication, and illuminating it with perceptive comment, evaluating it and helping the receiver to understand it and to enjoy it more?" He would ask this question not in an eristic or argumentative manner, merely for the sake of contradiction alone, but because the challenging question is a dialectical tool for forcing a response which will stimulate a counter-response and so forth, hopefully leading to a critical insight, a novel togetherness, which will act as a cell-firer in the critical mass. You have here the well-known dialectical rhythm of Plato, Kant, and Hegel, the three-beat thesis, antithesis, synthesis. The evocation of this rhythm is the true business of criticism, as it is of art, as it is of life.

When criticism is not seen in this light, its power is diminished. If a critic calls a work "good" or "bad," and tells me why, and sets it in its historical context, and examines its structure and texture, he may leave me informed, richer in my understanding of the work, and either in agreement or disagreement with him on his act of judgment. But if the critic has not himself made a truly novel discovery, as the result of the collision between himself and the work, then he has failed to fire my cell—or he has only succeeded in firing it at a comparatively low level of energy—and the contribution to the critical-mass chain reaction is null or minimal. A high-powered firing comes from a process in which neither explanation nor evaluation, exclusively or dually, is the only end of criticism—although both may be contained, and perhaps should be, in the final "nugget of meaning." It comes from a process in which description, analysis, and judgment are carried—as a carrier wave from a transmitter is modulated to carry the particular oscillations of a coded signal, a message; and that message, the symbolic meaning, so to speak, of the communication, is the "novel togetherness," the insight that has been produced in the collision between the critic and the thing criticized.

The significance of the three-and-one metaphor I have been describing is that unless it is applied to the specific job of criticism, the optimum cell-firing cannot be achieved. It is the essential process of the critical-creative act. The total process of criticism may be described in three stages; and within the second stage, the triple rhythm is indispensable. In the description of the total process, you find first a continuum, a random deductiveness, the endless horizon of the universe which exists for critical scanning. It is in itself a synthesis, or it appears as such; in any case, it is a multiplicity, a complexity, a unity incorporating separate parts in some assigned or undetected order of being.

Along this continuum the critic discerns a point, a particular object, and he focuses his attention upon it—a poem, a painting, a television program, an essay, anything. He hooks into it; he forms a combination, an interaction: the "doublet" is now there; it is destined to breed: the new synthesis that will be the fruit of it may or may not be a cell-firing: at the juncture this is unknown. The critic observes, reacts, feels, thinks; he pores over the object, he surrounds it, he researches it—his objective is to store up as much data as he can about the object. He is, in a sense, compiling a master-dictionary, a total language of given "facts," to feed into his critical computer.

The scope of his dictionary depends entirely upon the amount of time that he has to give to his acquisitions, upon the depth of his own awareness of the ambience of the particular object, and upon his understanding of the exact nature and function of this first stage in the dialectical process. The greater the lexicon and the amount of time in which to gather it, the greater are the possibilities for eventual cell-firing. This does not mean that all that the critic gathers in this first phase of research and exposure will eventually be used. As will be seen, a selective process will be set in motion: some data, as in the New Testament parable, will fall on good ground and bear fruit; other data will fall on stony ground and wither away. The tares will be separated from the wheat—to the fire or to the barn in the final architectural reckoning. It is not at all necessary, at this first stage, that the critic should jump to conclusions or to judgments. He should resist the temptation to do so. His reactions should be fed into the computer, along with all other data, for possible significance later. The input is all preliminary, and not decisive.

Since I am using the scientific term "data," I might as well take care to explain to the reader that I am not signifying merely independent "facts." As Abraham Kaplan points out in *The Conduct of Inquiry,* not all facts are "data." "Data," he writes, "are always data for some hypothesis or other . . . no one interpretation is necessitated by what is observed; there are always many ways of mapping behavior into data . . ." Nietzsche exploded "the dogma of immaculate perception." The pure spectator-spectacle condition is an illusion. The observer does not observe, he disturbs and enters into an interaction with the thing observed. He brings to it his preconceptions, his prejudices, even his peculiar linguistic distortions. "Observing," says Kaplan, "is a goal-directed behavior . . . the product of an active choice, not of a passive exposure."

For criticism, this means that the critic should be aware that he sees what, in a sense, it is necessary for him to see. He must remember that he is making a map, and that other people observing the same thing are making different maps. This awareness means that he shall be alert to the dialectical possibilities inherent in the maps of others and constantly check himself. Darwin, we are told by Kaplan, "kept a separate notebook to record observations counter to his theory, lest he overlook or underestimate them." A critic may be enthusiastically moved by first contact with his object, or repelled: this is merely to be noted—no more. People who share the reception of an art experience with a critic often turn to him immediately to ask, "What do you think of it?" The critic would be justified if he chose to answer "How do I know? I will try to find out."

The second stage in our descriptive triad is the period of incubation: this is the important stage. It is usually neglected or passed through in a hurry by critics who are unfortunate enough to have to deliver their criticisms under the gun of a strict deadline. That is why such criticism confines itself mostly to reporting and evaluation: it is unfair to ask the critic working under such conditions to do more.

As a producer of television programs, I often discussed outlines of programs with writers. Then they would go away and write and come back with the finished scripts. I remember one writer in particular who would not come back as quickly as the others. When I would ask him, "How's the script coming?" he would tap his brow and say with a serious expression, "The boys in the back room are working on it." He was in the incubation stage, the phase of digestion, of breaking down, of analysis, of cracking a former synthesis into a dissolved pattern of randomness.

There is a vast literature on this subject of the period of incubation. Probably the most comprehensive treatment of it is contained in Arthur Koestler's *The Act of Creation,* a study of the conscious and unconscious in science and art. Ghiselin's *The Creative Process,* referred to earlier, is another compilation of the experiences of artists, scientists, poets, musicians, and novelists in the wilderness area of what Koestler describes as "the blocked matrix"— a period of snow blindness, dreams, frustrated drives, of despair and of trial and error, of patience and plodding, of the sense of being lost in a dark tunnel. The experience may seem to manifest itself at a conscious or at an unconscious level; actually, it proceeds on both levels—the two levels being comparable to snakes at play—first one on top, then the other. The experience of Coleridge in composing *Kubla Khan* operated at the level of the unconscious, as the poet described it in a prefatory note to the poem. He was in ill health and was staying alone in a lonely farm house. He took two grains of opium to check a slight indisposition and fell asleep "for about three hours" (our old friend three again!). At the moment of his falling asleep, however, he had been reading a book in which he found the words: "Here the Khan Kubla commanded a palace to be built, and a stately garden thereunto. And thus ten miles of fertile ground were inclosed with a wall."

During Coleridge's sleep "all the images rose up before him as *things,* with a parallel production of the correspondent expressions, without any sensation or consciousness of effort. When he awoke, he immediately began to write down the visions, but was interrupted by a visitor; and when, an hour later, he returned to his composition, the visions had gone, all except eight or ten scattered lines." Of course, the whole of Coleridge's life up to that moment when he fell asleep constituted the underground mine that his unconscious explored, marvelously making associations, finding relationships, combining and re-combining linkages into novel togetherness. Sometimes one knows that one is working with "the boys in the back room." More or less of reverie may be active in this condition. The collision between the critic and the object has become a problem, a puzzle; and one searches in all directions, with every tool at his command, for the solution, the breakthrough into the new insight, the uncommon vision. Koestler calls it "bi-sociation," the linking of two formerly independent, autonomous matrices in a flash of recognition of something that may have been there all along, but which was unperceived. The special significance of the phrase "one in three" in *The Rime of the Ancient Mariner* is a case in point. I had not "seen" it, for all my years of reading the poem, until, as I was searching for the novel togetherness that would integrate this chapter, it suddenly "dawned" upon me, after a long period of random groping.

In scientific discovery, the time required for the bi-sociative linking, the flash of insight, the leap of the imagination, the "aha!" experience may be stretched to the passing of years. Einstein, at the age of sixteen, was struck by a paradox concerning the speed of light. Ten years later, years of "combinatory play" with the paradox, he got out of bed one morning and in a sudden moment of truth—there was his basic insight into the relativity of Time! When Einstein later replied to an inquiry about his method of work, he wrote:

Taken from a psychological viewpoint, this combinatory play seems to be the essential feature in productive thought—before there is any connection with logical construction in words or other kinds of signs which can be communicated to others.

So we have this "combinatory play," this playing handball with an idea against the wall of possible linkages, more or less at the level of reverie and the unconscious. Yet I believe that even at the level of the mind's underground, the game is played according to the three-beat rules: unities are dissolved and re-formed at paradoxically more complex, yet more simple plateaus; one paradigm is destroyed to be replaced by another.

In criticism, while there may be descents into the underground, the deliberately cognitive attack dominates the process. The dialectic is conscious. Dialectic is a wide word. It may mean the conversation, the dialogue between minds cooperating, not battling, with each other in a search for truth. It may mean the commitment to contradiction, as in Marxist dialectical materialism, where thesis, antithesis and synthesis describe the nature of the production arrangements of human societies, and where contradiction is the inevitable iron law of economic relationships. Dialectic may, on the other hand, seek for the elimination of contradiction; it has also been described as merely another method of inquiry, the method of trial and error. I knew very little about dialectic when I began writing about television and radio. In the course of my work, regularly facing the problem of writing short critiques, I slowly evolved my own particular "theory" of criticism: I called it "the three-beat theory." I had never come upon the words "three beat" used in this sense, until a few years ago, when I experienced delight in finding the following in Karl Popper's *The Open Society and Its Enemies,* Vol. II (Popper is referring to Hegel's conviction that "reason is nothing but the product of [our] social heritage, of the historical development of the social group in which we live, the nation"):

> This development proceeds dialectically, that is to say, in a three-beat rhythm. First, a thesis is proffered; but it will produce criticism, it will be contradicted by opponents who assert its opposite, an antithesis; and in the conflict of these views, a synthesis is attained, that is to say, a kind of unity of the opposites, a compromise or a reconciliation on a higher

level. The synthesis absorbs, as it were, the two original opposite positions, by superseding them; it reduces them to components of itself, thereby negating, elevating, and preserving them. And once the synthesis has been established, the whole process can repeat itself on a higher level that has now been reached. This, in brief, is the three-beat rhythm of the progress which Hegel called the "dialectic triad."

Let us back up here and remind the reader that we are using the three-beat notion in a double application—in a description of the whole process of critical-creative thinking, and in a statement of the nature of the second step in that process. In the description of the whole method, the first beat is the exposure and research phase, the saturation by data. The saturation phase varies in duration: it is best ended when the critic is convinced that he has, in his research, in his exploration of the object as it came to him along the critical continuum, reached the point of diminishing returns. Whatever else he accumulates, as knowledge about the object, its content, context, biography, circumstances, etc., is recognized as echoes of what he has already learned. This conviction, at best, is a feeling of rightness— no more; for there is an infinite regression of pertinent data that is possible for any object. Intuition alone, and the pragmatic limitation of time can circumscribe the boundaries of the research phase.

The second beat is the incubation-dialectic-combinatory play and reveries phase. The third beat is the discovery of the hidden connection, the novel togetherness, the thing that sent Archimedes hopping out of his tub and running down the street shouting "Eureka!" It is the flash of insight, the leap of the imagination, the sudden illumination.

There is a further extension of the three beats, as applied to the writing down of the fruit of the process: we will come to that later. Now our objective is to penetrate more deeply into the second stage of the three-beat process. The goal of this second phase is, quite literally, to find something to say, something that is *worth saying* to a busy and demanding audience. We can report and describe, judge and give the reasons for our judgment; but as we maintained earlier, why bother? If we are acting in a journalistic sense, this is functional. The critic scans the environment for the reader and supplies him with bits of information to keep his map of things up to date.

The question is: what does the reader do with the information? He stores it away in his memory bank, and that is that: he has had an additive experience but not a qualitative change, which results from an enlargement of his view, a new perspective, a critical proposition, so to speak, with which he can wrestle. This new way of seeing things, the critic's discovery, is his own, unique, uncommon vision. It transcends judgment: it is something more, something beyond. For if the critic judges something to be good, and if I agree with him, he flatters but does not enrich me. If I disagree with his judgment, and that is all there is to his critique, our communication is broken off. There is no interlocking of the minds, no engagement, no cell-firing. I am as before the critical encounter, with a few more "facts" in my bag of information, that vary in their degree of relevance to life. This is meritorious and serviceable, and not to be derogated; but it is not criticism as I understand it.

The critic's goal—certainly not always attained—should be to change his reader, such that he will never again see a given, perhaps a familiar object (which is the subject of his discourse with the critic) in exactly the same way that he perceived it before. A parable expresses this: I do not remember where I first came upon it; but I will paraphrase it:

> Once there was a pre-scientific man who lived in a forest, a
> primitive critic. Every day he walked a beaten track through
> the trees and passed by a clear pond. Whenever he chanced to
> look toward the center of the pond, he would see a small branch
> protruding through the surface of the water; and the branch
> was crooked at the water-line. One day something prompted
> him to leave the path, to walk into the pond, stoop down and
> with his hand to take the branch up out of the water—and lo,
> the branch, held in his hand in its full length, was straight.
> He had discovered the principle of refraction. Never again
> would he walk past that pond, or any other, and imagine, when
> he saw a branch protruding from the surface of the water, that
> it was half straight and half crooked. The world of this
> primitive critic had been irrevocably restructured.

He was not only a primitive critic, he was also a philosopher. As Herbert Marcuse writes in *One-Dimensional Man*:

> The intellectual dissolution and even subversion of the given facts is the historical task of philosophy and the philosophic dimension.

Marcuse also writes:

> Under the repressive conditions in which men think and live, thought—any mode of thinking which is not confined to pragmatic orientation within the status quo—can recognize the facts and respond to the facts only by "going behind" them. Experience takes place before a curtain which conceals and, if the world is the appearance of something behind the curtain of immediate experience, then, in Hegel's terms, it is we ourselves who are behind the curtain.

To pierce that curtain is the business of criticism. Claude Lévi-Strauss, in *Structural Anthropology*, asks: "Is it possible to conceive of the human mind as consisting of compartments separated by rigid bulkheads without anything being able to pass from one compartment to the other?"

His answer, of course, is "no." He asked the question in an essay on linguistics and anthropology in which he argued for correlations between the two disciplines; but the following quotation from that essay can be applied to our concept, in criticism, of breaking through rigid bulkheads and setting up correlations:

> If there were no relations at all, that would lead us to assume that the human mind is a kind of jumble—that there is no connection at all between what the mind is doing on one level and what the mind is doing on another level. . . . So the conclusion which seems to me the most likely is that some kind of correlation exists between certain things on certain levels, and our main task is to determine what these things are and what these levels are. This can be done only through a close cooperation between linguists and anthropologists.

I should say that the most important results of such cooperation will not be for linguistics alone or for anthropology alone, or for both; they will mostly be for an anthropology conceived in a broader way—that is, a knowledge of man that incorporates all the different approaches which can be used and that will provide a clue to the way according to which our uninvited guest, the human mind, works.

Kevin Van Nuys, in *Is Reality Meaningful?*—a work in which he develops a coherent, dynamic theory of reality as opposed to a static model—asserts that "nature's advance to the immeasurable complexities of design that she achieves," is the result of "a definite search for the novel and vivid experience, and a tendency to invent forms and structures that will efficiently subserve such experience . . ." He denies that "chance" can be the agent in this advance of nature; and he maintains that the Static Mechanistic Theory of Reality ignores "the ever-baffling riddle of why nature is not satisfied to remain on the first level of manifestation (hydrogen atoms) but insists on 'climbing up' the ladder of evolution." Dialectic is, in a sense, a "climbing up," a linear ascent. If we also perceive it as moving horizontally as well as vertically—even, perhaps, as exploding into the third dimension—we are getting closer to the three-beat notion of criticism. A metaphor employed by Kurt Lewin in speaking of the action of theory in systematizing and unifying our knowledge can also be applied to criticism: "The ultimate goal is to establish a network of highways and superhighways, so that any important point may be linked to any other."

The task of the critic is to think dynamically and relationally rather than statically. Karl Mannheim, in *Ideology and Utopia*, describing the emergence of the scientific essay in the sixteenth to the eighteenth centuries, writes:

The technique of the thinkers of that period consisted in leaping into any immediate problem which was conveniently at hand and observing it for so long and from so many angles that finally some marginal problem of thought and existence was disclosed and illuminated by means of the accidental, individual case.

The observation "from so many angles" is the critical dialectic, and no area of human experience, no realm of art, commerce, science, or theology is off limits to it. Gertrude Himmelfarb, the biographer, in *Darwin and the Darwinian Revolution,* remarked of the great naturalist that "he was able to give ultimate answers because he asked ultimate questions." And she adds:

> His colleagues . . . deliberately eschewed such ultimate questions as the pattern of creation, or the reasons for any particular form, on the grounds that these were not the proper subjects of science. Darwin, uninhibited by these restrictions, could range more widely and deeply into the mysteries of Nature . . . It was with the sharp eyes of the primitive, the open mind of the innocent, that he looked at his subject, daring to ask questions that his more learned and sophisticated colleagues could not have thought to ask.

In describing (in *The Act of Creation*) the steps by which Darwin made his discovery, Koestler explicitly speaks of the experience as having "three threads." The main thread, which Darwin had picked up from the evolutionists who preceded him, was the credo of the descent of the species as opposed to the single act of creation. The second thread, artificial selection, he picked up from "a careful study of domesticated animals and cultivated plants." But this led to a cul-de-sac: Darwin could not explain what agent or agency was active in the case of undomesticated animals or plants. After having gone through his first beat—the collection of facts—he had entered the "combinatory play" period, and in his dialectical reaching out for linkages, he had struck the snowblind condition. Writes Koestler:

> The deadlock lasted a year and three months. He tried a number of hypotheses, but none of them worked. He toyed with the idea of some universal law, according to which species were born, matured, and died, just as individuals do . . . but they were wrong guesses; and his thoughts kept running in circles in the blocked matrix . . .

Then he read Malthus' *An Essay on the Principle of Population,* which had been published more than forty years earlier, and "he saw in a flash the 'natural selector,' the causative agent of evolution, for which he had been searching"—it was the principle of the survival of the fittest. "Here then," wrote Darwin himself of this discovery, "I had at last got the theory by which to work." Concludes Koestler:

> He had found the third thread. Now the pattern of the theory was complete; what remained to be done was the elaboration— the weaving of the huge carpet which took him most of the rest of his life.

Darwin's third beat was his breakthrough into a new dimension, a higher plane encompassing the plane upon which he had labored earlier: it was a vertical movement; it was a horizontal movement; it was tri-dimensional.

We may ask what made him quit, how he knew that there wasn't a yet higher dimension to attain, a more embracing flash of insight. The answer is: it felt "good" to Darwin; it had coherence, elegance; it fitted other acceptable insights into the architecture of advancing science. Sufficient unto the critic is the insight that makes him "feel good." Mankind has been chewing on Darwin's restructuring of the history of species for more than a century. It may be that future times will see the swallowing up of the theory of evolution by a higher theory that will incorporate it as a special case, just as relativity and quantum mechanics have incorporated Newtonian mechanics as a special case, which is "true" for some aspects of physical laws, "not true" for others, and in either case, assuredly not the absolute, enveloping truth which Newton thought that it was. Even Einstein's special and general theories of relativity may prove to be special cases of still wider laws. W. P. D. Wightman ventured this prediction in *The Growth of Scientific Ideas*: "It is more than likely that history will repeat itself and Einstein's beautiful theory be found after all to be not quite 'true.'"

The third beat is the novel togetherness; it refreshes, clears, and satisfies the mind: and it enables the critic to assume the role of the Ancient Mariner—a man who has had a unique experience, one that he must perforce contribute to a mind that is a Wedding Guest at the world's busy feast of individual preoccupations. The "one of three" will be stopped by the collision; his cells will be fired, and he will come away with an energy incorporated into his processes of intellect and emotion, compelling him to rumination. What we have here is a bit of the two worlds of scientific method—the worlds of correlational and of theoretical procedures. Correlational thinking, according to Henry Margenau in *The Nature of Physical Reality,* is the comparison of surface data, empirically collected and observed. A theory, on the other hand, is born when the surface of mere correlation is broken and subsurface explanation begins. "The contingency of correlation," Margenau writes of such an action, "had given way to logical necessity. This statement remains significant even if it recognized that the necessity is not absolute but hypothetical, dependent on the validity of the Euclidean premises."

Speaking of "Bohr's proof of the Balmer formula, in 1913" in which "a theory of the atom was born," he remarks: "An internal luminosity suddenly shone through the empirical formula." In our context of critical method, the collection of the data lies in the first beat; the comparisons, the correlations are preliminary probes. Beams of inquiry looking for hooks, and dialectical, combinatory play make up the second beat. In this beat, subsurface connections may be discovered progressively, but they must continually be subjected to challenge and debate, and referred to other data, until the master metaphor is seized—"the internal luminosity," which is the third beat. Margenau observes that:

> Historical evidence indicates that all sciences start upon the correlational level and evolve progressively toward the theoretic stage. At any given stage, no science is entirely correlational, and none is entirely theoretic. Nevertheless, if there is a significant methodological distinction, it is this, that a science is either predominantly correlational or predominantly theoretic.

Margenau asserts that within the theoretic structure "lies the key to physical reality."

I maintain that, in a similar fashion, the key to the critical method lies within its theoretic, third-beat aspect, although the total method is also a combination of both ways of developing critical insights. Two further examples, one from the field of the historiography of science, the other from the field of psychoanalysis and human development, will indicate the universality of the three-beat process in innovative, critical thinking. Thomas S. Kuhn, in *The Structure of Scientific Revolutions,* asserts that new theories are developed in science by the creation of new paradigms for old, at times of "crises," when problems can no longer be solved by reference to accepted conceptual frameworks. Science, he explains, is never quite the same again after it has gone through the procedure whereby paradigms change:

> Discovery commences with the awareness of anomaly, i.e., with the recognition that nature has somehow violated the paradigm-induced expectations that govern normal science. It then continues with a more or less extended exploration of the area of anomaly. And it closes only when the paradigm theory has been adjusted so that the anomalous has become the expected. Assimilating a new sort of fact demands a more than additive adjustment of theory, and until that adjustment is completed— until the scientist has learned to see nature in a different way —the new fact is not quite a scientific fact at all.

We have, in the above process, a tension induced by contradiction or anomaly, an exploration of that tension which is more than "additive," and its final result—the scientist's learning to "see nature in a different way." I find a comparable process outlined in Erik H. Erikson's description of three dimensions "of the psychoanalyst's job" in *Childhood and Society.* "The first dimension," he writes, "extends along the axis of *cure-research,*" which is pursued in the clinical situation, the interpersonal relationship between doctor and patient: this is analogous to the initial superficial interaction between critic and object criticized. "The observer's frank and self-observing participation in this job marks the second dimension: *objectivity-participation.*"

> The clinician's knowledge . . . must ever again yield to interpersonal experiment; fresh impressions must ever again be regrouped into their common denominators in configurations; and the configurations finally, must be abstracted into sugges-

tive conceptual models. The *third dimension* of clinical work, therefore, is ordered along the axis of *knowledge-imagination*. By using a combination of both, the clinician applies selected insights to more strictly experimental approaches. (italics in original throughout)

Kant, it has been remarked, had a tendency to make unbridled generalizations, transcendental leaps from noting that certain traits are common in experience to claiming that they are necessary conditions for all experience. I wish to make it clear that no such transcendental leap, no law, no categorical imperative of criticism is being offered here. This whole three-beat concept is merely an individual construct of mine, thrown out suggestively, with the accompanying comment that there is something provocative in the fact that the triad, in its critical-creative connotations, has been found manifesting itself rather universally, in consistent outcroppings across the human scene. A critic might reply that we are simulating profundity by making much of the obvious—namely, the hoary, Aristotelian tradition of a beginning, a middle, and an end.

Maybe. I recall, in this connection, an amusing experience that I had once with a Madison Avenue account executive, when I went to his office to tell him the outline of a television program that I had been commissioned to write. He was round and energetic; he wore a Madison Avenue account executive's then fashionable checkered waistcoat, and he strode vigorously around his commodious office, as he proclaimed in a booming voice: "You don't have to tell me your outline. It isn't necessary. There's only one thing, and one thing only that I demand from a story. Without it—you have nothing; with it—everything. The only thing that I demand from a show is that it have"—he paused dramatically, then raised his voice a boom higher and slammed the big fist of his right hand on the walnut desk—"is that it have a beginning, a middle, and an end!"

Every narrative, of course, has this triad, except, perhaps, modern anti-plot novels that abjure the conventional unities of space, time, and scene. Narratives conventionally are organismic in growth, partaking of dynamic development. They generally unfold inductively however, allowing the third beat to reveal itself only at the very end, although it may be said that the third beat exists, *a priori* as it were, in the author's mind before the narration commences. In criticism, the third beat ideally should be announced at once, as is the thematic statement in a symphony. It is a deductive proposition that reverses the inductive process by which the third beat has been achieved.

This will be explained shortly; now I wish to remind the reader that we have been developing the notion of the third beat as the discovery of an uncommon vision, something that is worth saying to a reader. In the field of science, Kaplan (in *The Conduct of Inquiry*) speaks of such visions as *"invisible data . . .* retrospectively seen to be perfectly obvious and even striking manifestations." For criticism, we may borrow the concept of "the paradigm observer," the ideal critic, so to speak, as described by N. R. Hanson in *Patterns of Discovery*:

> The paradigm observer [is] not the man who sees and reports what all normal observers see and report, but the man who sees in familiar objects what no one else has seen before.

J. Bronowski, in his brilliant "The Abacus and The Rose: A Dialogue after Galileo" (in the *Nation,* January 4, 1964), superbly discusses this notion of the uncommon vision in criticism. The characters in the dialogue, three Englishmen, are participating in an East-West conference on cultural matters in Switzerland. They dine together one evening at sunset, and the two younger members of the trio, Dr. Amos Harping, representing "the literary furies," and Professor Lionel Potts, representing science in the contest between "The Two Cultures," move, in their conversation, to a sharp debate on the beauty of the sunset. Harping, the man of letters, rebukes Sir Edward Albish—the eldest, Establishment member of the trio—for saying that the sunset is beautiful.

> HARPING: No, Sir Edward, you must not [say that it is beautiful]; you must not, if you want to use words sensitively. Beauty is not measured, like splendor, by a comparison with the commonplace. It is felt in each of us by what is most individual in him . . . And when we, the critics . . . discuss beauty in a work of art or of nature, we are looking for what is

uncommon, what is personal, what we can see and someone else cannot. We are using the occasion, each of us, to search into our own individual gifts of appreciation.

SIR EDWARD: Why? You may be engrossed in your private exercise; but why should I be? Why should I attend to what you, Amos Harping—you and no one else—have to say about a poem or a sunset?

POTTS: He may be a better judge of them than you are, Sir Edward.

HARPING: No, Potts, no, no—or rather, yes and no. Yes I am a better judge because no I am not a better judge—because I am aware that no one is a better judge. Why did you ask me about the sunset, Sir Edward? Do you think me a better judge of sunsets than you?

SIR EDWARD: No, Harping, I do not.

HARPING: Then why did you ask me?

SIR EDWARD: Because I wanted to hear what you would say.

HARPING: Of course; and that is the nature of critical appreciation. You want to hear what I say, not because it is better than what you say, but because it is different—minutely, subtly different, different in this personal foible or in that glimpse of another mind. And these differences, these small flashes of light behind the outline, they illuminate and enrich your own vision. You wanted to hear what I had to say, Sir Edward, because now that you have heard it, you will make it your own—a shift of emphasis, an infinitesimal enlargement of your apparently sacred and settled opinion of sunsets.

I find in Harping's position a minor clash between his insistence on "the uncommon vision" and his statement of the "slightly different" flashes of light. A "different" vision can also be commonplace. If, however, we take the liberty of using what Bronowski wrote for our own purposes; and if we interpret his minutely, subtly different glimpses of another mind as representing Whitehead's "creative advance into novelty," which is something more than mere difference; why, then, we have a progressively more penetrating insight into the third beat. For the reader must remember that what the critic is seeking is something that is worth saying; and in our scheme, the mere fact of subtle difference falls short of the goal of critical worth.

The problem comes down to a criterion for testing "worth." The exercise of this testing process occurs in the second beat of the critical method. Essentially, the process may be called *To Criticize the Critic*—which is the title of the lecture delivered by T. S. Eliot at the University of Leeds in 1961. In this lecture, Eliot turns his powers of criticism on his own literary criticism of "the last forty-odd years." He observes that his earlier essays made a deeper impression on the world than his later ones, and he attributes this partly to "the dogmatism of youth":

> When we are young we see issues sharply defined: as we age
> we tend to make more reservations, to qualify our positive
> assertions, to introduce more parentheses. We see objections
> to our views, we regard the enemy with greater tolerance and
> even sometimes with sympathy. When we are young, we are
> confident in our opinions, sure that we possess the whole truth;
> we are enthusiastic, or indignant. And readers, even mature
> readers, are attracted to a writer who is quite sure of himself.

Eliot makes age or maturity—the critic; it acts as a countervailing force to the critic's own dogmatism. In the second beat of our critical method the critic must function as his own critic. He must adopt a posture of estrangement, detachment, distance, reflection—after the manner of a Brecht drama. He must employ what Marcuse, in *One-Dimensional Man,* has called "the rationality of the negative." Marcuse has also called it "the Great Refusal—the protest against that which is." "Contradiction," he asserts, "is the work of the Logos." "Poetry, in its cognitive function," he maintains, "performs the great task of thought." And he quotes Paul Valery, the French poet: "le travail qui fait vivre en nous ce qui n'existe pas" ("the effort which makes live in us that which does not exist"). Marcuse continues:

> Naming "the things that are absent," is breaking the spell of
> the things that are; moreover, it is the ingression of a different
> order of things into the established one—"le commencement
> d'un monde."

Plato, it has often been held, was the great dogmatist, the philosopher with the closed mind, the absolutist, the idealist: but in the *Parmenides,* the dialogue in which that Eleatic philosopher teaches Socrates a more subtle dialectic than mere interrogation, Plato was the first critic to criticize his own ideas. Benjamin Jowett, in his introduction to the *Parmenides,* puts it this way:

> The method of the *Parmenides* may be compared with the process of purgation, which Bacon sought to introduce into philosophy. Plato is warning us against two sorts of "Idols of the Den"; first, his own Ideas, which he himself having created is unable to connect in any way with the external world; secondly, against two idols in particular, "Unity" and "Being," which had grown up in the pre-Socratic philosophy, and were still standing in the way of all progress and development of thought.

In analyzing our ideas according to the method of the *Parmenides,* Jowett concludes, we trace their history, criticize their perversion:

> We see that they are relative to the human mind and to one another . . . They come to us with "better opinion, better confirmation," not merely as the inspirations either of ourselves or of another, but deeply rooted in history and in the human mind.

This is the dialectical method of Parmenides. The Eleatic philosopher explains to Socrates that it is a sort of mental gymnastic, in which one considers not only what will follow from a given hypothesis, but what would follow from a denial of it, to that which is the subject of the hypothesis, and to all other things. Parmenides concludes the description of his method to Socrates thus:

> In a word, when you suppose anything to be or not to be, or to be in any way affected, you must look at the consequences in relation to the thing itself, and to any other things which you choose—to each of them singly, to more than one, and to all; and so of other things, you must look at them in relation to themselves and to anything else which you suppose either

to be or not to be, if you would train yourself perfectly and
see the real truth.

Zeno, Parmenides' friend, adds with a smile: "Most people are
not aware that this roundabout progress through all things is the
only way in which the mind can attain truth and wisdom." One
must read the words "truth and wisdom" here as approximations.
Plato, according to Jowett, never pretended to "settle" the per-
plexities of the "one" and "the many," which are the subject of the
Parmenides. Nor have they been settled in modern times by philosophers or by critical realists of the scientific schools who still are
unable to separate the strands of the logic of truth and of reality.
"To settle a question," it has been said, "is to dismiss it." The critic's
discovered plateau of "novel togetherness" is merely the launching
pad for a new ignition process. For the critic, the immediate work is
over; he can go on to other puzzles; for the reader it could be the
compelling seed, the "stunning" blow, as he walks away from
the Ancient Mariner.

The critic must criticize himself—the second beat of our critical
method. He must engage in a dialectical process. He must talk to
himself, self-deprecate, needle, challenge, scorn, and provoke. He
must stimulate, repudiate, query, refuse, oppose—in a phrase, he must
continually say to himself: "So what?" Does it really matter that the
critic "likes" a drama, for example? Is not "taste" completely subjective? Random correlations, we have said before, are not "data" in
the critical sense. Suppose that the critic can give good reasons for
his preference for an actor's performance, a well-directed scene—what
then? Is this substance or shadow? A reader may be enlightened in
a small way by the critic's sharper angle of vision; but does that
justify stopping the Wedding Guest at the door of the feast?
Furthermore, the announcement of a preference is an action on
a single dimension—"I like it." "I like it, because . . ." is still the
same, single dimension, merely elaborated. The elaboration may
go on for pages; but the length is not to be mistaken for dynamic
development.

"I like it, because . . ." is the "settling" of a question, its dismissal. It hooks into nothing more dynamic than agreement in the
reader's universe. If the reader likes "it" too, there is a reassuring

echo; if he does not like it, there is a closing of a door between two rooms. What can you do with the collision of two subjectivities? In any case, the announcement of a preference can be stated very quickly—the reader catches on quickly—whereas the object of the game is to get on with it. "I like it" terminates the game. How then is the next plateau to be reached, the penetration into a fresh dimension that will keep the dialectical tension alive? We must "carve at the joints," as Plato said; we must look for the "linkages" to other things, to other constellations or clusters of relevance. The search is for the bi-sociative matrix, in Koestler's vocabulary of creativity. Warner Fite, in *The Examined Life,* has written:

> To think of a given object, I would point out, is always to think
> beyond it; and therefore to think of possible other, and possibly
> preferable, objects in place of it. And thus to think is inevitably
> to question; and the depth and significance of the question
> is measured by its range of imagination.

Henry James, in his preface to "The Spoils of Poynton," a short story, gives a charming account of one way in which this "thinking beyond," this "linkage," can occur. He was dining with friends in London on a Christmas eve; and a lady seated next to him related the true account of a friend who was "at daggers drawn with her only son" over the ownership of the furniture of a fine old house, left to the young man at his father's death. As James's dinner companion chattered on, giving the true facts of the case, which were utterly useless to the novelist, he suddenly winced at the "prick of inoculation" carrying the "germ" of a story. James had come upon, quite suddenly, "the rich pasture that at every turn surrounds the ruminant critic." The real center of the story, as James later wrote it, was "the Things, always the splendid Things . . . the cabinets and chairs and tables." What actually "became" of them was "a comparatively vulgar issue":

> The passions, the faculties, the forces their beauty would, like
> that of antique Helen of Troy, set in motion was what, as a
> painter, one had really wanted of them, was the power in them
> that one had from the first appreciated.

James had thought "beyond" the bare bones of the facts of the case. He had penetrated into a new category—the furniture. This was his "nugget," his unique relationship to the subject. This was what he now felt compelled to relate to his readers. To be thus passively inoculated is a happy event. The "thinking beyond" comes harder usually in the business of criticism. Stephen Spender, in *The Making of a Poem,* comments on the extraordinary kind of concentration required for creative writing:

> It is a focussing of the attention in a special way, so that the poet
> is aware of all the implications and possible developments of his
> idea, just as one might say that a plant was not concentrating
> on developing mechanically in one direction, but in many
> directions, towards the warmth and light with its leaves, and
> towards the water with its roots all at the same time.

The critic reaches out in all directions. He asks of the object of his critical attention, What does this mean? What is interesting about it, significant? What can I discover about it that no one else has seen? Is it a representative of a known category or an innovation? Does it break with precedent or cast tradition in a new light?

What possible connections may it have to other realms of human endeavor? Does it reveal something about institutions? Does it distort history? How can we escape from the prison of the limitations that the object of our observation would set up for us in our act of observing it? Has it an origin? Does this give us a clue to a higher level on which we may operate? What are the motives of its creators? Is there a sociological linkage, a political, psychological, military, existential, philosophical point of entry? If an answer comes back, "Yes," one engages it dialectically at once. The weapon is always the dialectical challenge, So what? Suppose that it has this particular connotation: is that significant? What if it has, and if others have already remarked upon it? Is it worth the Wedding Guest's time to sound an echo? Why not? Perhaps the Wedding Guest has not yet heard that particular echo? This is a rationalization; the critic must suspect it. The claim that he stakes out must be, so far as he knows, original. If, beyond his knowledge, it turns out that others have staked out the very same claim, this merely sets his own discovery in a multidimensional setting, but it does not diminish one whit the discovery that he has made.

There is, in each particular case of criticism, the "secret" of that particular case, which exists for the critic alone, and which he alone must find. Another critic, regarding the same case, must find in it another "secret." The critical universe represents an infinity of secrets—that is its splendor: each, like a star, is a marvel unto itself; that is why, in a sense, the object of the critique is born again whenever it is transmuted in the fires of the critical imagination. For each consciousness a new universe—the same yet different. Such an experience is not accomplished by an opinion or a judgment but by the discovery, perhaps the *invention* of what the critical object most completely expresses for the critic.

The secret perhaps never reveals itself at the beginning of the dialectical search. It must be stormed through whirlpools of confusion, blocked matrices, and often in despair of finding a solution. "The poet," wrote Jean Cocteau, on the process of inspiration, "is at the disposal of his night. His role is humble, he must clean house and wait." Poems are rarely written to order; critiques usually are. There must be something of the Cocteau recipe in the critic's job; but above it, there must also be the plodding patience, not only of the ruminant but also of the importunate critic, hammering doggedly at the door of his master metaphor until it is opened from some mysterious within or he is tendered the key.

The master metaphor hardly ever resembles the vague notion that is thrown upon the dialectical gaming table at the outset. That first notion suffers a sea-change: it is shuffled and bartered about for more promising fare; sometimes it returns in novel forms, only to dissolve again, to put on new disguises. It resembles a ladder of ascending generalizations, each more complex than the former but subsuming it, as the sapling incorporates the acorn. I have often thought of it as a sort of Jacob's ladder as described in the Old Testament (Genesis 28), with the angels ascending and descending on it, between earth and heaven, until Jacob, the critic, asleep on his stone pillows, found his third beat and awoke to realize that he was not in a state of guilt-ridden exile but veritably at the gate of heaven.

The angels, in the critic's experience, become "angles," perspectives illuminating incongruity. The angles, like packages of insights, are patiently set alongside one another, fragmentary, seemingly unrelated. It is a laying about of building blocks for a house whose design and specifications remain unknown. Eventually, as we have insisted, there is a "click," a "snapping together," the appearance of a pattern, a holistic field. As if thrust about by a magnetic force, the elements now whip themselves into the ultimate composition. Those elements that belong to, go with the newly discovered center of things, dress-parade themselves almost in military fashion. A hierarchy is established, a grouping assembles; the elected angels now march precisely, each in his place, to their appointed position in the logical development. The excess falls away, unwanted; but many blocks, formerly remote and having little apparent relevance, now become basic and shine with new importance.

This is how it was necessary, destined, the critic now sees. Was it a push or a pull that produced the novel togetherness? Like the cosmos, this is a metaphysical mystery. The angels walking up and down Jacob's ladder, in their dream choreography—were they pushed from behind toward an unfolding climax or were they attracted by the luminous presence at the top of the ladder? Do "things" shape themselves organically to an open end or do the ends shape them? For a critic it seems both, a push-pull; but it is really the click-click that matters to him. Such a critical method appears to be hard work, a reader observes silently; why bother? One must savor the process to judge its value.

The second beat, which we have been attempting to describe, comes to fruition in what Kenneth Burke has aptly called "the chordal collapse," which represents a unified sounding of all the relevant, individual notes of the chord that have been struck during the "arpeggio" that has led up to the collapse. I call it the third beat or *the critical proposition*. It is a treasure that has been mined; and it has been arrived at through an inductive process, an empirical building up, as it were, of layer upon layer of meaning, as a composer builds up the richness of a musical texture by successive platforms of tonalities. When the chordal collapse has been discovered, the critic ought to sound it at once, as quickly as possible, in his address to his readers. It sets the dominant tone, the resonant feeling of his piece at the very outset, declaring unequivocally, and with authority, what the critical communication is all about. And in his development of the composition, the critic unfolds the arpeggio, the constituent elements of the chordal collapse, *in reverse* and *deductively*. Thus, in retrospect, he recaptures the basic notes of the chord: and we should not be surprised to find that they are three in number—the tonic, the perfect third, and the perfect fifth of the major.

Carried along on the arpeggio are any number of "minor" or lesser variations. To the critic, who knows the chordal collapse and the notes that went into it, the arpeggio (the "angels") will now constitute a descending action on the ladder; to the reader, it will appear to be making an ascent—a climbing up; and the penetration to new levels, plateaus, or dimensions will seem an unfolding, a widening of the lens, a reaching out to more inclusive generalizations. Thus the reader should, in a manner of speaking, retrace the inductive course which the critic has run, but which he is now replaying deductively. Sometimes it happens that the critic, in the deductive act of stating the chordal collapse and developing the arpeggio, discovers a yet more inclusive meaning or critical proposition at the very end of the actual writing of his composition. He may then go back and begin again with this new and higher chordal collapse; or he may be content to leave the ascent open-ended, suggestive, for the reader's rumination. This is a matter of critic's choice.

CHAPTER THREE

From Process to Ethics

IN THE PREVIOUS CHAPTER, I described the ideal working of the method of my "theory of criticism." One often falls short of the ideal, and the critique is flawed, when measured against the model. The rewards are greatest, both for the critic and the reader, when the specifications are met. A trained observer in the sciences would, I trust, adopt a kindly tolerance for the use of the word "theory" as applied to the notions here given of criticism. "Theory" is an awesome word; one associates it with profound thought, empirical care and validity and verification. I use the word with modest intentions yet with confidence. My ideas about criticism are still evolving; but they constitute an attempt to make a generalization, a synthesis about the work of a critic of the mass media.

Loren Eiseley, writing about Charles Darwin in *Lives of Science,* said:

> Almost every great scientific generalization is a supreme act of creative synthesis. There comes a time when an accumulation of smaller discoveries and observations can be combined in some great and comprehensive view of nature. At this point the need is not so much for increased numbers of facts as for a mind of great insight capable of taking the assembled information and rendering it intelligible. Such a synthesis represents the scientific mind at its highest point of achieve-

ment. The stature of the discoverer is not diminished by the fact that he has slid into place the last piece of a tremendous puzzle on which many others have worked. To finish the task he must see correctly over a vast and diverse array of data.

If we scale down the magnitude of this description to an appropriate level for the discussion of mass media criticism, Eiseley's comments may be usefully applied. People say that they have a theory about something when they attempt to explain it by referring to some essential organizing principle. Philosophers of science build complex and very specialized structures of thought when they elucidate theory-building.

I have noted in my reading many definitions of theorizing; but I will quote here from Abraham Kaplan's *The Conduct of Inquiry* a few sentences which get to the heart of the matter so far as my own use of the word "theory" is concerned:

A theory is a way of making sense of a disturbing situation so as to allow us most effectively to bring to bear our repertoire of habits, and even more important, to modify habits or discard them altogether, replacing them by new ones as the situation demands . . .

To engage in theorizing means not just to learn by experience but to take thought about what is there to be learned . . .

A theory is more than a synopsis of moves that have been played in the game of nature; it also sets forth some idea of the rules of the game, by which the moves become intelligible . . .

A theory must somehow fit God's world, but in an important sense it creates a world of its own . . .

The acceptability of a theory will in any case be a matter of degree—more or less weight will be assigned to it, and it will always have a more or less limited range of justified application . . .

The value of a theory lies not only in the answers it gives but also in the new questions it raises . . .

Theory systemizes and unifies our knowledge. Kurt Lewin's metaphor is, I think, particularly apt: "The ultimate goal is

to establish a network of highways and superhighways, so
that any important point may be linked with any other."

When I advance my alleged theory of criticism under the
umbrella of the above generalizations about theory-building, I suppose that I am suggesting notions along the following lines. I am
attempting, first of all, to understand and to be able to explain just
what is going on when someone criticizes an object or reads a criticism. I want that explanation to be coherent, to correspond with as
wide a range of observable or imagined data as is possible. I want,
if I wish to make a judgment, to be able to give sufficient grounds
for that judgment, to defend it. If I say that a thing is good, bad,
or indifferent, I want to know just why it is one of these three. I
want to be able to tell the reader how he can discriminate between
the so-called bad and good, in the esthetic realm, the moral, the
political, the social, and so forth.

Now, if I wish to do this in any thoughtful manner (note that
I do not say "serious" manner; for playfulness and mental, even
physiological, fun, are important components of criticism as I understand it) I have to have what the philosophers call *a theory of
value*. But judgment, in my view, is merely one small step in authentic criticism: a theory of value must go deeper and find a ground
in *a theory of being*; in other words, you have to enter into the
metaphysical labyrinths of the mind and decide for yourself what
is real and what is not, what is meaningful and what is not. The
"oughtness" of a thing is inextricably bound up with the "isness"
of it—whether that "isness" be a matter of appearances, as with
Plato's concept of sense testimony, or of divine, eternal essences, as
the great image-maker of Socrates believed, or of a dynamic, evolutionary ascent, never-ending, of parts to wholes to even greater
complexities, and so on, *ad infinitum*—as if ultimate truth were a
pair of parallel tracks that did meet at the horizon, only to cross
and assume once again their parallel lines and directions.

Strike a critic who has gone down into the valley of values and
descended into the pit of being, and you collide with an attitude
that rings solidly. Strike one who hasn't taken the time or the trouble
to relate his criticism to his values and to his notions of reality, and
you mush around in shifting sand. The hardness of the first strike,

doubling back on your own penetration, will set up a tension. If you stand upon a rock yourself, the clash will be invigorating; if your foundation shifts with the sand, you may be overwhelmed—which is not a contest, and not much fun. Or you may be frightened by the response and quit the connection, sacrificing what you might have gained, if not further loosening the grains of sand upon which you uncertainly stand.

That the most learned, perhaps the wisest men have been engaged, at empyrean levels of intellect, in wrestling with the thus-far humanly unfathomable problems of the nature and the meaningfulness of reality; that they have been at the job for at least twenty-five hundred years since Pythagoras, Xenophanes, Socrates, Plato, and Aristotle undertook the Western world's first recorded gropings into science and metaphysics; and that the modern inheritors of their tradition of intellectual inquiry are still merely unraveling the first threads of possible first principles—all this should intimidate no one. In the end, every man who attempts to think must deal with the same problems and find his own answers. Men of more adequate credentials ought, surely by now, to have enlisted for the job of relating the field of epistemology to the mass media. That they have not done so is in itself an incitation to fools to enter where wise men disdain to go.

Perhaps inadequacy will blaze a small trail for more qualified minds to enter the forest. In any case, this effort is addressed to anybody anywhere who has taken some thought about the matter at first hand, and wants to share something—even degrees of ignorance. The tentative propositions offered about criticism in this book are not those of a professionally trained philosopher. No systematic discipline produced these assertions except, perhaps, the discipline of two decades of just having to compose critical pieces regularly, weekly, for a demanding audience. The field has fascinated me and drawn me deeper and deeper into its radiating forces —to question, to seek out, to cogitate upon. If more competent critics or students of criticism can find here any food for contemplation, that will be satisfactory. If not, I will be only half disappointed. I am trying to make, as they say in the trade, a contribution.

There are multitudes of critics and a healthy variety of methods of focusing attention on literary or artistic products in order to extract from them the gold of pleasure, or richer appreciation, or support for various ideological positions in the realms of economics, government, and religion. The reader who has not read widely in literary criticism should be warned at this point that there are thoughtful critics who take a dim view of all this talk of values, of theories of being, and of metaphysics. A critic should confine himself, they assert, to what he can find in the thing that is before him to criticize. You don't have to know anything about what comes before or goes after it. Concentrate on "it"; that's all. Other thoughtful critics maintain that putting esthetics together with politics, sociology, religion, or any other field is nonsense, confusing, unfruitful —and anyway no one critic has the necessary intellectual equipment to deal with such a rich variety of subjects.

T. S. Eliot, who practiced both the crafts of poetry and criticism, developed attitudes toward criticism that shifted, from time to time, among the lodestones of the field. In 1956, for example, in *The Frontiers of Criticism* he said:

> We can therefore ask, about any writing which is offered to us as literary criticism, is it aimed toward understanding and enjoyment? If it is not, it may still be a legitimate and useful activity; but it is to be judged as a contribution to psychology, or sociology, or logic, or pedagogy, or some other pursuit— and is to be judged by specialists, not men of letters . . .
>   If in literary criticism, we place all emphasis upon understanding, we are in danger of slipping from understanding to mere explanation. We are in danger even of pursuing criticism as if it was a science, which it never can be. If, on the other hand, we overemphasize enjoyment, we will tend to fall into the subjective and impressionistic, and our enjoyment will profit us no more than mere amusement and pastime.

In 1961, however, while Eliot still held to a distinction between "pure literary criticism" and "other types of criticism," he made the following statement (in *To Criticize the Critic*):

> I have suggested also that it is impossible to fence off *literary* criticism from criticism on other grounds, and that moral,

religious and social judgments cannot be wholly excluded. That they can, and that literary merit can be estimated in complete isolation, is the illusion of those who believe that literary merit alone can justify the publication of a book which could otherwise be condemned on moral grounds.

If the poet who wrote *The Waste Land* refused to place a fence around literary criticism, which concerns itself with works that aspire to be art, how can one justify a type of criticism directed at the "vast wasteland" of broadcasting which isolates that phenomenon from the great web of society that radiates both into and out of it? A neat thrust at the kind of criticism offered in this book was delivered by Richard Poirier, writing in the *New Republic* (May 20, 1967). Though the following excerpt deals with Eliot's poetry, I do not hesitate to apply it to his works of criticism as well. It suggests another interesting possible stance for a critic who chooses none of the critical tracks of understanding, enjoyment, or socially oriented communication, and who insists on avoiding any rigorous, demanding, hard-think approach to criticism:

> [Eliot's] poetry is about the difficulty of conceiving anything. Never merely expressive of ideas already successfully shaped in the mind, his poems enact the mind's effort even to form an idea . . . This Eliot . . . is secure in "the kind of pattern we perceive in our lives only at rare moments of inattention and detachment, drowsing . . . in sunlight." Eliot exists for understanding at an impossible remove, perhaps from the kind of mind, the liberal-orthodox mind of the "new" as much as any old left, for whom thinking and even suffering, consists in the abrasions of one abstraction on another.

Another attack, a delightful one, on the sort of criticism that we offer is made by C. S. Lewis in *An Experiment in Criticism*. Lewis believes in the value of "the primary literary experience." "A system," he writes, "which heads us off from abstraction by being centred on literature in operation is what we need." With this value uppermost in his scheme, he attacks what he calls "the Vigilant school of critics":

To them criticism is a form of social and ethical hygiene.
They see all clear thinking, all sense of reality, and all fineness
of living, threatened on every side by propaganda, by adver-
tisement, by film and television. The hosts of Midian "prowl
and prowl around."

They labor to promote the sort of literary experience that
they think good; but their conception of what is good in
literature makes a seamless whole with their total conception
of the good life. Their whole scheme of values . . . is engaged
in every critical act.

Nothing is for [the Vigilants] a matter of taste. They admit
no such realm of experience as the aesthetic. There is for them
no specifically literary work. A work, or a single passage,
cannot for them be good in any sense unless it is good simply,
unless it reveals attitudes which are essential elements in the
good life. You must therefore accept their [implied] conception
of the good life if you are to accept their criticism. That is, you
can admire them as critics only if you also revere them as
sages.

Lewis suspends judgment as to the good this school can do,
but he sees signs that it can do harm. I would agree with his warning against the critic's "armed and suspicious approach . . . the
dragon watch with unenchanted eye," that is determined not to
yield or surrender to any possibly meretricious appeal; but his approach to criticism leaves me dissatisfied: he fails to state his ultimate
ground of being whereupon he builds his theory of value in criticism. The end of literature, he argues, is the extension of "the
privilege of individuality." "In reading great literature I become a
thousand men and yet remain myself," he asserts. "I transcend myself; and am never more myself than when I do." Transcendence,
to be sure, is an element in the business of dialectics; but Lewis
fails to say *why* transcendence is good, except that it "feels good."
I would disagree and argue that the psychological test is insufficient.
Lewis, I believe, senses this insufficiency, but he is content to leave
the question of the *value* of any activity—as distinguished from the
activity itself—"to what Aristotle would call 'a more architectonic
inquiry . . .'" Lewis then adds:

We must not "take too much upon ourselves." There may even be a disadvantage in bringing to our experience of good and bad reading a fully informed theory as to the nature and status of the literary good. We may be tempted to fake the experiences so as to make them support our theory. The more specifically literary our observations are, the less they are contaminated by a theory of value, the more useful they will be to the architectonic inquirer.

I am aware that, in the previous chapter, in the discussion of how Darwin found his third beat—natural selection as the causative agent of evolution—I said that he accepted his discovery as the end of his search because the notion of natural selection felt "good" to him. "Sufficient unto the critic," I added, "is the insight that makes him 'feel good.'" Why, then, do I now find Lewis' good feeling to be an insufficient test of his argument in favor of strictly literary criticism? The answer, I venture, is that Lewis has merely asserted the usefulness of "specifically literary" observations to the architectonic inquirer, without justifying this new proposition. He has, in short, begged the ultimate question. He could, of course, respond that the new proposition "feels good" too, but this would lead down an endless road of good feelings. The right mix is not only the psychological satisfaction that is produced by an elegant proposition but also the statement of that satisfaction combined with some dialectical taking into account of contradiction.

To all theorists of criticism who follow roads other than the "architectonic" one mapped out in this book, I say welcome to your private compartments as you journey, and a fervent romance between you and your readers. The world of criticism is wide enough to contain many gardens; I hoe my own. I do not, after this fashion, however, subscribe to the notion of inevitable relativism in criticism. Karl Popper, in *The Open Society and Its Enemies* (Vol. II), has dealt with this controversy so well, in my opinion, that to illustrate my point I will quote him at some length:

> So each of us sees his gods, and his world, from his own point of view, according to his tradition and his upbringing; and none of us is exempt from this subjective bias . . . Thus it is of the

utmost importance . . . to give up cocksureness, and become
open to criticism. Yet it is also of the greatest importance not to
mistake this discovery, this step towards criticism, for a step
towards relativism. If two parties disagree, this may mean that
one is wrong, or the other, or both: this is the view of the
criticist. It does not mean, as the relativist will have it, that
both may be right. They may be equally wrong, no doubt,
though they need not be. But anybody who says that to be
equally wrong means to be equally right is merely playing with
words, or with metaphors . . . Thus self-criticism should not be
an excuse for laziness and for the adoption of relativism. And
as two wrongs do not make a right, two wrong parties to a
dispute do not make two right parties.

If there is such a thing as a final critic of critics, an ultimate
critic at the end of an infinite regress of critics—the eschatological
critic, if you will—he will say who is right and who is wrong. Meanwhile, in my view of criticism, it is not so important to be right as
it is to say: "Right or wrong, this is my sense of right; I am ready to
teach and to learn from your own sense of right in a joyous critical
dialectic. Let us see what we have to give each other in our approximations of truth, questing for ever closer approximations." And to
attain these closer approximations, it is necessary for the critic to
cross and recross many bridges; to traverse the networks and super
highways that Kurt Lewin mentioned—in short, to inquire into
ever widening sets of relationships.

This is why, in my concept of criticism, esthetics cannot be
split off from morality or economics or government or metaphysics.
If I am to be consistent, and if my theory of criticism calls for
criticism as a way of life, why, then my concept of criticism must
be bold enough to encompass all of life to the limit of my present
capacity to reflect it. And this is particularly why criticism of television and radio, or mass media criticism—because broadcasting is
increasing its predominance over all mass media—this is why mass
media criticism must, with modesty but with courage and daring,
touch all the human bases that it can possibly use. For television
and radio today everywhere in the world are the total human environment, the mental ecological field where mankind's destiny is

being shaped. Let the intellectual who despises and scorns television and radio as the pablum of the comic-strip masses, ignore them as he will and fix his gaze on more noble objects of attention—yet the commonalities as well as the particularities of his life are impinged upon by the mercurial power of these media.

The world is being globalized and homogenized by the electromagnetic culture: this is a common observation, readily verified. Governments rise and fall on media images; international relations are affected; aspirations are fired and visions accommodated and contained by the controllers of the media in every country. When you look at or hear a single program or a short newscast, you are in the presence of a system, a network of interests, actions, and conflicts that involves every sector of humanity today. The "touch-points" in this web may be closer for citizens of the industrialized nations than they are for people who inhabit the materially poorer parts of the planet (nations that we euphemistically call "underdeveloped"); but the relentless enterprise of the owners and managers of the world's advancing communications technology (soft as well as hardware) is swiftly closing the gaps between the points. In Marshall McLuhan's terms, the "implosion" of the international message-systems, doubling back on the originators, is rapidly overtaking the "explosions," the outward reaches themselves.

To gaze upon this dynamic complexity and to delimit one's attention to merely the esthetic (or any other single aspect of it) is to indulge one's passion for precision and particularity (an undeniable right)—but, in my view of criticism, it is analogous to flicking a piece of lint off a seamless garment. Two thousand years of literary criticism in western thought, it must be said, have much to give to the mass media critic by way of introduction to his special problems; but literary criticism, unfortunately, generally shuns television and radio. The men in history who weighed matters of taste, value, nobility, and delight in the scales of literary criticism were elites addressing themselves to elite audiences. They rode like petals on the crests of waves of non-reading multitudes in the seas of illiteracy.

The mass media are phenomena that transcend even the broad worlds of literature. They call for the discovery of new laws, new relationships, new insights into drama, ritual, and mythology, into the engagement of minds in a context where psychological sensations are deliberately produced for non-imaginative ends, where audiences are created, cultivated, and maintained for sale, where they are trained in nondiscrimination and hypnotized by the mechanical illusion of delight. When the symbols that swirl about the planet Earth are manufactured by artists who have placed their talents at the disposition of salesmen, criticism must at last acknowledge that "literature" has been transcended, and that the dialectics of evolutionary action have brought the art to a new level of practice and significance.

Perhaps the critics of tomorrow, who have been nurtured at the altar of the television idol worshiped in living rooms around the globe, will come more naturally and deliberately to the task of criticizing the mass media. I have long hoped that critics with more notable credentials would address themselves to the critical quantum leap that mankind has made with the creation of the mass media; but I have come slowly to realize that the phenomenon is too new for anyone to have acquired the requisite credentials. Exploring critically the mass media is exploring mankind, in an atmosphere far more pregnant for human destiny than the lunar landscape. Unlike the astronauts, the author was not chosen to make his exploration—he volunteered. If not capacity, then at least audacity.

I know intimately the process of criticism that I have described. I have endured its agonies and relished its satisfactions. In the beginning it was far less painful—and, if memory does not cheat me, less rewarding. In fact, it was easy; I enjoyed it. As I worked at it, learning my trade, finding out new things about the craft, it became progressively more difficult but also more satisfying. It is entirely possible that the whole edifice that I have reared in my mind is merely the consequence of a mechanical, technical necessity—namely, the fact that, in writing for a magazine which operates on an eighteen-day deadline for manuscript copy, I was faced with special problems. A television critic, reviewing or "covering for the record" a program, writes and thinks differently, on a daily basis, from a critic who knows that when his critique finally appears in print, the event that inspired it will probably have receded down the horizon of the past almost beyond the memory of most readers. Much of what television broadcasts is as ephemeral as it is trivial. Fairly sophisticated readers who wish to keep in touch with a medium that they rarely watch demand to be told what is significant; and since space is at a premium, they must be told in pressurized columns of print, tersely.

The requirement, in the critic's mind, that he say something worthy of the reader's attention, something beyond the mere "record" of a television event, or even beyond a judgment of it (for mostly it is a case of "who cares?")—this requirement undoubtedly was the force that impelled me, in writing my critiques, to practice the discipline of "thinking beyond," of groping for the uncommon vision: and the consequence of the discipline was the gradual development in my mind of my critical theory and method. It may be said that the opportunities for the expression of such critical thinking about the mass media are very limited in today's market of ideas; at best, the whole business may have only an exotic interest for a very small group of critics-in-being. I believe, however, that the market will grow larger. I am optimistic about the future of criticism. I see public understanding of the mass media in a technological society standing today at about the same point, comparatively speaking, where the public understanding of the economic theory of society stood when Marx and Engels fashioned their critiques of capitalism.

Ideas have their ripeness historically: the time for criticism is, I hope, coming soon. If this coming is an illusion—if Marcuse, in his more pessimistic moments, is right, and if the containment of the critical spirit will grow more repressive and universal as the rationality of a technological mass civilization marches side by side with the myth of equality, with control of mass message-systems concentrated in the hands of elites, of exclusively economically motivated managers in an iron hierarchy—then criticism must more and more stand upon the Great Refusal, the negation of the negation, however few the refusers and the negators. Those who are born to be critics will never be content with idling motors. There is always the waiting energy of the critical mass. As for my own theory of value and of being, and as for my criteria for the judgment of the "good," these will become plainer in the pages that follow, as I attempt to apply my notions of criticism to critiques which I have written. As I criticize my own criticism, I will try to overcome, to whatever degree is possible, the problems of subjectivity; and where possible, I will naturally benefit from my "inside" knowledge of the critic that I am criticizing—myself.

A book of this sort, if it be honest, cannot avoid being, to an appropriate degree, a confessional. Therefore I will say straightforwardly that the process of criticism which I have learned has "deepened" my life: it has made me a less dogmatic and a more inquiring person. It has exposed to me the illusion of "objectivity"; but it has, at the same time, compelled me to be more comprehensive and just, and to attempt—if not always to achieve—some degree of genuine compassion in the exercising of my privilege of dealing, in public discourse, with the works of people who have devoted their professional careers and energies to labor in the broadcasting industry. T. S. Eliot, in *To Criticize the Critic,* wrote, toward the end of his career:

> As the critic grows older his critical writings may be less fired
> by enthusiasm, but informed by wider interests, and, one hopes,
> by greater wisdom and humility.

CHAPTER FOUR

The Critic as an Agent for Change

I saw a third . . .

ONE ALMOST HEARS trumpets in this phrase, which begins line 508 of *The Rime of the Ancient Mariner*. Is it mere coincidence that the transcendent third occurs at this climactic moment in the narrative? I think not: it powerfully suggests to me the conscious intent of the poet. Study the poem carefully, and you will find that the explicit use of the third occurs most often at affirmative moments. It is an active third, a comprehensiveness embracing and overleaping dualities. Consider the actual setting of *The Rime of the Ancient Mariner*. The dreamlike adventure unfolds in the duality of two seas, the Pacific and the Atlantic. Prominent and of significance, I believe, in the mind of Coleridge, is the movement of the ship back and forth across "the line," the Equator. Geographically, the fate of the Mariner is affected suspensefully by the pendulum-like swing of the ship away from and toward the South Pole, as beneficent and revengeful spirits battle for the Mariner's life.

Coleridge's fascination with philosophy as well as poetry is fully documented not only in the events of his life (he studied transcendental philosophy in Germany, coming heavily under the influence of Kant's idealism) but also in his own philosophical writings. In the twelfth chapter of *Biographia Literaria,* his account of his literary life and of his poetic principles, he sketches a system of philosophy which he promises to elaborate and publish later (he never did). The sketch represents his ideas on the reconciliation of the objective and the subjective, the self and the other, the fusion of knowing and of being. The concepts of "the line" as a point of division, and of "the poles" as opposite tendencies which must be united—a triad—occur again and again. Speaking of "The spirit of sectarianism [which] has been hitherto our fault; and the cause of our failures," Coleridge writes: "We have imprisoned our own conceptions by the lines which we have drawn, in order to exclude the conceptions of others." And again:

> For if all knowledge has, as it were, two poles reciprocally required and presupposed, all sciences must tend towards the opposite as far as the equatorial point in which both are reconciled and become identical.

Critics who have seen in *The Rime of the Ancient Mariner* merely a horror-story, constructed by Coleridge purely as an act of the poetic imagination and reflecting no conscious philosophical or religious meaning, might have considered the possibility that his poetry and philosophy are two aspects of the same critical intelligence. The identical creative, critical problems are confronted repeatedly in his poems and his philosophical treatises, as well as in the lay sermons that Coleridge wrote. For him, as for others, wholeness is significance, containing but not obliterating particularity: the one and the many, the concrete and the universal. Indeed, the most humanly wrenching scene of *The Rime of the Ancient Mariner* occurs when this "third," this wholeness, is dramatically, tragically absent. In Part V of the poem, after the Mariner has blessed the water-snakes and, in immediate consequence, has been freed of the dead Albatross that his fellow crewmen hung about his neck; after he has slept and been refreshed by rain—then, the becalmed ship mysteriously begins to move again, and the bodies of his dead shipmates are reanimated by a troop of angelic spirits.

No breeze blows, but they work the ropes, this "ghastly crew"; and then, the Mariner tells the Wedding Guest:

> The body of my brother's son
> Stood by me, knee to knee:
> The body and I pulled at one rope,
> But he said nought to me.

Two are present, but there is no *communication* between them, no possibility for any transcendent third. Community has been lost; there is apartness without togetherness. It is a depth of social alienation more profound even than the sense of the abyss suggested by the lines:

> Alone, alone, all, all alone,
> Alone on a wide wide sea!
> And never a saint took pity on
> My soul in agony.

Humphry House, in *Coleridge,* his Clark Lectures, makes explicit the full meaning of the Mariner's apartness in his particular social context:

> This brings home, as nothing else does, the horror of the deaths, the violation of family ties which the action has involved; it dramatizes to the Mariner's consciousness the utter ruin of the merry, unified community which had set out on the voyage. The curse in the stony eyes (lines 636–41) is made far more appalling by this specially intimate experience of the fact that intimacy was forever gone.

"I saw a third . . ." The Mariner aboard the ghostly ship, his curse at last expiated, approaches home and the harbor bar. The triplet sounds:

> Is this the hill? is this the kirk?
> Is this mine own countree?

He sees a boat appear—the Pilot and the Pilot's boy: and then:

I saw a third—I heard his voice:
It is the Hermit good!
He singeth loud his godly hymns
That he makes in the wood.
He'll shrieve my soul, he'll wash away
The Albatross's blood.

The Rime of the Ancient Mariner is one of the three great poems that Coleridge wrote (*Kubla Khan* and *Christabel*). It continues to be enjoyed, studied, and evaluated as probably the greatest romantic poem written in English. A myriad of interpretations, critiques, and commentaries have been written on it. It is fascinating, ambiguously transpartent and obscure: therein lies one of its chief attractions. It invites every reader and critic to find in it whatever suits his own purposes. Biographical, Freudian, Jungian, biological, and mythico-symbolic patterns have been discovered in it. I hope that the reader will not take exception to another small addition to the interpretive chorus. Obviously, I have already found in the poem succulent food to feed my own purposes—and I will fatten on yet more—but at this point, the Hermit is the special object of my appetite.

He'll shrieve my soul, he'll wash away
The Albatross's blood.

If *The Rime of the Ancient Mariner* is understood—as it has been in many interpretations—as a myth of crime and punishment, then the Mariner's expectation of his relationship to the Hermit should give no one any pause. It is a confessional experience, pure and simple, a giving of absolution qualified by penance. This, to be sure, is the primary meaning of the word "shrieve," which, according to Webster, is a "pseudoarchaic version" of "shrive." But *The American Heritage Dictionary* ferrets out a much more interesting possibility, peculiarly adapted to our own purposes in the context of an explication of criticism. This dictionary includes an appendix which gives the Indo-European roots of many languages, including Sanskrit, English, German, Latin, Greek, and Russian. An assumption of the modern science of comparative linguistics is that the words of the Indo-European language group may be traced back to roots in proto-Indo-European, a common prehistoric language which is ancestor to all of them.

After listing the conventional definitions of "shrive," *The American Heritage Dictionary* says: "See *skeri*—in Appendix." When we do as we are told, we find that a "reconstruction" of the original root yields its basic meaning: "To cut, separate, sift." At once we are presented with cognate words which denote "description," words such as "scratch, write, ascribe, describe, transcribe." Further on we get such words as "sieve, riddle, crime and judgment," which would lead directly to the sense commonly ascribed to "shrieve" in the poem. But then the trail gives off a more intriguing scent as we find, from the Latin and Greek, such reconstructions as "decide, discern, secret," and finally, from the Greek again, "crisis, criterion and—*critic*" (italics RLS). Ultimately even the Russian is there, *krai*, meaning "edge, brink."

What have we here, then? Did the Mariner, when he thought to himself, of the Hermit, "He'll shrieve my soul . . ." expect that the godly man would do something different from, or more than, the act of giving him Christian, penitential comfort? Did Coleridge, in arcane fashion, hide his real understanding of the Hermit's role in the poem? Since the Mariner spoke his own mind only through the mind of the poet, we may fuse the two and speculate on Coleridge's intention—a single clear meaning of "confession," or a double meaning, the first part manifest, the second latent. Not a shred of evidence, so far as I know, exists for my peculiar speculation. Whether or not Coleridge had another meaning in mind, however, is of no moment: what is here being ventured is put forward entirely for my own purposes. The function of the Hermit, indeed, in the poem, was to play the role of *critic to the Mariner*.

In the small galaxy of meanings welling up from proto-Indo-European for the word "shrive" as traced back to *skeri*, its radical, original sense, we are struck, for our purposes, with the dialectical quality of all of them. In this microcosm we find a qualitative condensation of the macrocosm of dialectical criticism. First, there is the purely descriptive level—the symbolic event to be criticized. It comprises a coherent pattern, a concrete entity.

Then, the deeper meanings suggest the second beat, that of combinatory play, the antithesis to the first thesis. It is a taking apart, an analyzing, a seeking for relationships. The words "riddle" and "secret" suggest that there is a significance waiting to be discovered behind the confusing, disintegrated, fragmented but moving scene of sign-events in dynamic flux. And finally we have the decisive words, the chordal collapse of the third beat—"crisis, criterion, critic" —the sudden illumination, the "aha!" experience, the critical proposition. The Russian *krai*, with its meanings, "edge, brink," can be understood as a suggestion for "beyond," the tentative nature of the new discovery, susceptible of another diffusion, on its way to yet a higher step. We may hear in it an echo of the peculiarly Russian experience of apparently limitless steppes, stretching away to an unreachable horizon, dividing yet ever beckoning.

When the Mariner, rescued as in a dream from his ghostly ship which sinks in the harbor, finally comes ashore and cries to the Hermit, "O shrieve me, shrieve me, holy man!" may we not read his appeal as a dramatic statement of his intense need to grasp the significance, the "So what?" of his experience? An additional meaning derived from the Indo-European root, *skeri,* is that of "hypocrisy." This word suggests a feigning of reality, a falseness of appearance, a mask or a stage play, which is not what it appears to be. The Mariner, in confronting the Hermit, was hungering for "the point" of his strange adventures. His experience was more than "a sign"; it was "a sign-event," a concrete event which symbolized a purpose. "Divine that purpose," he entreated the Hermit.

In *Symbols and Values: An Initial Study,* John E. Smith provides an analogy to the critical process in his description of how two persons, trying to communicate with each other, must use symbols understood by both to bridge the "chasm which exists between two selves":

> This can be done only through a dialectical process lasting through time in which each self attempts to understand the meanings and intentions of others by reading their symbolic expressions.

We may say that a dialectical process of criticism is set in motion between the Hermit and the Mariner when the latter makes his request for clarification, for tracing relationships, for "thinking beyond" his experience. This is an extrinsic dyad: but the dialectical process may also go on in one person's mind, between ego and alter ego. In this sense, we could conceive of the Hermit and the Wedding Guest as one person seeking the significance of a sign-event. In Coleridge's poem, the characters are never presented in detailed human dimension; they are superficially representative, functionally identified—the Mariner, the Wedding Guest, the Hermit, the Pilot, the Pilot's boy.

In the context of our chain reaction of critical motors revving at different speeds, some faster, some slower, the Wedding Guest is the critical energy at its lowest, most common level; he is introduced, symbolically, at the Wedding Feast. One is reminded of the unflattering, elitist description of the common man in Plato's *Republic,* Book IX, in which he speaks, through Socrates, of "the life of the many, . . . their pleasures mixed with pains":

> Those then [says Socrates to Glaucon] who know not wisdom
> and virtue, and are always busy with gluttony and sensuality,
> go down and up again as far as the mean; and in this region
> they move at random throughout life, but they never pass into
> the true upper world; thither they neither look, nor do they
> ever find their way, neither are they truly filled with true being,
> nor do they taste of pure and abiding pleasure . . . For they
> fill themselves with that which is not substantial, and the part
> of them which they fill is also unsubstantial and incontinent.

The Mariner, we may assume, was the Socratic equivalent, more or less, of the Wedding Guest—that is, *before* his voyage. Coleridge never mentions the cargo or the destination of the ship— it is immaterial to his intentions—but the poem contains evidence which suggests that the crew was a representative company of sailors, in some medieval time, bent on a normal, this-worldly, commercial venture. After the voyage, the Mariner is a different man, shaken in spirit; and he will, in turn, shake the Wedding Guest with his compelling, disturbing narrative. The Hermit is the third— a critical motor revving at a higher level than that of either the Wedding Guest or the post-voyage Mariner. There are three, also, in the boat that approaches the doomed ship: the Pilot's boy, the Pilot, and the Hermit. Here, too, we may ascribe to the trio an ascending order of critical energy: the first (youth); the second (maturity); and the third (wisdom). Let us examine Coleridge's description of the Hermit, as the Mariner pictures him to the Wedding Guest:

> This Hermit good lives in that wood
> Which slopes down to the sea.
> How loudly his sweet voice he rears!
> He loves to talk with Marineres
> That come from a far countree.
>
> He kneels at morn, and noon, and eve—
> He hath a cushion plump:
> It is the moss that wholly hides
> The rotted old oak-stump.

On its face, this is a quick drawing of a medieval holy man, an ascetic, given to the meditative life. But this is no "solitary" man. He has not chosen the path of withdrawal from the world. He lives, Coleridge specifies, "in that wood/ Which slopes down to the sea. . . . He loves to talk with Marineres/ That come from a far countree." The wood which slopes down to the sea suggests "the line," the equatorial point on the mental map, where opposites meet to be reconciled. It is a port, a place of entry and exit; it indicates a busy place. In the language of cybernetics and modern systems theory, it is "an open system." Gordon W. Allport, in *The Open System in Personality Theory*, pieces together four criteria for an open system, after combing the alternatives:

> There is intake and output of both matter and energy; there is the achievement and maintenance of steady (homeostatic) states, so that the intrusion of outer energy will not seriously disrupt internal form and order; there is generally an increase of order over time, owing to an increase in complexity and differentiation of parts; finally, at least at the human level, there is more than mere intake and output of matter and

energy: there is *extensive transactional commerce with the environment.* (italics RLS)

The Hermit is a "relational" man. He is well grounded in his own faith—this critic's theories of value and of being are clearly conceptualized—but he represents an adaptive system. Edward Sapir, in *Encyclopedia of the Social Sciences,* writes that such systems are "characterized by a great deal of shifting variety" ("booming, buzzing confusion"):

> While we often speak of society as though it were a static structure defined by tradition, it is, in the more intimate sense, nothing of the kind, but a highly intricate network of partial or complete understandings between the members of organizational units of every degree of size and complexity . . . It is only apparently a static sum of social institutions; actually it is being reanimated or creatively reaffirmed from day to day by particular acts of a communicative nature which obtain among individuals participating in it.

Our critic-Hermit loves to talk; and his voice may be loud but it is also "sweet" (an adjective which all critics will modestly acknowledge as accurate and appropriate). The partners of his perpetual dialogue are "mariners," and the tales that they tell, the cargoes that they bring, are discoveries, some familiar, some rare. These tales must be examined, sorted, combined, and recombined: and the end of the dialogue is to make them yield up their hidden treasures of sudden illumination, of reality reconstructed, of novel togetherness. The Hermit's tool is the question. To the Mariner's cry for shriving, his instant response gets to the crux of the matter:

> "Say quick," quoth he, "I bid thee say—
> What manner of man art thou?"

In literary criticism of *The Rime of the Ancient Mariner*, the Hermit's demand has been interpreted as his fear that the strange figure fallen to its knees before him may be a drowned body reanimated by a demon or by the Devil himself perhaps, as the Pilot's boy suggested when the Mariner, awakening as if from the dead to find himself in the boat, seized the oars and began to row toward shore. For me it purports a different meaning: "I observe the appearance," the Hermit may be said to declare, "but I demand the reality, the core, the inner significance of the outer symbol that I perceive with my optical sight: I want the in-sight, the secret of the unique identity of the experience that lies behind the deceptive mask of its outer appearances." Coleridge, in his *Biographia Literaria*, gives his masterly account of the principle of penetration beyond the surface appearance of things, when he contrasts "nature" with "intelligence":

> The necessary tendency therefore of all natural philosophy is from nature to intelligence; and this, and no other, is the true ground and occasion of the instinctive striving to introduce theory into our views of natural phenomena. The highest perfection of natural philosophy would consist in the perfect spiritualization of all the laws of nature into the laws of intuition and intellect . . . Thence it comes that . . . the more the principle of law breaks forth, the more does the husk drop off . . .

Coleridge's philosophical and religious explorations throughout his life constituted his effort to equatorialize the two poles of reason and love. It was Coleridge, we must remember, who originally commented that all men are born either Platonists or Aristotelians; and though he veered often, in this dyad, from one pole to another (as thinking men often do), in the final reckoning there is no doubt into which camp he fell. His idealism, his sense of something beyond the natural world (reflected not only in the supernatural powers that he personified in his poems, but also in the Christian sense of an "intelligence" beyond nature) marked him a transcendentalist, a vitalist in the tradition which led from Plato through the Neoplatonists, the Christian mystics, and Kant to Bergson, Santayana, and Whitehead, as opposed to the more skeptical tradition of Democritus, Bacon, Locke, Hume, Voltaire, and Bertrand Russell.

The Hermit then, we are insisting, symbolizes the critical

spirit at its highest, scrutinizing the object of criticism—in this instance, the Mariner's experiences. The experiences, by themselves, may be understood; they may even be interpreted or commented upon; but the term "criticism" is reserved exclusively for the primary function of discovering and indicating significance: and this is done by relating, transacting, as it were, the sign-events to larger contexts, and evoking from the dialectical inter-subjectivity—the emergent uniqueness or the critical symbol behind the events. The area between the sign-events and the culminating symbol in *The Rime of the Ancient Mariner* is not elaborated. We are given only the first and the third; the second beat is missing. Do I deliberately press my purposes a bit too far when I find this second domain, the searching for connections, suggested in the verse that follows the Hermit's question to the Mariner: "What manner of man art thou?"

> Forthwith this frame of mine was wrenched
> With a woeful agony,
> Which forced me to begin my tale;
> And then it left me free.

What was the "freedom" that the Mariner found if not the *significance* of his tale? Coleridge does not immediately give that significance: he reserves it for a later, more climactic moment— namely, the Mariner's transmittal, in an ongoing chain of knowing and acting, of the significant discovery that the Hermit made. The Mariner repeats the tale to the Wedding Guest, but this time its point is "seen" and expressed succinctly. That wrenching, "woeful agony" suggests the ordeal of the second beat, for which Coleridge himself coined a name that has never resonated in literary criticism: "esemplastic power," meaning "molding into unity." It occurs as a one-line preface to the thirteenth chapter in *Biographia Literaria,* where the poet briefly states his much-quoted distinction between "fancy" and "imagination," affording the former a lesser function in poetry than the latter. For "poetry," in our context, read "criticism"; and the pertinence is unqualified. Coleridge prefaces his terse definitions of fancy and imagination with a three-page discussion whose substance is usually not given in anthologies of English poetry and criticism; it is of such stimulating importance to my own theory of criticism that I will pay some careful attention to it.

First, Coleridge affixes to the head of the chapter some lines from Milton's *Paradise Lost* (Book V). I quote the lines here in full, and invite the reader to say whether or not Coleridge recognized, or discovered, in them his own sense of the three-beat rhythm and process of creation:

> O Adam! One Almighty is, from whom
> All things proceed, and up to him return
> If not depraved from good; created all
> Such to perfection, one first nature all
> Indued with various forms, various degrees
> Of substance, and in things that live, of life;
> But more refin'd, more spiritous and pure,
> As nearer to him placed or nearer tending,
> Each in their several active spheres assign'd,
> Till body up to spirit work, in bounds
> Proportion'd to each kind. So from the root
> Springs lighter the green stalk; from thence the leaves
> More airy: last, the bright consummate flower
> Spirits odorous breathes. Flowers and their fruit,
> Man's nourishment by gradual scale sublim'd,
> To *vital* spirits aspire: to animal:
> To intellectual!—give both life and sense,
> Fancy and understanding: whence the soul
> Reason receives, and reason is her *being*,
> Discursive or intuitive . . . (italics in original)

Coleridge then begins the body of the chapter with these words:

> Des Cartes, speaking as a naturalist, and in imitation of Archimedes, said, Give me matter and motion and I will construct you the universe. We must of course understand him to have meant, will render the construction of the universe intelligible.

In the three ideas "matter, motion, and the intelligibility of the universe" we find the critical triad.

Coleridge then speaks of the dynamic interaction of the three ideas, in this fashion:

> Now the transcendental philosophy demands, first, that two forces should be conceived which counteract each other by their essential nature ... The problem will then be to discover the result or product of two such forces ... When we have formed a scheme or outline of these two different kinds of force, and of their different results by the process of discursive reasoning, it will then remain for us to elevate the Thesis from notional to actual, by contemplating intuitively this one power with its two inherent indestructible yet counteracting forces, and the results or generations to which their interpenetration gives existence, in the living principle and in the process of our own self-consciousness. By what instrument this is possible the solution itself will discover, at the same time it will reveal to and from whom it is possible.

Then he concludes that the power acting in the two forces is

> ... inexhaustibly re-ebullient; and as something must be the result of these two forces ... and as rest or neutralization cannot be the result; no other conception is possible, but that the product must be a *tertium aliquid* ... Now this *tertium aliquid* can be no other than an interpenetration of the counteracting powers, partaking of both.

Summarizing the three pages from *Biographia Literaria*, we find provocative evidence of a critical theory which involves the one and the many, singularity and plurality, a process of creation which is dialectical in nature, and an explosion that is intuitively generated from the collision of the dialectical forces into a reconstituting idea, a third beat, which recombines the generating forces in a novel togetherness. "Matter, motion, and intelligibility"—in terms of *The Rime of the Ancient Mariner,* the Mariner's raw experiences constitute the matter; the motion is embodied in his dialectical collision with the Hermit-critic, a collision which has as its goal the discovery of the "tertium aliquid," the third beat, "inexhaustibly re-ebullient," that is, capable of being further recombined, related, exploded, and so on, in the infinite chain reaction of the organismic, critical sense of life. In explaining his "esemplastic power," which he also called "the imagination," Coleridge reiterates the threefold, ascending order of creativity and criticism. He splits "imagination" into two phases, and relates both to "fancy."

Fancy is at the lowest level, the material level, the level of raw experience. Fancy, says Coleridge, "has no other counters to play with but fixities and definites," the flux of the senses immediately, sensuously perceived, fragmented, and divided, a buzzing, confounding confusion. When concentrated in a sign-event, an object in space and time, a target for the critical faculty, fancy appears to have coherence, but it is a mask hiding significance. Fancy can only manipulate "fixities and definites." Its cell-firing potential is of the "mechanic" variety. The secondary level of the imagination (the esemplastic power molding into unity) begins to move, in Milton's words, the "body up to spirit . . . in bounds proportion'd to each kind . . ." It is matter infused with motion. Coleridge says of it:

> It dissolves, diffuses, dissipates, in order to recreate; or where this process is rendered impossible, yet still, at all events, it struggles to idealize and to unify. It is essentially *vital*, even as all objects (*as* objects) are essentially fixed and dead.

Again, in a lecture on Shakespeare, Coleridge speaks of the secondary power of the imagination, the dialectical phase, in these words:

> Still mounting, we find undoubted proof in his [Shakespeare's] mind of imagination, or the power by which one image or feeling is made to modify many others and by a sort of *fusion to force many* into one . . .

His most detailed account of the creative-critical process is given in Chapter XIV of *Biographia Literaria*:

The poet, described in *ideal* perfection . . . diffuses a tone and spirit of unity that blends and (as it were) *fuses,* each into each, by that synthetic and magical power to which we have exclusively appropriated the name of imagination. This power reveals itself in the balance or reconciliation of opposite or discordant qualities; of sameness, with difference; of the general, with the concrete; the idea, with the image; the individual, with the representative; the sense of novelty and freshness, with old and familiar objects; a more than usual state of emotion, with more than usual order; judgment ever awake and steady self-possession, with enthusiasm and feeling profound or vehement . . .

The process, finally, is analogous to continuous process, which is God's creation, as Coleridge implied in commenting on the third and highest level of the ascending order:

The primary IMAGINATION I hold to be the living power and prime agent of all human perception, and as a repetition in the finite mind of the eternal act of creation in the infinite I AM.

If the infinite resonates in the finite, if the ideal unity is the mystery and secret of disparate multiplicity, then it is the universal which is exploded from the singular by the critic. Coleridge writes:

The medium by which spirits understand each other is not the surrounding air, but the freedom which they possess in common, as the common ethereal element of their being, *the tremulous reciprocations of which propagate themselves even to the inmost of the soul.* (italics RLS)

What was it, we may ask, which gave the Hermit-critic the power to perceive in the Mariner's adventures the unifying notion which left him "free"? Delving again into the proto-Indo-European root of the word "hermit," we find the cognate meanings "desert, solitude, empty, desolate, bereft." The Hermit, too, has been "separated"—

that is the sense of the Indo-European root, *ere*. He has been "full of empty space, rare, having intervals between."

Did the Hermit himself, after some agonizing experience in which he, too, felt "alone, alone, all alone on a wide, wide sea," cut off from community, suffering an apartness bereft of togetherness—did he meet, find, or come suddenly into collision with another Hermit, another Mariner, who had known the same essential unawareness and had "shrived" him by a critical insight, a penetration into the universal ground of things? Had the Hermit then taken up his own post "in that wood which slopes down to the sea," the point of inter-subjectivity with others, to minister reconciliation, dialogue, and life where there had been only life-in-death? The desert experience in human life is so overwhelmingly universal, it has been so endlessly documented and recorded in art, literature, and psychology, that I need not labor it here; but I will borrow a short quotation from Coleridge, and ask the reader to note how the poet relates emptiness with lack of dialogue and the void of meaninglessness:

> Where the spirit of a man is not filled with the consciousness of freedom . . . he wearies himself out with empty words, to which no friendly echo answers, either from his own heart, or the heart of a fellow being . . .

Emerson, speaking of the art of painting, wrote in a journal entry:

> . . . highest behavior consists in the identification of the Ego with the universe, so that when a man says I think, I hope, I find—he might properly say, the human race thinks, hopes, finds . . .

What the Hermit actually celebrates in "freeing" the Mariner is a ritual of initiation, a cell-firing ceremony in which he admits the wanderer into a community of critics, whose task it is to keep the critical chain reaction going, to accelerate it into an ascending explosion of critical masses. Such a community is truly a nuclear group, possessed of very great power. I have always been amused by the fact that, if we playfully rearrange the first three letters of the word "nuclear," we get "unclear." To clarify experience, vice versa, is to render it dynamically energetic.

That there exists such a critical community must become apparent to artists, philosophers, scientists, critics, scholars, journalists—to all who, impelled by their own intellectual activity and relentless curiosity, are constantly, through their reading, conversation, and observation, inter-subjectively vibrating in the element of "tremulous reciprocations." The telltale signs of the community are to be found everywhere in the writings of estheticians and philosophers concerned with the companion problem of ethical behavior. Merely a few examples (readers surely could put together their own collections) will suffice. Erik H. Erikson, in *The Study of Lives, Essays on Personality in Honor of Henry A. Murray,* writes:

> Each man calls his own a separate body, a self-conscious individuality, and a personal awareness of the cosmos; and yet he shares this world as a reality also perceived and judged by others and as an *actuality* within which he must commit himself to ceaseless interaction.

John E. Smith, in *Symbols and Values: An Initial Study,* draws from the same well in his description of the ongoing religious community:

> The original experiences, sign-events, crucial occurrences out of which Biblical religion emerged, were, to be sure, individual experiences, experiences of the great men of faith, but they did not and could not remain merely individual . . . Furthermore, not only did these individuals seek to interpret their own experiences for themselves and in so doing express them in symbolic form, but their experience, in becoming the basis for a community, came to be interpreted by others who in turn sought to interpret it for still others and so on without end . . .

Finally, these passages from Karl Jaspers' *Man in the Modern Age:*

True nobility is not found in an isolated being. It exists in the
interlinkage of independent human beings. Such are aware
of their duty to discover one another, to help one another
onward wherever they encounter one another, and to be ever
ready for communication, on the watch, but without
importuncy . . . This solidarity extends even to an enemy
when selfhood comes into genuine opposition with selfhood.
Thus there is realized that which, for instance, might exist
even in political parties across all divergencies as a solidarity
of the best . . . The unity of this dispersed elite is like the
Invisible Church of a *corpus mysticum* in the anonymous
chain of the friends from among whom, here and there, and
through the objectivity of individual activities, one selfhood
is revealed to another and perhaps distant selfhood. In this
immaterial realm of the mind there are, at any moment, a few
indwellers who, entering into close proximity, strike flame
out of one another by the intimacy of their communication.
They are the origin of the loftiest, soaring movement which is
as yet possible in the world. They alone constitute true
human beings.

The philosopher speaks in a very high and mighty manner
here of a community of elite spirits, of which he himself is undoubtedly a member. The notion that such a community is of the
"few," and not of "the many," has a long and honorable (or dis-
honorable) heritage beginning, at least, with Plato. It is the myth
of the saving remnant, the good seed that took root where the bad
seed withered: it is the spirit in which Joseph, in his coat of many
colors, elevated himself in his dream above his brethren. The many,
the mediocre—it has been argued by the few—hold together against
the creative minority.

Coleridge stated the opposition in terms of "the immediate,
which dwells in every man" as set off against the "original intuition,
or absolute affirmation of it (which is likewise in every man, but
does not in every man rise to consciousness)." I cannot evade the
reader's correct suspicion that, as a critic espousing a theory of criticism founded on the kind of special function that I have been
advancing, I number myself among the described community. In

candor, and hopefully in honesty, I presume to speak for that whole community, when I assert that the posture is not one of "elitism" as commonly conceived—namely, privileged superiority. I read Jaspers' "mediocrities" in Coleridge's sense, as the potential of "the original intuition" not yet risen to consciousness. The cells are all at varying levels of fired activity: I do not see how the human mind can, in its finitude, free itself from the sense of hierarchy: but the effort is always made to understand hierarchy in the sense of quality and not of quantity; to exclude no man from the infinity of the potential of all men, but merely to note that in the real, the practical, world we see this potential dynamically in relativity.

The challenge of the dialectic is always the problem of ending it. Hegel faltered on an ending and so did Marx: their versions of historical utopia ended for one, in the Prussian state, and for the other, in the finality of ultimate communism. The transcendent revelation either must transcend itself in non-being, a divine stasis, which is beyond logical comprehension, and even defies "original intuition": or it must escape its cul-de-sac in the organismic notion of life, the miracle of negentropy, of infinite rebirth and renewal. Thus the leap must inevitably be made from the quantum to the spirit, over a gulf which eternally divides the Platonists from the Aristotelians, the vitalists from the mechanists. The critic who accepts initiation into Jaspers' *corpus mysticum* accepts, along with that initiation, an axiology (theory of value) as well as an ontology (theory of being). He may go all the way with the overt religious impulse and, with Coleridge and the mystics, expostulate for the metaphysical Divine: or he may come somewhat short of the Hebrew-Christian sense of the Divinity, like Whitehead in his own cautious formulation, in *Process and Reality*, of the miraculous nature of creation:

> Thus the universe is to be conceived as attaining the active
> self-expression of its own variety of opposites—of its own
> freedom and its own necessity, of its own multiplicity and
> its own unity, of its own imperfection and its own perfection.
> All the "opposites" are elements in the nature of things, and are
> incorrigibly there. The concept of "God" is the way in which
> we understand this incredible fact—that what cannot be, yet is.

For Whitehead, God is "not *before* all creation, but *with* creation":

> Thus the actuality of God must also be understood as a multiplicity of actual components in the process of creation. This is God in his function of the kingdom of heaven.

Across the century that separated them, Coleridge, the poet, and Whitehead, the philosopher, acknowledge each other graciously. Writes Coleridge:

> In order to obtain adequate notions of any truth, we must intellectually separate its distinguishable parts; and this is the technical *process* of philosophy. But having done so, we must then restore them in our conceptions to the unity in which they actually coexist; and this is the *result* of philosophy.

Whitehead, at his station on time's bridge, writes of God:

> He does not create the world, he saves it: or, more accurately, he is the poet of the world, with tender patience leading it by his vision of truth, beauty and goodness.

Thus, the philosopher transcends the "intuitions of Greek, Hebrew and Christian thought [which] have alike embodied the notions of a static God condescending to the world . . ." But Whitehead speaks favorably of the Galilean origin of Christianity, as not emphasizing either "the ruling Caesar, or the ruthless moralist, or the unmoved mover. It dwells upon the tender elements of the world, which slowly and in quietness operate by love . . ."

Hierarchy and multiplicity are different aspects of the same mystery and miracle of the one and the many, the apart and the together, the individual and society, Man and God. It is incredible, as Whitehead puts it, that they should be the same, and yet the mind amenable to Henri Bergson's concept of creative evolution accepts the incredibility as the fusion of being and value. Nicolai Hartman, a modern German realist in metaphysics, a philosophical humanist who would dispute the idealistic views of both Coleridge and Whitehead, as well as monism, medieval supernaturalism, and forms of theism, nevertheless has written (in *Symbols and Society*):

> In a certain sense one may say that everything which exists somehow falls under the category of values, that everything in the world, even the most remote and indifferent, is in the perspective of positive or negative worth. The same universe, which in its totality underlies ontological phenomena, belongs also in precisely the same totality to ethical phenomena. It is no less a world of good and evils than of things and their relations. At least it is as radically the former as it is the latter.

What I am maintaining here is that, for the creative critic, his values, the touchstones by which he makes his individual discriminations and judgments, when confronted by the concrete sign-events or objects of criticism, are the inevitable outcome of his vision of reality—what man is, what the universe is. He has but three major ontological choices, three great *Weltanschauungen,* world views, which underlie the varied systems within philosophy—Naturalism, Humanism, and Theism. If he elects to be grounded in the naturalistic vision, wherein the universe is seen as a continuum of disparate lumps of matter lacking any transcendent, spiritual quality, his values (axiology) will tend to be relativistic and subjectivistic, both in the realms of esthetics and ethics; for value implies a sense of the good, and how can one have a sense of the good without some teleological understanding, some notion of ends, purposes, and goals? If one has no sense of direction, any path is as attractive or as unattractive as any other. Even critical standards, in such a blind determinism, may be regarded as the mere mechanical consequences of other mechanical antecedents.

In the second *Weltanschauung,* Humanism, man is neither mechanically continuous with material Nature, nor yet (though possibly he may be) shaped by some Divine Being behind the cosmic scenes. There are certain absolute values, but they inhere in the *entelechy,* the inner nature of things that determines their development; and man is capable of esthetics and ethics because, through reason, he is able to grasp these fundamental values. A humanistic critic may declare for truth, beauty, goodness, for love, loyalty, kindness, service, and social justice, and may seek to shape the world in the direction of the universal activity of such essences and qualities.

The theistic critic (in many varieties) would postulate, assert without proof, that man has a special worth and destiny; that it is either given from without or is an immanent agency in the world; and that the universe and man are characterized by the miraculous or paradoxical fusion of both reason and love. Such a critic would tend—like the humanist but acting from different principles—to join the *corpus mysticum,* the modest elite of Jaspers, and to become a Hermit-critic, or a cell-firer in the world, perpetually activating himself and others to higher penetrations that reveal the "beyond," the dynamic behind the static husk, the significance behind the sign-event, the esemplastic third beat, which creatively renews itself in the pursuit of community, mutuality, and love. The worldly implications of this view would be a continuous inter-subjective dialogue, which sought to transcend conflict by an evolving series of reconciliations in the secular life of men and nations. Such reconciliations, in which one opposite did not survive at the price of obliterating the other, but in which both would find a novel togetherness, enabling each to maintain and strengthen its own apartness, would be the fruit of significations and clarifications, "shrivings" and ascendent "freeings."

The use of force, William Ernest Hocking wrote (in *Strength of Men and Nations*), is essentially uncivilized: "[it] is itself an abandonment of the issue of justice, perhaps a confession of *inability to think the question out!*" A friend told him in 1938: "Economics is no longer a closed science: there are no economic solutions without ethical solutions"—to which Hocking added "nor without metaphysical solutions." In our theory of criticism, metaphysics is the fabric of the seamless garment on which all the particularities of man's secular concerns and interests are woven. There are literary critics who have deprecated such ambitious views. One was George Moore, who, in his introduction to *Anthology of Pure Poetry,* advocated "art for art's sake" against "large, noble and eternal truths about humanity." "Shakespeare never soiled his songs with thought," Moore wrote; and he contrasted "innocency of vision" to "the hub of an empire." "So perhaps," he mused, "the time has come for somebody to ask if there is not more poetry in things than in ideas, and more pleasure in Gautier's *Tulipe* than in Wordsworth's ecclesiastical, political and admonitory sonnets."

Such poets, and critics, refuse to be comforted by old beliefs, by Magical Views, which are falling away. I. A. Richards, in *Science and Poetry,* asserted that ". . . experience is its own justification; and this fact must be faced, although sometimes—by a lover, for example—it may be very difficult to accept." But Richards immediately added: "Once it is faced, it is apparent that all the attitudes to other human beings and to the world in all its aspects, which have been serviceable to humanity, remain as they were, as valuable as ever." Thus even Richards, the "new" critic, grounded rather in humanistic psychology than in religious humanism, refuses to separate his ontology from his values. His own definition of value, psychologically oriented, is clear, as he gives it in earlier passages of his book. There, speaking of how "we," as friendly observers, would wish to see a hypothetical individual living, he writes:

> If we are to approve of his experience, it must not only be full
> of life and free from conflict, but it must be likely to lead to
> other experiences, both his own and those of other people,
> also full of life and free from conflict.

The concept of mutuality then, the concern for "the other," for his personality as a symbol of dignity, worth, and love, may inhere, in varying degrees, in critical postures which are grounded in dimensions of the naturalistic, humanistic, and theistic theories of being. The more theistic the foundation, the more it partakes of a sense of the immanence of the transcendental in man and the universe, and the more intense the concern for mutuality is likely to be: for the naturalistic view, as stated earlier, has no recognition of teleological end or purpose, and therefore has the least justification for one mode of action over another. The humanistic view admits of uncertainty and may, consequently, be subject to doubts, incoherence, and waverings, whereas the theistic view, whether it be organismic (within space and time), as in Whitehead, or religiously creative (outside space and time), as in Coleridge, is founded on a coherent conviction which integrates the critic and enables him most affirmatively to act as well as to know. "Most affirmatively" is, of course, a hierarchical judgment, and as such, it is open to dispute. But any encounter of such a judgment with other and opposing judgments would, in itself, if pursued in the Hermit-critic spirit, be a dialectical engagement and valuable: for the end of such an engagement should be, could be, a deeper clarification of one's own views, if not a mutual reconciliation of opposites in a higher meta-beat.

The meta-beat of *The Rime of the Ancient Mariner* is given in the final stanzas of the poem:

> Farewell, farewell! but this I tell
> To thee, thou Wedding-Guest!
> He prayeth well who loveth well
> Both man and bird and beast.

> He prayeth best, who loveth best
> All things both great and small;
> For the dear God who loveth us,
> He made and loveth all.

This is the Mariner's parting message to the Wedding Guest, presumably the repetitive burden of his penance. Coleridge appends it as the moral of the poem. To be sure, it comes as no evolutionary climax to the Mariner's adventures: it does not explode from within with a dramatic inevitability. Critics have not looked favorably on this ending: many have regarded it as a tacked-on, Sunday-school jingle, not at all commensurate with the imaginative power of the poem itself. Coleridge himself is reported to have spoken somewhat lightly of it in a conversation, but the circumstances of that conversation are not decisive.

On the other hand, it may be argued that the literal moral is precisely what Coleridge meant to signify by the poem, which is a myth of community and cosmology. The Mariner sets sail on his voyage in a communal atmosphere, which continues until the Albatross, a communal bird, is murdered, apparently without motive, by the Mariner. Then follow the ghastly experiences as supernatural forces work their vengeful will on the ship and its crew, for the crew assumes some complicity in the Mariner's act. The Mariner is freed of the carcass of the Albatross only when he blesses the water snakes, by the light of the moon:

> They moved in tracks of shining white,
> And when they reared, the elfish light
> Fell off in hoary flakes.
>
> O happy living things! no tongue
> Their beauty might declare:
> A spring of love gushed from my heart,
> And I blessed them unaware:
>
> The self-same moment I could pray;
> And from my neck so free
> The Albatross fell off, and sank
> Like lead into the sea.

The praying and the blessing, expressions of community, are what break the curse for the Mariner: in the end, the praying and the blessing restore to him a new and higher sense of community—one in which bird and beast are included, as well as man. Value (ethics) has been reunited with ontology (being): the dialectical encounter has yielded a higher, more inclusive sense of love, in which all natural things have suddenly been invested with quality as well as with quantum. Whence came this transformation of the Mariner's *Weltanschauung*, from unthinking, uncritical, self-focused, exclusive, and fragmentary existing into critical, mutual, and encompassing knowing and acting? Coleridge gives us no direct clue; we are to infer that somehow the Mariner concluded, intuited it from his experiences. In my view, we can find an explanation by touching again the critical function that the Hermit serves in the poem. The reconstruction of the Mariner's universe was the work of the man who "shrived" him, who clarified and showed him the significance of what he had lived through.

The moral of the poem undoubtedly, in the modern temper, has a "sweetness and light" connotation: it smacks of the homily and the little-ones sermon. But words are masks: they often, as we have seen before, conceal even as they reveal. To pray, in the conventional religious sense, is to beg, to ask, to entreat, to attempt to modify an anthropomorphic deity who, presumably, is capable of capricious or considerate response. In the proto-Indo-European root of the word "pray," however, lies a clue to a richer meaning for our purposes—in which we use the Hermit as a lodestone for criticism. The *American Heritage Dictionary* Appendix leads us from "pray" to "perk"—where we arrive at the root word "expostulate," which is defined "To reason earnestly with someone in an effort to dissuade or correct: remonstrate," even "to object, . . . to demand strongly." Returning with our deeper definitions to the Mariner's homiletic jingle, what do we find? He (any man) reasons, argues, remonstrates, objects, and dissuades best who loves best.

If we reiterate our notion that the Hermit-critic (by his dialectical signifying to the Mariner of the meaning of his voyage) initiates him into the universal community of more critically alive individuals, we find, then, that the Hermit also gives him the secret "grip," the code, the formula for behavior that is the mark of the critical brotherhood. The highest degree of criticism is that which is inseparable from the highest value placed upon mutuality, upon insights whereby we strengthen not only ourselves but all others, as our own voyages, our experiences, afford us the opportunity. We are able to do this because our axiology is consistent with our ontology; we can love because loving is making: the metaphysical first principle, the very ground of being, is the essence of every act of Hermit-criticism.

What Coleridge has done here is to unite knowing and acting: for acting, in the human realm, requires choice; choice is freedom of will, discontinuous with Nature (and therefore either humanistic or theistic). Where there is choice, there is value, and in the value of love, of mutuality, is also its epistemology, its theory of knowledge. The critic who breaks through, in his intellectual and affective life, to this transcendent vision never becomes a recluse, a contemplative withdrawer from society, an esthetician exclusively, in some poetic or magical disillusioned trance, indifferent to or helpless before the worldly problems of his community. The Mariner, after he "stuns" the Wedding Guest, is "gone": gone where? Presumably to travel from land to land, overtaken, at uncertain hours, by his penitential agony, and compelled to fix with his glittering eye some other hapless Wedding Guest who will hear his monotonous tale—a rather dark and brooding destiny.

The Mariner, some critics have speculated, is none other than the Wandering Jew, the legendary figure condemned to roam the earth till Jesus returns. Indeed, J. L. Lowes, in *The Road to Xanadu,* cites evidence to show that the medieval legend of the Wandering Jew (Cain is an older version of the same mythical theme) was much in Coleridge's mind. J. B. Beer, in *Coleridge the Visionary,* quotes a newly discovered fragment of Coleridge's conversation which confirms Lowes's opinion:

> It is an enormous blunder . . . to represent the Ancient Mariner as an old man on board ship. He was in my mind the everlasting Wandering Jew—had told this story ten thousand times since the voyage, which was in his early youth and 50 years before.

I detect no qualitative consistency between the joyous content of the Mariner's own final interpretation of his adventures and the gloomy image of the elderly literary epileptic pictured in Gustave Dore's illustrations of the poem (first published in 1875). The Ancient Mariner, after his initiation into the critical community by the Hermit, became in turn a Hermit-critic himself. The Hermit chose his own cell-firing "where the wood slopes down to the sea." The Mariner elected to fish for critics along the wider networks of inter-subjectivity: each man selects his own piece of ground, sea, or sky, upon which to rest his lever to lift the planet of human consciousness. The point is that the metaphysics pays off in the ethics, and the dialectic stands watch over all to make sure that inter-subjectivity faints not nor falters nor freezes, perhaps, into the rigidities of self-possessed dogma, which fails to take into account "the other."

This structural relationship of being, valuing, and double-checking is most happily stated in the Latin epigraph which Coleridge affixed as a preface to *The Rime of the Ancient Mariner*. It was written by Thomas Burnet, in his *Archeologiae Philosophicae* (1692). The poet must, obviously, have approved of Burnet's thoughts, found himself in agreement with them, and recognized in them significant coincidences of meaning that related to the meaning of *The Rime of the Ancient Mariner* itself: otherwise he could not have so crucially identified the epigraph with his poem by choosing it as a preface. In Coleridge's own translation, it reads as follows:

> I readily believe that there are more invisible than visible Natures in the universe. But who will explain for us the family of all these beings, and the ranks and relations and distinguishing features and functions of each? What do they do? What places do they inhabit? The human mind has always sought the knowledge of these things, but never attained it. Meanwhile I do not deny that it is helpful sometimes to contemplate in the mind, as on a tablet, the image of a greater and better world, lest the intellect, habituated to the petty things of daily life, narrow itself and sink wholly into trivial thoughts. But at the same time we must be watchful for the truth and keep a sense of proportion, so that we may distinguish the certain from the uncertain, day from night.

To deal with the epigraph, let us separate it into three parts; the first part ends ". . . but never attained to it." Here we find Burnet addressing himself to the problem of being. He asks dialectical questions, contrasting "invisible" to "visible" Natures. He echoes Coleridge's own distinction between "fancy" and "imagination," between unfolding unities as opposed to unredeemed empirical facts, common sense, and one-dimensional phenomena. The questions about the "family of these beings," their "ranks and relationships and distinguishing features and functions . . . What do they do? What places do they inhabit?" may again intimate the dialectical mode of inquiry in its search for insights, significations, uncommon visions, the bi-sociation of matrices—third beats.

In the second part of the epigraph, which begins "Meanwhile, I do not deny . . ." and ends "sink wholly into trivial thoughts" we have the value dimension, given in the essential phrase "the image of a greater and better world." The word "greater" may denote quantity exclusively, suggesting larger universes of discourse; but one can hardly read "better" in any but a qualitative sense. Two weeks before he died, in 1834, Coleridge, commenting on his failure to write the systematic statement of his philosophy to which he aspired in *Biographia Literaria,* protested:

> For, as God hears me, the originating, continuing and
> sustaining wish and design in my heart were to exalt the glory
> of His name; and, which is the same thing in other words,
> to promote the improvement of mankind.

In the last sentence of the epigraph, we return again to the saving grace of the dialectical taking into account of "the other," whether it be in accord with our own deepest beliefs or opposed to them. To be "watchful for the truth" is to be ever on guard against accepting or settling for what, in the absence of careful examination, may be less than the truth. To keep "a sense of proportion," is wise counsel to a critic, which exhorts him not only to persist in the critical negation of his own critical insights and to hold all judgments tentatively, but also to recognize that, in human discourse, even criticism that transcends, "goes beyond," may, in its own turn, be itself transcended by a higher meta-criticism. In the Kantian critique of pure reason, the noumena are unknowable: a theory of being becomes an act of faith—a mode of belief and action, an "as if"—based on statements about the nature of man that are subject to proof only within the boundaries of the theorist's own epistemology.

Dialectical criticism, then, is this: motion. Motion itself is the miracle, the negentropy, the vitalism—motion is good, continuous, spontaneous, never ending. In Bergson's conceptualization, motion is that which we can know not in actual, clock-time, which separates matter into discrete lumps—there being no bridges between them— but which we know only in psychological time, which endures and does not pass away, which is a succession without distinction.

Dialectical criticism is a "miraculism" (we borrow the term from John Crowe Ransom, who uses it in *The World's Body* to describe Metaphysical Poetry, which he places higher than either Physical Poetry or Platonic Poetry):

Specifically, the miraculism arises when the poet [read critic] discovers by analogy an identity between objects which is partial, though it should be considerable, and proceeds to an identification which is complete . . . scientific predication concludes an act of attention but miraculism initiates one. It leaves us looking, marvelling, and revelling in the thick *dinglich* substance that has just received its strange representation . . . It suggests to us that the object is perceptually or physically remarkable, and we had better attend to it.

The attending to it, furthermore, is unending. Fred Hoyle, the British astrophysicist, gave us the theory of continuous creation in the universe, a miraculous process in which the comos is unlimited, as opposed to the theory which holds that the universe began with a "big bang." The dialectical counterpart is, of course, the notion that there will never be a "big finish." We are left with the miraculous, self-perpetuating notion of the "big in-between": for wherever there is an allegedly static "one," it is merely a way-station to a new dissolution into fluid apartness; wherever there is an older pattern in flux, there is the inevitable recombining in a new togetherness. The "leap of the imagination" which fuses a creative advance into novelty can never be known in advance. Thus there can never be a static utopia, an ultimate end to historicity. Yet, even in Bergson's vision of creative evolution, there remains an implicit sense of some great consummation of his *élan vital;* for it would seem that the human mind needs a sense of goal, needs a meaning that transcends even the notion of infinite process. Thus we arrive at the mythico-symbolic action of "as if." The goal recedes as we approach it; the "second coming" never comes.

Nevertheless, the individual visionary critic, the cell-firer, *must act as if it were coming;* and in each dialectical encounter (criticism) he evokes the idea or the feeling of the consummatory event. In each act of criticism he celebrates, with his Wedding Guest, the ritual of miraculous consummation. The "isness" of life coexists with the "oughtness" of life—that is the truth of the combined being and goodness—but it must be symbolically reenacted over and over again, as if the very reenactments, though small and perhaps obscure and transient events, have the power to hasten the desired consummation. In this sense, dialectical criticism—imbued with the vision of Coleridge's "better world" and "the improvement of mankind"—is a continual martyrdom. Each critical contact that the Mariner makes is an "agony" that returns; and until "the tale" is told, the "heart within him" burns.

I am indebted for some of the thoughts that I have just expressed to a very stimulating unpublished paper, "Metaphysics, Myth, and Politics," by Peter Bien. He sees the ritualistic, creative martyrdom in "all campaigns which have a mythic character because the hoped-for goal is infinite and sublime":

> George Sorel, speaking of the Wars for Liberty in France, calls them "truly Homeric conflicts," for "on the battle-field the leaders gave an example of daring courage and were merely the first combatants, like true Homeric kings . . . If we wished to find, in these . . . armies, what it was that took the place of the later idea of discipline, we might say that the soldier was convinced that the slightest failure of the most insignificant private might compromise the success of the whole . . . All things [were] considered from a qualitative and individualistic point of view . . . Battles under these conditions could, then, no longer be likened to games of chess in which each man is comparable to a pawn; they become collections of heroic exploits accomplished by individuals under the influence of extra-ordinary enthusiasm."

The miraculous nature of this "as if" criticism includes the faith that it is creative, that truth is formative. Coleridge wrote: "The heart should have *fed* upon the *truth*, as insects on a leaf, till it be tinged with the colour, and show its food in every . . . minutest fibre." He was speaking of art, but we substitute "criticism," and read that art (or criticism) is more than "an expression of feeling"; it seeks to inform, broaden and develop feeling—to arouse "that sublime faculty by which a great mind becomes that on which it meditates." Each Hermit-critic has his Mariner, and each Mariner his particular, at-the-moment Wedding Guest. They fire the network, keep the motion going; and—in genuine dialectical fashion—the system is open at both ends. When the Ancient Mariner stopped "one of three," what of the other two? To assume that they are outlanders, alien to the self-firing network, is to invalidate the whole theory. No one is excluded.

Coleridge is silent about the other two; but we may speculate that each of them could have been a Wedding Guest or a Mariner or a Hermit. No figure in this triad is a closed system unto himself: he is always dynamically in motion. The motor may idle to the point where we cannot even hear it, but it does not die; neither does the accelerating motor tear itself apart with its high speed energy. The Wedding Feast, the ship, the wood that slopes down to the sea, and the land-to-land map of the cell-firing Mariner are all symbolic points on everyman's compass. We may assume that the Hermit, at his fixed vantage point in the poem, partook of dialectical infusions from the "marineres" with whom he talked, who came "from a far countree." In *The Critical Spirit, Essays in Honor of Herbert Marcuse*, M. I. Finley writes, apropos of the word "Utopia":

> The initial letter "u" stands for the Greek "ou" ("no," "not") and hence Utopia is Nowhere. But by the exercise of a little imagination the "u" can also stand for the Greek prefix "eu" ("good," "well") and then we get "good place," "ideal place."

The good and ideal place, the beckoning of a better mankind, may be nowhere in the future, but "as if," critical cell-firing articulates its reality. Criticism strives to shape man's future: it does not merely contemplate it. The dialectical critic is an agent for change. "A man gains awareness of what he is," writes Karl Jaspers, "through his selfhood in a world in which he plays an active part." Jaspers' comments on the role of the journalist in society can be applied to the particular function of the mass media critic:

> The journalist [read critic] can realize the ideal of the modern universalized man. He can merge himself in the tension and the reality of the day, adopting a reflective attitude towards these. He can seek out that innermost region where the soul

of the age takes a step forward. He deliberately interweaves his destiny with that of the epoch. He takes alarm, he suffers, and he balks when he encounters Nothingness. He becomes insincere when he is content with that which brings satisfaction to the majority. He soars towards the heights when he sincerely fulfills his being in the present.

"He takes alarm . . . suffers . . . balks": what active, vigorous words these are, describing particularly the ideal function of the mass media critic! For where, in the contemporary scene, is there more at which to take alarm, to suffer and to balk, than in the utterly non-dialectical world of broadcasting which is dominated by the manipulation for consumerism of man's biological instincts of fear, suspense, anger, sex-interest, contest, violence, revenge? The critic, as we recall from our proto-Indo-European explorations in essential meanings, not only discerns, reasons, persuades; he also deprecates, imprecates. Irony, contempt, paradox are weapons in the armory of the dialectical critic, as he seeks to shape the medium to his own particular vision of the good, the ideal place.

Nevertheless, even in his rebellion, he seeks to obey Camus' injunction: "the only original rule of life today: to learn to live and to die, and in order to be a man, to refuse to be a god." In the struggle to be alive, to clarify reality, the critic is the "pro-active" rather than the "re-active" man. Learning, he maintains, is the unfinished business of every critic: he exhibits the "true humility of the audacious questioner." He reminds himself continually that, in the wholeness of the cell-firing network within which he operates, the selfhood of the one is essentially the selfhood of the many. Even Plato, in his most sublime, self-critical insights, took into account contradictions of his own assertions. In Book VI of *Republic* he took a more hopeful view of "the multitude" which, in elitist manner, he soundly scorned in Book IX. Socrates, after disparaging the many for looking "coldly on the subtleties of controversy," declares to his dialectical partner:

O my friend . . . do not attack the multitude: they will change their minds, if, not in an aggressive spirit, but gently and with the view of soothing them and removing their dislike of over-education, you show them your philosophers as they really are . . . and then mankind will see that he of whom you are speaking is not such as they supposed—if they view him in this new light, they will surely change their notion of him, and answer in another strain. Who can be at enmity with one who loves them, who that is himself gentle and free from envy will be jealous of one in whom there is no jealousy? Nay, let me answer for you, that in a few this harsh temper may be found but not in the majority of mankind.

For who can look about the world today, its wholeness apparently sundered, its idealism frozen by the ice of cynicism, without shuddering, Sisyphus-like, at the hellish prospect? Benedetto Croce, in *The Defence of Poetry,* summarized the contemporary world's "woeful agony" in eloquent passages driving home the crucial criticism:

> Our civilization is technically perfect and spiritually barbarous; ravenous of wealth and indifferent to good; utterly insensible to all that ought to move the human conscience.

And yet, he continued:

> In point of objective truth, it is easy to see how much exaggeration and illusion there is in such a picture of the modern world . . . To paint a true picture of the whole process [critics] would have to include themselves, and many like themselves, who resist it or work in an opposite and complementary sense, not to mention that mute, inglorious host of good and honest men who are the underlying fabric which holds human society together. Instead of this, in the strife and fury of passion they forget both themselves and these others; their imagination sees the whole field occupied by the triumphant and ravaging hordes of the enemy.

It is not their imagination that sees such a prospect, I would assert, but their fancy; for the gloomy portrait is dialectically unrelieved, adrift on a sea of "fixities and definites." It cries out for the esemplastic molding of unity, for an inter-subjective collision which will transcend the darkness with the very counter-light that Croce introduces. It cries out, in short, for dialectical criticism, in the motion of its process and its ethics. Croce concludes his defense of poetry (and we conclude this sketch of our theory of criticism) with some final words on motion:

> It may be said, in discouragement of vain hopes and over-confidence, that the world is hard and heavy, and needs more than individual good-will and poetic fancies. But we know that, all the same, this hard and heavy world moves, or rather that it only exists in movement, and that it is moved by nothing but our united efforts; that each of us, great or small or tiny as he may be, in his relation to all the others is answerable for the world. If we too, as lovers of poetry [read criticism] exert what strength we have, we shall have done the duty of our station.

Wasn't it another Italian critic, who, when forced to abjure his heliocentric third beat—namely, that the earth moves around the sun—apocryphally transcended his own recantation with the counter-dialectical whisper: *"E pur si muove!"*—"Nevertheless, it *moves!"*

CHAPTER FIVE

Biographical Interlude

I pass, like night, from land to land:
I have strange power of speech; . . .

THE MARINER, when first he commands our attention, is a man with a history. He exists in space, has duration in time, and, we may assume, he has experienced growth in consciousness. He does not emerge, *ex nihilo,* out of nothing. Even as a purely literary creation, an effect of the imagination, we know, from Lowes's examination of its origins in depth, that the poem is a developmental phenomenon, owing its form and content to Coleridge's education and reading and to the network of his personal relationships, embracing good and ill fortune. The Mariner has been—to employ a metaphor—on the trail for an unknown time. The Wedding Guest that he stops in the poem is not the first upon whom he fixes his glittering eye: nor will he be the last. We may infer that there has been a long line of Wedding Guests; and that the critical brotherhood has been substantially enlarged, in many and varied scenes, wherever he has told his tale, engaged in a piece of critical activity, and fired a cell.

We know, too, that there was a time in his life when he was not consciously a cell-firer. There is a gay, worldly and unconcerned naivete about the Mariner and his shipmates as they begin their voyage:

> The ship was cheered, the harbor cleared,
> Merrily did we drop
> Below the kirk, below the hill,
> Below the lighthouse top.

Here is no crew of a contemplative few, but a group of convivial, operative men, representative of the many, going about the ordinary business of their lives at an idling motor level. Certainly their sense of ethics is not very highly developed, for when the Mariner shoots the Albatross, they have no clear sense of the rightness or wrongness of the act. At first they judge that the Mariner has done "a hellish thing," and that "it would work 'em woe." But when the fog which accompanied the Albatross lifts, and "the glorious Sun uprist," they all aver that " 'Twas right . . . such birds to slay/ That bring the fog and mist."

It is a state of consciousness which Coleridge depicts at the poem's beginning, and the Mariner shares it with his shipmates. His sense of inter-subjective linkages is weak; he does not see that the bird is related to him in any significant way: he is a man closer to the "apartness" end of the continuum of humanity–nature than to the "togetherness" end. He is part of a collectivity but not of a true community. The purpose of his adventure, which transforms him, is to replace his collective identity with his communal identity, to give him a higher sense of the dialectical tension between uniqueness and mutuality. When the Hermit radically changes the Mariner's sense of being and of value, and makes him a critic–cell-firer in the world, the latter's "strange power of speech" is at a very low point on its energy curve. We may assume that the Mariner, too, like his chain of Wedding Guests, is "stunned" at first when he receives the impact of the Hermit's signification of the meaning of his experience. The Mariner rises and goes, and begins his passing from land to land (from one level of dialectical awareness to another), a sadder and a wiser man, but one who is certain to intensify the sadness and the wisdom, as he clarifies them simultaneously on the contemplative (theoretical) and operative (practical) levels of his ongoing experiences—not only at wedding feasts, but also in market places, schools, churches, sports arenas, and theaters, along the roads and in homes.

If we extend the Mariner, from the fixed point in space where we meet him in the poem, and project him into time, we cannot accept the notion that he repeats, parrot-like, the identical lines which Coleridge wrote for him. Such a conclusion would satisfy us at the *fancy* level. At the level of *imagination,* we are persuaded by the thought that, like any autonomous teller of tales, the Mariner cannot simply repeat memorized words by rote. He must embellish the facts, change a detail here and there, reconstruct an episode ever so slightly, until the tale itself becomes a dynamic entity with a life of its own, taking over, controlling, and steering the Mariner from within. Nevertheless, it is the same tale essentially, with the same protagonist, agony, and moral—a theme with variations. And all the while that the Mariner changes his tale in time, making small creative advances into novelty with each telling, he himself is dynamically changing, passing from phase to phase of his own consciousness, which is developing organically, as it interacts in time, space, and history with others. The Mariner of the first Wedding Guest is different from the Mariner of the second and the third, and so on. May he not meet Wedding Guests who do not silently rise and go, but who stand and condemn the Mariner, or debate with him, reject his propositions, call him a fool, an idiot, or a charlatan?

The Mariner is not dialectically "home free." He must react to his Wedding Guests' reactions, be molded and altered by them in turn, just as he molds and alters them. In this collision of subjectivities, his convictions are challenged, tempered, modified, or strengthened. Nor do his tale-tellings, his dyadic encounters, take place in a contextual vacuum; he and his Wedding Guests are historical beings, reciprocating at particular moments in unique social systems which are characterized by ideological storms, biophysical phenomena, divisions, conflicts, routs, and rallyings, as the human race on spaceship earth pendulates between progress and regression—at times frenetic, at times paralyzed.

Paradigms, both intellectual and material, blast at the cell-firer and his targets, circumscribing their common visions of reality and shaping their mentation and action without their being aware of the unsuspected forces. "You cannot step twice into the same rivers," said Heraclitus, "for fresh waters are ever flowing in upon you."

The Mariner's "strange power of speech," his dialectical criticism, is, like all things, in flux. He clarifies his theory in practice, and his clarified theory modifies his practice. He succeeds or fails in harmonizing the two; he learns or does not learn from his failures and successes; he meets every new Wedding Guest with senses poised for collision and the hope for more novel advances, more dialectical motion, more community.

So, too, the dialectical critic (and here I leave my metaphor and speak plainly of myself) is a man with a history; and the reader should know me as such. I had my precritical origins in an early commitment to broadcasting as the prime professional area of my work. I worked as a writer-producer-director for both commercial and non-commercial broadcasting networks, stations, and related organizations. My critical instincts, of course, helped shape most, if not all of my creative work in programs. Anecdotally, I recall that my first informal critical pieces were written while I was an executive producer at CBS during World War II. To keep its producers and directors in touch with the entertainment world, the network administrators encouraged us to go to the theater at corporate expense. Like good administrators, however, our superiors in the chain of command required a *quid pro quo* for the free tickets. We were asked to submit short reviews of the plays that we had seen, along with our requests for reimbursement. I would come into my office the morning after having been to the theater and sit down at my typewriter; after a few moments, a notion would strike me, and I would write a few paragraphs. Even then, I remember, I was unwilling to set down my "opinion" of the play without detecting some central point about it. Around this central organizing concept, I would build a short debate with the play's author or director, or discern high quality to appreciate. Mr. James Seward, then an administrative officer at CBS, was the executive in charge of the staff's expense accounts (later, before he retired, he rose in the CBS hierarchy to become an important figure in the radio network, a close friend of Edward R. Murrow and the administrator of the newsman's estate). Jim would drop in to my office occasionally to tell me that he had read my review and wanted to talk about it. That would bestow upon him the peculiar, rather dubious, distinction of being this critic's first Wedding Guest.

It was not until 1950, after I had left CBS, that I began to write, under a critic's by-line, for *The Christian Science Monitor*. I had been asked to write a special series of eight articles for the international daily newspaper by John Beaufort, who was then editor of the feature magazine section. The subject was television's impact upon children. After the series had appeared in print, the paper asked me to become its first television-radio critic: and I wrote biweekly pieces for the *Monitor* for about a year. The eight articles were published in a small book by Longmans, Green and Company, under the title *Television and Our Children*. What intrigues me about that book—which was essentially a journalistic, investigatory account of a new and sensitive area in broadcasting, with a modicum of critical analysis—is the fact that I used Robert Browning's poem *The Pied Piper of Hamelin* as the central organizing concept, placing much of the burden of the movement of the articles on actual lines from Browning's work. Since I have repeated the exercise in this book, using Coleridge's poem, I am compelled to wonder what experience, in my early education and reading, would account for this almost instinctive reaching out to striking poetic imagery (usually involving elements of blessing and cursing, loneliness and shattered community) as dialectical hooking-up points for my critical activity.

While still writing for the *Monitor*, I was invited by William D. Patterson, publisher of *Saturday Review* (he was then associate publisher) to write regularly for the magazine on television and radio. During the period of my association with SR I have continued also to be involved in the creation and production of both television and radio programs for the major networks and for public broadcasting organizations, as well as in the writing and production of documentary records and sound tapes for the American Heritage Publishing Company.

Like the Ancient Mariner, I began in space, so to speak, as a critic, with a personal, precritical mentality. I extended my critical activity in time, as I moved from one Wedding Guest (critical cell-firing) to another, in a chain: and all the time, I have experienced the dynamic development of my total critical consciousness, as the world and its many Hermit-critics have had their cell-firing effects upon me. I have learned to appreciate ever more strongly how greatly indebted we all are to cell-firers whom we often meet and sometimes forget along the way—authors, teachers, friends, colleagues, students, family, even minds that we encounter with inexplicably immediate, mutual hostility. To take criticism seriously, one must indefatigably scout the frontiers of human thought, especially in one's reading. Critics cannot grow dialectically unless they are voracious readers, interested in every aspect of human activity, however remote one particular area may seem to lie from the daily preoccupations of a critic who works exclusively in a single field. The pacemakers of intellectual history, contemporary and classic, must be avidly sought and explored. Nothing should be alien to the mass media critic, whether it be literature, science (natural or social), religion, philosophy, or metaphysics. A Hermit, ready to shrive, may lie waiting in every unexplored page. A critic, almost by definition, is a generalist; and a mass media critic ought to be the most general of generalists. "Criticism is the youngest of all literary forms," wrote Anatole France, and then he speculated: ". . . it will perhaps end by absorbing all the others."

When the publishers of this book first suggested that I put together a collection of the pieces that I had written, my own sense of Coleridge's "esemplastic" necessity for unity rejected the notion of an anthology unredeemed by any thematic organization. By that time, I had become so deeply committed to the dialectical search for novel togetherness, for some discovery that would become a critical proposition, that a collection of "fixities and definites," a mosaic-like assembly of existing bits and pieces, lacked appeal. Coleridge seems to have had a similar experience when, in March, 1815, he was preparing a collected edition of his poems, for he planned to include "a general preface . . . on the principles of philosophic and genial criticism." Later this preface became his extended *Biographia Literaria,* which consists of two main parts—his "literary life and opinions, as far as poetry and *poetical* criticism [are] concerned, and a critique of Wordsworth's theory of poetic diction." Coleridge, in short, expostulated his theory of criticism and turned its batteries toward a critique of Wordsworth's poetry. I have elected to train the guns of my own critical theory on my own criticism, for this is the one area in which I can lay some in-depth claim to expertise. Except for T. S. Eliot's paper *To Criticize the*

Critic, in which he comments on his own contributions to literary criticism, I know of no other critic's comparable examination of his own body of works.

The attempt, of course, is by no means its own justification. My hope is that, by commenting on some of my critical pieces that were written over a period of twenty years, I may throw some light on criticism generally, on my own applications of my theory, and on the art of dialectical criticism, as well as on the broadcasting scene that has been so intimately and profoundly involved with the experience of contemporary Americans during a period of true crisis in world history. My intention, then, in the following chapters, is to play Mariner to my own Wedding Guest, or Hermit to my own Mariner. I am impelled to grasp the significance, if at all possible, of what I have written at particular moments in particular contexts, as well as their integrative meanings, if these exist and can be detected. I have an obligation to attempt this, it seems, both to myself and to the reader. In order to do this, I have had to overcome my distaste for introducing the personal note. I hope that the reader will be tolerant in this respect, and seek with me only that personal commentary which has transfer value and can be generalized in terms of issues that are relevant to criticism.

The assumption that I ask the reader to make is that the cell-firing Mariner-critic is out there somewhere, passing, like night, from land to land, from one single critical action to the next, from one state of mind to another; that each action represents one Wedding Guest, one cell-firing, one attempt at an "aha!" experience. I will begin at the beginning, and will make a selection of pieces that I have written since then, according to a variety of criteria. I will follow the Mariner's critical trail, inquiring into his basic themes, his variations on those themes, his involvement with the world as an agent of change, and as a practicing dialectical critic clarifying his art and his ethics. In so doing, I will attempt to be candid about achievements and shortcomings, and to illuminate critical principles with biographical experiences that are appropriate to the self-critique.

As a personal adventure, the prospect offers valuable insights to me. It will, I hope, prove useful to other Hermits and Mariners, and even to Wedding Guests—whose motors idle at authentic critical levels—"stunning" them with cell-firing insights. These, in turn, may be targeted at others in the open-system, recycling network which is the potential of the critical mass, aglow with ever more critical energy, in whole and in part—advancing creatively into the anticipated but never attained utopia where no counter-criticism breaks the nondialectical stillness of non-being, non-value, and non-life.

Part Two

The Theory Applied—
Selected Pieces and Critical
Commentary

CHAPTER SIX

Chicago Between New York and Hollywood

I FIND it curious, upon noticing it, that my first TV-radio column, which appeared in *The Christian Science Monitor,* was filed from Chicago. Lake Michigan's biggest city is neither the spiritual nor the geographical center of the United States; but to most people who pass through it on their way from one coast to the other, it serves as a sort of equatorial line, a frontier where the East and West merge, an apartness-and-togetherness point for the polar opposites of the states of mind that we call Hollywood and New York. It appears to me now to be of some significance that my first assignment as a working critic was to do a story on Chicago: for what happened to Chicago in the development of television is symbolic of the tension between the one and the many in broadcasting, of the struggle between individuality and mutuality, and of the replacement of community by mere collectivity.

TOYNBEE, TV, AND CHICAGO   June 3, 1950

CHICAGO

It is a long way from Television to Toynbee, but somewhere in between lies Chicago. Television, as the toastmasters say, needs no introduction. Arnold J. Toynbee has not had so wide a press. The English historian is, however, reasonably renowned as the author of a recent work of extraordinary scholarship and, surprisingly something of a best seller, *A Study of History.* Mr. Toynbee's main idea is that civilizations rise and fall in the measure of their success or failure in responding to great natural or social challenges.

Now, Chicago, with which this article is chiefly concerned, has made considerable impact on television in the United States. Some of the new medium's most original ideas have come from the city where the wind blows 'round the Loop. Interested observers have wondered about this phenomenon—and even Chicagoans have been puzzled by it. To examine the cause, I spent some time visiting Chicago's two chief centers of television production—the Merchandise Mart, where the studios of the National Broadcasting Company are located, and the Civic Opera House, where some of the shows of the American Broadcasting Company originate. I spoke to the men and women who create and are producing Chicago's top programs; I watched them in rehearsal and on the air; and as a result of the inquiry, I venture one more theory to explain the phenomenon of Chicago TV. Mr. Toynbee provides the key.

The epic propositions of the Toynbee hypothesis are, of course, too grand to be caught in the net of a coaxial cable. They cannot cavalierly be applied. But a light touch of analogy cannot possibly harm Mr. Toynbee's stature—and it may in some remote way help television.

The English historian declares that, when the "cake of custom" is broken—and, as a result, a civilization emerges from a primitive society—this emergence is not due to any superior racial qualities possessed by the emerging people, nor to a particularly "easy" environment. Instead—so speaks Mr. Toynbee—the achievement is the response of the emerging group to a challenge of special difficulty, which rouses it to an unprecedented effort. In short, adversity has its virtues. There is a great deal more to it, naturally. Mr. Toynbee, a scholar of prodigious capacity, has taken all of ten volumes to develop all the ramifications of his theory; but for our purposes the propositions summarized will serve.

Applying Toynbee to Chicago as a TV center, we can reasonably argue that Windy City producers have simply responded with special efforts to meet and overcome the challenge which confronted them.

Ted Mills, producer of NBC–TV's Sunday night show "Garroway-at-Large," told something of how the challenge was met as we sat in the scenery-crowded nineteenth-floor reception room at NBC.

"Chicago," said Mr. Mills, "can't compete with New York or Hollywood for top name talent. We can't afford the prices. So we have to put our accent on quality, originality, ingenuity, cleverness, taste, low-cost production."

"This doesn't mean that we value these things in themselves," Mr. Mills continued. "In New York, they have what I would call a cynical approach. Their shows are money-built. They quiver with pace and rock with speed, lushness, and excitement. They are of the zim-zam-zowie variety. If I were in New York, I would be producing that kind of a show. But I'm in Chicago—our economic position doesn't permit it. Therefore we are forced to think our way out of being an economic underdog, and come up with a new kind of programming, which is essentially a frame of mind, an attitude, a way of looking at television entertainment. This approach produces shows that are warm, friendly, relaxed, simple."

Burr Tillstrom, creator and star performer of NBC–TV's "Kukla, Fran, and Ollie," further illustrates how Chicago's poor-relation status compelled it to emphasize these qualities. "Kukla, Fran, and Ollie" is a puppet show which was originally designed for children, then attracted adults, and now is a delightful national favorite with TV's young-in-heart of all ages.

"It's difficult to imagine New York production chiefs giving a show like 'Kukla, Fran, and Ollie' a chance," said Mr. Tillstrom, a young man with a subtle wit, a Puckish insight into the weakness and strength of human character, and a crew haircut.

"But in 1947, Captain William Crawford Eddy, a local TV program manager, was encouraging new ideas. Captain Eddy said I had something fresh and wholesome. He told me to go ahead, experiment, and let the idea grow. And that's exactly what I did, with the help of my producer, Beulah Zachary, and a company of artists who rebelled against the cliches and formulas of the entertainment world. 'Kukla, Fran, and Ollie' has sincerity, spontaneity, and joy, and that's the way it will remain. Its geography is not Chicagoan or metropolitan—it's Kuklapolitan!"

Backstage at the Civic Opera House, Donald F. Killian added further detail to the Chicago TV picture. Mr. Killian is program director for the American Broadcasting Company in Chicago. We were watching a rehearsal of "Super-Circus," an ABC Sunday afternoon program—a fast-moving children's show.

"Assembly line production—that's the only way we can compete with New York," said Mr. Killian. "Mass production means using basically interesting ideas, which is cheaper than hiring people. You've got to have producers and talent who are close to the public, unspoiled by big city sophistication, not ashamed of corn—at low cost."

Thus, Chicago's three national television shows—"Garroway-at-Large," "Kukla, Fran, and Ollie," and "Super-Circus"—are the big city's answer to the problem of being an in-between production center without the big money of New York and Hollywood.

Each of the three programs through which Chicago speaks to America's TV audience possesses its own approach. Each responds differently to the challenge presented. For one thing, Mr. Tillstrom would probably not agree with Mr. Mills that a New York-based show must of necessity represent the approach "cynical." For another, it certainly cannot be said that "Garroway-at-Large" and "Kukla, Fran, and Ollie" are "grass-roots" in the sense that "Super-Circus" strives to be.

Messrs. Mills, Garroway, and Tillstrom have all worked in New York. They are definitely sophisticates. Sophistication, however, does not preclude taste, imagination, or even simplicity. In the case of Garroway and Kukla, it is sophistication consciously working for the essential, the honest. "Super-Circus," deliberately avoiding sophistication, achieves a clean, wholesome zest. That all three shows have found national audiences is clear evidence of their individual, appealing qualities.

Chicago TV is not only born but growing. Once an active radio center, Chicago was the originating point of the interminable daily serial as well as the home ground of such great radio stars as Fibber McGee and Molly, Amos and Andy, Vic and Sade, Lum and Abner.

Then, not so long ago, the Windy City suffered a slump. Chicago's setback in radio may well have contributed stimulus to its resurgence in television.

At this fluid moment in 1950, in television homes throughout the United States, there is cause for gratitude that even television producers can respond to difficult challenges by tapping deep, fresh springs of imagination and skill.

"Toynbee, TV, and Chicago" is the piece that suggested to "Pat" Patterson, of *Saturday Review,* that I might be the person that the magazine (then in its early transition from an exclusively literary to a departmentalized periodical) was seeking to write a regular TV-radio column. The hooking-up of Toynbee, whose monumental *Study of History* was then a best seller, exciting controversy among historians, with Chicago television and the programs, "Garroway-at-Large," "Kukla, Fran, and Ollie," and "Super-Circus," had a literary flair and a claim to in-depth treatment of the medium. I accepted SR's offer; and for a year or so, I wrote concurrently for both the magazine and the newspaper. The audiences were different; and I have noticed, in rereading the old pieces, how the same subject matter was invariably treated differently—an affair not only of content but of tone and basic assumptions: the *Monitor* pieces tended to be reportorial and relatively free from overt value judgments, whereas in the SR columns I would not hesitate to adopt a forthright editorial posture. There were never any direct instructions from either of the two editorial offices; and the varying emphasis was entirely a result of my own unverbalized assumptions. The experience was a valuable lesson which illuminated the manner in which we tend to adjust our messages according to the subtleties of our relationships with the receivers of those messages.

If connecting Toynbee to Chicago television was an interesting discovery, the piece itself, as I now view it in retrospect, does not achieve an authentic third beat. One bit of evidence that testifies to this failure is the fact that, although the Toynbee allusion begins the piece, it disappears almost entirely as the treatment progresses, returning only as a faint echo, too faint, in the very last sentence. This is almost always a sign of faulty architecture, of a dialectic carried not far enough. If we skeletonize the structure, we get the following pattern:

1. Toynbee's thesis of challenge and response explains Chicago's successful television programs.

2. We illustrate the thesis by examining the three shows in

detail, and noting how they are all responses to an identical challenge.

3. There is cause for gratitude in the Toynbee-Chicago phenomenon.

If, however, we look for the "critical proposition"—namely, what it is, tersely, that the piece is saying, we find this pattern:

1. We ought to be grateful that Chicago produces successful shows by responding to its peculiar challenge.

2. We describe the shows.

3. We restate weakly the essential proposition. By asking, "So what?" the reader exposes the fact that the piece has only two beats, not three. There has been no breakthrough, no penetration to a fresh level of novel togetherness. If I, as a reader, should disagree with the critic about the alleged quality (in his estimate) of the programs, the only bridge between us is the challenge and response metaphor. Somehow the article has an unfinished feeling, a one-dimensional tone. The association of two unrelated universes (Toynbee and Chicago television) is there; but there is no counter-dialectic, no negation challenging the first response of association.

The critic failed to "take into account" this lack of negation: he rested too swiftly content with the first blush of his discovery. If we ask, "What should he have done?" the response to that challenge can only be: "I don't know; the only way to find out is to go into the dialectical trance and see if I can find out." The very essence of the idea of novel togetherness is that it is completely unpredictable: herein lies its vitalist as opposed to a mechanist character. To enter the free-floating combinatory play, the creative-dialectical trance, is never to be assured that there will be a payoff. Sometimes the effort must be abandoned and a fresh start made; sometimes we settle for less than the optimum because there are cutoff points, deadlines, beyond which we are constrained not to venture. In the Toynbee-Chicago piece, however, there is a clue; and let's pick it up.

In the second and third from the last paragraphs, the critic tells us that Chicago was once "an active radio center," the originating point of daily serials and popular shows. Then it suffered a slump; but television has stimulated its resurgence. If that is true, then the critic should ask: "May it not happen again? Why did Chicago break down as a radio center?" Actually, if the critic had been sophisticated enough to ask these questions, the piece would undoubtedly have taken a different turning: for the expert knowledge of radio's economic history would have told him that Chicago, in Toynbee's own terms, is a perennial victim of the phenomenon of universal states and their relationship to provinces. In the formative stages of the emergence of a civilization (read broadcasting industry), facilities appear, life surges forward in diverse forms at many places; there is an atmosphere of freedom and unfoldment, of personal choice and the capacity to affect one's own local destiny. Chicago had that experience in radio's formative period, as did Detroit, where successful programs also flourished and were distributed along the national networks.

But when the activity of growth consolidates, it gravitates to the true power centers—in this case, New York and Hollywood. The key executives who make the crucial decisions are located in these two cities, at the networks, the advertising agencies, and at the talent unions. Economic factors dominate: radio costs were possible for local production centers; for television, the costs are of a larger order of magnitude. In Chicago's early days, the costs and the presence of the talent and of the local decision-makers were in appropriate balance; but then the universal state took over. "Time," as Toynbee wrote of disintegrating civilizations, "works on the side of the barbarians." The barbarians for Chicago were Hollywood and New York; and the critic should have asked: "In time, will the pattern not repeat itself in television?" The critic would then be obliged to scan the scene for forces that might oppose the alleged inevitability of the disintegration of Chicago's television civilization.

He might have postulated, again in Toynbee's terms, "a creative minority" that would lead the Chicago majority to survival in the new challenge. He might, on the other hand, have predicted Chicago's inevitable, eventual demise in television as in radio. Somewhere in the play of this dialectical opposition, he might have found a true third beat, which would have enabled him to complete the superficial Toynbee metaphor. In short, he might have concluded: "Toynbee—meet Darwin." Time, of course, was indeed on the side of the barbarians. In 1953, I wrote an SR piece about "Miss Frances from Chicago," and her NBC success with the memorable daily program for preschoolers "Ding-Dong School." I closed the piece with this sentence: "The wind that blows again from Chicago is welcome and salubrious after a long winter of childhood-TV discontent." In 1957, however, an SR piece entitled "A Knell for Ding-Dong School" recorded NBC's jettisoning of their "darling little 'Ding-Dong School,' to which they once pointed with such fatherly pride." It seemed, then, that NBC could make more money with "Home," a women's-magazine-type program that replaced "Ding-Dong School" on the morning network schedule.

And in 1958, there was a piece called "Chicago's Local TV Corpse," which reported that local Chicago personalities were being cut off the air, as a result of "orders from New York." Finally, in 1959, the SR piece "A Deadly Calm in the Windy City" wiped the equatorial center off broadcasting's globe: it reported that the talent unions were asking the Federal Communications Commission to hold public hearings, "to determine whether network owners had lived up to their promises of performances made when originally obtaining their franchises, and whether the networks in their recent cut-back of local talent shows in Chicago had not faulted their 'public-service' local programming responsibilities." The barbarians *had* triumphed; and Mr. Darwin bestrode Mr. Toynbee. The critic, of course, should not be rebuked for his lack of foresight. He is not expected to be a soothsayer; but had he, in those early days of television in 1950, had more expertise, a better sense of history, and a deeper respect for scrutinizing his own initial critical insights more carefully, his first Wedding Guest might have left him a little sadder, a little wiser, and not quite so filled with momentary enthusiasm. He might usefully have responded to the challenge of Toynbee's sobering concept of "the mirage of immortality"—an illusory halo, often worn for a time by "moribund universal states."

CHAPTER SEVEN

The United Nations, the Mafia, and Paradise Lost

Day after day, day after day
We stuck, nor breath nor motion,
As idle as a painted ship
Upon a painted ocean.

THESE ARE probably the most widely known lines of *The Rime of the Ancient Mariner*: they represent the static pole in the spiritual geography of the poem, which oscillates continually between movement and immobility. The ship, motionless on the ocean, awaits the winds that will move it. As the sea rots and the deck rots, and the dead men lie still, the Mariner watches "the moving Moon" going up the sky, "And a star or two beside." Beyond and within the shadow of the ship the water snakes coil and swim and move in tracks of shining white. It is then that the Mariner blesses the sea creatures; and the blessing frees him from the Albatross. He sleeps, and when he wakes, the rain falls, a roaring wind arrives, and the ship moves on. Nothing moves, then, until the Mariner himself moves upward, *within himself*—the act of blessing is the inner motion that transcends the outer immobility.

"Mariner, move thyself" becomes the critic's task. Make your own discovery—for only there is the ultimate cell-firing energy, which can afterward be targeted at other points of fixity. Toynbee, in *A Study of History*, characterizes the growth of a civilization by the symptom of "etherialization, . . . the evocation of a spiritual meaning out of a material one." Underlying this process, he writes, is a movement "towards a transfer of the field of action from the macrocosm to the microcosm." It is such a movement which can be found in the rebirth of civilizations: the response to a challenge, the really powerful response, must be within. The television critic who elects to be an agent for change—in the context of a national policy which determines that the medium be used primarily for the movement of information and entertainment at a profit to the movers—is destined to learn this lesson. The industry seems always motionless, an idle ship upon a painted ocean. One cries alarm; one rebukes, pleads, cajoles, employs wit, sarcasm, irony, satire: it seems all to no avail.

"Day after day, day after day/ We stuck . . ." The years pass; and the small gains, the transient enthusiasms, the aroused hopes all seem to turn back upon themselves, heavy with the weight that gravitates to dead center. It is a serious occupational hazard for a critic; and the learning of it and the way of coping with it comes quickly or slowly, depending on the sophistication of the critic when he takes up his labors. In my case it came slowly. I was forever, in the early days, flashing Toynbee's metaphor of challenge and response: the challenge was mine (presumably reflecting that of an alleged creative minority); the response should have been the business of the lords of broadcasting. It was a business to which they seemed never to attend. As another early example of the challenge and response routine, I submit Wedding Guest Number Seventeen (the pieces cited hereafter are all from *Saturday Review* unless otherwise indicated).

AN OPEN LETTER TO THE TELEVISION INDUSTRY
April 7, 1951

THE KEFAUVER SENATE CRIME INVESTIGATING COMMITTEE hearings are continuing in Washington, D. C., at this writing, after their two lively weeks in New York. No doubt the inquiring senators on their home grounds in the national capital will continue to provide TV audiences with the same bewitching brew of entertainment and information that lured millions of citizens to TV sets during the Committee's sessions in New York's Foley Square. No

current or future testimony, however, is likely to rival the
revelations so dramatically made in the town of the "Prime
Minister of Crime," Mr. Frank Costello. The Costello-Hill-
O'Dwyer parlay hit the jackpot, if we may mix two gambling
metaphors; the rest is anticlimactic.

The television industry did its job brilliantly. There is no
detraction in saying that there was really nothing for it to do:
merely turn cameras on the show, and let it unfold. Television,
however, did cover the hearings, cancel programs, recapitulate the
day's testimony in the evenings, go all out.

Neither does it mar the industry's performance to say that
public demand for the televising of the hearings was too great to be
ignored or denied. The public-service responsibility was clear. The
issue of whether or not the presence of cameras at such hearings
constitutes a dangerous invasion of a witness's constitutional rights
seems fairly on its way to being settled. Support is growing steadily
for the opinion that TV ought to be granted the same privileges
as those accorded press and films, provided that the fullest
consideration is given to witnesses acting in good faith and that the
atmosphere of a spectacle is avoided.

The American people have had a profound community
experience in the Kefauver crime hearings. The event has revived
in some measure the ancient, original form of Athenian democracy,
in which all citizens of Athens participated directly in public
affairs. The excitement of sitting in intimate judgment on the
officially exalted and the glamorously corrupt, and the thrill of
having powerful figures, customarily remote or mysterious, make
personal account to the viewers, each has been exhilarating.

Substantially, the hearings have spelled out in concrete detail
abstractions that we all have known. No one is shocked that some
politicians are iniquitous, that many hoodlums are wealthy, and
that specimens of both genera are invariably bosom-serpents. There
are a few of us, however, who know what it all adds up to.

On the one hand you hear: "Nothing will come of it. It's just
shrewd politics. It won't go too far up. It will have to stop short of
where it really hurts." On the other hand you attempt to come to
grips with the essence of the matter. This is a problem in crime,
you reason: the criminal is always with us. Will the deportation of

Costello, the election of "reform" candidates who shoulder fresh brooms, the passage of federal laws dam this too familiar flood of improbity?

The government official and the police officer are tempted by the racketeer's lucre; the gambler lives on the two-dollar bet. The syndicate waxes fat on the unexorcised impulse to wager that is respectably satisfied at church socials, lodge parties, and veterans' meetings. The barber's "on-the-nose-to-win" is legal at the pari-mutuel window—an offense off the track; the stenographer's "snake-eyes" at the gaming table is O.K. just across the county line—but a raid risk inside city limits.

How shall one regard this old social scourge of crime, in the light of the Senate upturnings? What can be done about it?

A reporter, traditionally, does not attempt to answer such questions; they belong on the editorial page. But why? There is no other subject upon which the broadcasters could more expediently editorialize. I should be much, much obliged to the networks if they followed up the Kefauver hearings with several enterprising and well-thought-out documentaries that really got down to cases on the subject, that were broadcast at favorable times, and publicized even slightly after the Kefauver fashion.

I want to know what to think about what I have seen. I want leadership and direction by the experts—criminologists, psychologists, sociologists, statesmen, yes, even philosophers. I want to know whether the Senate crime hearings were merely the whoppingest circus I ever saw—or whether this thing called television can really make a positive dent in our national mores. This is the investigation's ultimate challenge; and no other communication medium has demonstrated a greater capacity to meet it than TV, as the hearings have amply proved. Will television grasp the opportunity or will it rest on its well-deserved Kefauver laurels? We shall follow the industry's response to its greatest challenge.

With a semi-detached attitude, after an interval of years, I find some flaws in this piece. If the reader were to graph or skeletonize it, the message would run tersely as follows: The recent televised hearings, from New York, of the Kefauver Senate Crime Investigating Committee were a great show. The television industry acted responsibly in covering the hearings during the day, at the expense of canceled shows, and in recapitulating the testimony in the evening. It was an American community experience; it presented no new shocks of awareness; most of us know the depth and extent of corruption in the affiliations of racketeers and government officials. We also know how deeply embedded such corruption is in the common mores of respectable citizens. The problem is: what do we do about it?

At this point in the piece, the critic challenges the networks to go beyond mere reporting of the news, and to present documentaries, in depth, that will "make a positive dent in our national mores." He tells the lords of broadcasting that he, the viewer, wants to know what to think about what he has seen. Television has the power, obviously, to accomplish this miracle of behavior change; but will it grasp the opportunity or rest on its laurels? Tune in . . .

It is clear, however, that the critic has done no homework of his own. He has dealt with the "fixities and definites" of the events; he has seen no more than what other perceptive viewers, upon taking the same time and thought, would also have observed. He has added to the material nothing more enlightening than his own unanswered questions. Whatever interest the piece may have for a reader, it falls significantly short of any third beat. A reader could politely and reasonably respond: "So what?" Two weeks before the SR piece appeared in print, I covered the Senate crime hearings for the *Monitor*. For the newspaper I wrote a detailed account of the exciting moments of testimony as captured by the television cameras.

SENATE CRIME HEARINGS FURNISH REAL-LIFE
DRAMA   *March 20, 1951*

THE UNITED STATES SENATE may become television's top supplier of realistic drama.

Televising of the Senate Crime Investigating Committee hearings, currently in New York on its national tour, has raised delicate issues regarding the legality and general propriety of allowing TV cameras to focus on public inquiries. But, should these questions ultimately be resolved in favor of camera-covered investigations, America's august body could undoubtedly continue indefinitely putting on TV programs that no professional broadcasters could rival.

The Senate can command story materials created by the fabulous complexity of the nation itself, principal characters who are playing out part of their own life dramas, and an endless assortment of supernumeraries.

All of this unequaled material can be televised without extra cost or time charges, against legislative and judicial settings exclusively owned by the government.

In terms of audience interest, the impact is unbeatable. The fourth day of televised Kefauver hearings was typical. The first three days had been sensational enough, with the "headless" testimony of Frank Costello, kingpin underworld target of the investigation. The Costello "ballet of the hands" was something new in television.

Costello had complained about the TV cameras as he testified. Senator Kefauver, mellifluously, with gracious southern consideration, had ordered the cameramen not to televise the witness's face. But the ingenious technicians had covered their star from the neck down, catching his eloquent hands as they twirled a pair of horn-rimmed glasses, circled a water glass, or drummed a tattoo on the courtroom table.

Thus, the Kefauver hearings resulted in camera techniques that defied studio custom. The bane of directors in conventional TV is an "unframed" shot. Here was the senate committee helping to break Camera Rule No. 1—and getting undreamed-of effects.

The testimony of Samuel Levine, an agent of the Bureau of Narcotics, produced equally unorthodox and arresting results. Mr. Levine was not shown at all, in order to keep his identity a secret, and we TV spectators had a scene in which the key figure was offstage for his entire testimony.

Senator Charles W. Tobey (R) of New Hampshire played what in fiction drama would have been the "colorful character" role in the investigation drama—a forthright, salty, New England Diogenes, with "a touch of evangelism and a fund of biblical and literary aphorisms." He had quoted John Greenleaf Whittier, the

poet, and fervently moralized on the corruption that was being
unfolded.

The remaining committee senators; Rudolph Halley, the committee's chief counsel; the stenographers, witnesses, attendants,
privileged spectators; and the anonymous hands, arms, shoulders
and faces which passed with almost rhythmic irregularity before the
cameras—all these had performed excellently, holding attention,
building mood, creating suspense.

But no one—perhaps not even the committee itself—was
prepared for the dramatic climax that was to erupt "ad lib" on the
investigation's fourth day. Frank C. Bals, a former New York City
Deputy Police Commissioner, took the stand—firmly erect, gray-
haired, a distinguished-looking erstwhile guardian of the law.

The tale he reluctantly unfolded of police connections with
gamblers was bizarre enough to wring from Senator Tobey the
comment: "O. Henry in all his wonderful moments never conceived
of such a silly story as this!"

Few professional writers would have dared to perpetrate upon
an audience Mr. Bals's "clincher" to his story. Solemnly, he
affirmed that a certain underworld figure accidentally fell to his
death from a hotel window, while playing an innocent jest on six
husky policemen who had been detailed to guard him. The officers
were all oddly asleep in the same room at the identical moment
during which the witness played his grim "prank."

The hearings were full of theatrical contrasts. There were the
flat, unemotional, official readings of lines by such witnesses as
agent Levine and former Commissioner Bals. There was the
diffidently given testimony of Philip B. Stephens, business manager
of the New York *Daily News*. Mr. Stephens testified to an
unsuccessful attempt by a mysterious group of longshoremen to
extort $100,000 from his paper, as tribute for unloading a shipment
of newsprint.

In the next to final scene, the committee placed a "surprise"
witness, Mrs. Virginia Hill Hauser. The saga of Mrs. Hauser,
from Bessemer, Alabama, to Foley Square, New York, is material for
a legend. Dressed in a silver mink stole, pretty and defiant, Mrs.
Hauser will not soon be forgotten by the TV audience that saw her

give the representatives of the United States Senate a piece of her astonishing mind.

The third act held another climax. Frank Costello, the almost unseen star, hoarsely, speaking somewhat less than the king's English, took in stride the committee's warnings of arrest and a contempt citation and refused to testify. Pleading poor health, he asked for a postponement, which was not granted. He walked off the scene at precisely the moment he was expected to reveal the exact state of his bank account and the ultimate nature of his relationship with high political figures.

Television's mighty technological revolution continues apace. But with the United States Senate outdoing Alfred Hitchcock—where will it end?

The difference between the sr and the *Monitor* pieces may be explained by the critic's unwillingness to repeat himself. It is interesting, though, that for the *Monitor* I wrote essentially a reporter's report, with a framing fillip about the Senate as a possible supplier of top realistic drama on television, while for sr I assumed that the audience knew the details of the show, and directed my attention to thoughts beyond the event itself. Perhaps writing for a magazine, with its more leisurely deadlines, invites contemplation to a degree not practicable in filing newspaper copy. In any case the *Monitor* piece is less a cell-firing candidate than the sr column.

Once again, as in the Toynbee–Chicago television piece, the counter-dialectic is missing. The question is put: "Will the networks take up the challenge?" but no consideration is given to a possible answer of "no." And once again, time provided the answer. Thumbing the years swiftly, I find at least ten pieces which deal with network coverage of spectacular hearings or with comparable emergency sessions of the United Nations. In 1958 an sr tv-radio column, *"Time,* Popeye and the U. N." (August 30, 1958), defended the three networks' unscheduled preemptions (mostly of regular daytime programs) in order to cover United Nations Security Council debates on the crisis in Lebanon. *Time* magazine had reported belligerent phone calls and letters from regular tv viewers who resented the interruption of their enjoyment of such shows as

"Woody Woodpecker," "Zorro," "Circus Boy," "Mickey Mouse," and "Queen for a Day."

The critic had conducted his own poll of viewer response to the U. N. programs; having found evidence of enthusiastic reception, he wrote:

> Not all American housewives, it seems, were frightened, bored, and seeking anxious escape or ersatz fulfillment from TV. Television managers must bear their fair share of the diffused responsibility for whatever anger was loosed by the U. N. coverage; you cannot feed an appetite and then play the astonished innocent when you suddenly cut off the food supply and the hungry turn on you. But those who are for the networks' "higher destiny" are as many (perhaps more) than those who are opposed. True, the United Nations debates are very formal, very cerebral stuff. But there are many "publics" in the United States, and it is dangerous to forget that it is usually the "smaller" public that votes and makes crucial decisions for all of us. If we are to accept *Time*'s image of ourselves, then the American show is over—for everyone, networks and sponsors included. Hopefully, it "just ain't so."

Thus, to the question, "Will the networks respond to the challenge of preempting money-producing programs in order to present long periods of public events?" (cerebral as in the case of the U. N. sessions; theatrically exciting as in the case of the Kefauver crime hearings), was added a related question: "Does the television public want such programs carried at the cost of their opportunity to watch their favorite entertainment programs?" The latter question, that very year, 1958, was already producing (or reproducing) a familiar schism in TV's soul. Several weeks before "*Time,* Popeye and the U. N.," I did a piece called "The Mystery of the Peppermint Candy Men" (SR, August 9, 1958) in which no less an important industry figure than Sylvester L. (Pat) Weaver, Jr., former vice president, president, and chairman of the board of NBC, was quoted as accusing TV of "failing to reflect as a communication medium the whole richness and pluralism of our society ... as the networks abdicate certain areas of culture and information that they have been in . . ." But the SR piece went on to quote Richard Salant, vice president at CBS, in a counter claim:

> We've let ourselves get pushed into agreeing that "public interest" really means that kind of program in which not much of the public is really interested . . . let's admit that we're in business to entertain. If we do that, perhaps that will end this attempt to make us over in the image of the BBC, but with advertisers.

Two years later, as reported in the critic's "Danger Signal" (SR, November 4, 1961), it was William S. Paley, Chairman of the Board of CBS, who spoke out for "quality" in broadcasting as opposed to "popularity"; and it was *Broadcasting* magazine, the industry's leading trade weekly, that voiced a conflicting view in an editorial (October 16, 1961). Reflected the CBS Chairman of the Board at a network affiliates meeting:

> They [the people] may be temporarily intrigued by the cheap or the gaudy. But the cheap or gaudy runs its course fast, and the competition for enduring acceptance and solid growth is based on the courageous rather than the brazen, the satisfying rather than the tantalizing, the moving rather than the shocking.

Broadcasting, on the other hand, reported a slight drop, in 1961, in evening viewing in all television homes (from 45.3 per cent in 1959 to 44.9 per cent in 1961). "It is conceivable," said the editorial, "that we may be seeing the first effects of the rising volume of public service programing that critics have been clamoring for."

Two years later (1963), the question: "Out of which sides of their mouths do responsible industry spokesmen speak?" had become academic. Twelve years had gone by since the electric excitement of the Kefauver crime hearings on television, with their swelling promise of theater in the capital, and of profound, mores-altering community experience for the American people, Athenian fashion; and now, an even graver question had come to town, implicit in the critic's report and commentary on another celebrated congressional hearing that investigated organized crime in the United States.

CONGRESS AND THE COSA NOSTRA   *November 9, 1963*

TELEVISION'S HANDLING of the testimony of Joseph Valachi before the Senate Subcommittee on Investigations is an example of self-defeating rigidity in network program structure. The complete coverage of the mild-mannered mobster's fingering of the Mafia was easily the best show of the new season, yet only CBS News carried unabridged telecasts of the hearings in Washington (and these were shown during the daytime in the first week only). All nets had excerpts in their evening newscasts, plus boiled-down specials for the workaday worldlings who couldn't watch "Congress and the Cosa Nostra" morning and afternoon. But such compressions couldn't begin to catch the full flavor and fascination of the nearly forty-year saga of the New York West Side school drop-out who became a lowly killer-soldier or "outside button-man" in the army of Vito Genovese, "boss of all bosses." It was superb entertainment and important public information, yet none of the networks would or could clear away chunks of prime time at night for Valachi's unedited singing exercise, despite the fact that the telecasts would probably have piled up impressive ratings.

Radio, which so often stimulates the listener's imagination, proved a distorting medium in the case of Valachi. A friend who heard the proceedings on his car radio in Washington was struck by the vividness with which Valachi fulfilled the stereotype of the hoodlum—coarse, uneducated, sinister. The camera revealed an anti-stereotype mobster. Here was a confessed burglar, loan shark, narcotics dealer, and murderer, yet paradoxically he impressed television viewers as the prototype of the kindly immigrant fruit peddler. He caught on quickly to congressional testifying, and seemed ahead of several of his inquisitors.

Often he would patiently lecture the committee members, solicitous in his query: "Do you understand, Senator? Want me to explain it further, Senator?" He was the lower class in the Capitol, but he was mentally agile. Even tough-minded viewers might speculate how different this man's life could have been if the breaks

in a more rational society had fallen his way more softly. His revelations of secret oaths and blood-pricking at Cosa Nostra swearing-in
ceremonies were touched with comic opera, and humor was rampant
through this morality play—with middle-class judgment at one side
of the table and the locked-out, no-status criminal at the other. The
supporting cast was great. Offstage, in Valachi's memoirs, the figure
of "Buster," who looked like a "collegian" and carried a violin case
with a concealed submachine gun, was the incredible fusion of
truth and a "Little Caesar" movie of the thirties. On stage, the collision of Valachi's mob jargon with Senator John McClellan's
Arkansas accent was spectacular Americana. If there was a villain
in the piece, it was the chairman himself, whose incessant inter-
ruptions of the witness were maddening. One could only conjecture
that he wanted to make sure his constituents back home in the hills
understood this fellow from New York's underworld: that's why he
persisted in translating every word, no matter how clear, for the
television audience. The show even had charts showing the prolifera-
tion of the mob dynasties. And when the chairman, at one juncture,
recessed the hearings until after lunch, he announced (in next-week
trailer fashion) that Valachi would be back in the afternoon with
the details of three murders in which he participated.

All such vigor, and more, was bled away in the truncated
versions of the hearings that the networks showed at night.

It's rich human documentary, and perhaps some imaginative
ETV station can get the video tapes and show them complete for
future nighttime audiences. Knowledgeable analysts from several
disciplines would enrich such telecasts. Among them might be
Daniel Bell, the sociologist at Columbia University, author of *The
End of Ideology,* an excellent collection of essays in a Collier Books
paperback. In one chapter, "Crime as an American Way of Life,"
Mr. Bell wrote in 1953 (and let stand in 1962) the view that the
Mafia was a myth. "Unfortunately for a good story," he noted,
"—and the existence of the Mafia would be a whale of a story—
neither the Senate Crime Committee in its testimony, nor Kefauver
in his book, presented any real evidence that the Mafia exists as a
functioning organization." I'm sure it would be both engrossing and
instructive to watch Mr. Bell—for whom I bear a high respect—
eat whale.

The critic, this time, had a point and he went directly to it in his first sentence, with the key phrase of the critical proposition: "self-defeating rigidity in network program structure." "Easily the best show of the new season . . ." he wrote, "yet none of the networks would or could clear away chunks of prime time at night for Valachi's unedited singing exercise, despite the fact that the telecasts would probably have piled up impressive ratings." The critic, by now, had soberly forgotten all dreams that the networks would respond to the challenges of such hearings by carrying them in full in prime time and by following them up with reflective, in-depth documentaries, in an attempt to expose the social roots of crime and to modify the mores of the nation. "Perhaps," the critic was willing to settle for, "some imaginative ETV station can get the video tapes and show them complete for future nighttime audiences. Knowledgeable analysts [the dream dies hard!] from several disciplines would enrich such telecasts."

The final paragraph about the sociologist who had denied the existence of the Mafia was merely an appendage to the piece—too good to be resisted, but having no connection with the heart of the matter. The critic was still looking for someone to respond to his challenges, but his gaze had turned away from the commercial networks to the new boys in the game, the educational broadcasters. In Toynbee's terms, he was still unwilling to transfer his field of action "from the macrocosm to the microcosm," from the response of the broadcasters to his own response. He had made no genuine movement within himself, in transcending the unwillingness of the broadcasters to respond to his challenges. His range of vision, twelve years later, had been enlarged enough to comprehend the dialectical negation of his first, fond hopes that the networks would bring viewers not only great events in their completeness in time, but also great third beats of those events—their significations: but he stopped short of evoking a fresh insight out of the collision of challenge and no response.

By 1964, coverage of the United Nations moved over to the commendable efforts of the Xerox Corporation to translate the meaning of the world council into entertainment terms, in a series of filmed programs that cost willing Xerox shareholders a reputed $4,000,000. As for coverage of the Cosa Nostra, the FBI took over that job (and is still at it as of this writing) on the ABC network, Sunday evenings, in the fictionalized triumphs of FBI agent Lewis Erskine. In 1967, when William S. Paley, at CBS, had to choose between a network program chief who wanted to carry reruns of "I Love Lucy" and a network news chief who insisted on carrying the Senate Foreign Relations Committee's hearings on Vietnam—not in prime time, which was unthinkable, but in the daytime—he chose "the cheap and the gaudy, the brazen rather than the courageous, the tantalizing rather than the satisfying, and the shocking rather than the moving." The word "moving" is marvelously fortuitous; for the idle ship is still idle upon its painted color TV ocean. There is hardly a breeze anywhere; and the critic ought to know that he can never get it moving by macrocosmic maneuvers. He must expostulate inwardly, move himself to a novel togetherness that transcends the question of outer movement or immobility; and by his transferring the breath of that cell-firing to other cells and moving them, perhaps the wind that never comes can approach with a loud roar after sleep and gentle rain.

In Milton's *Paradise Lost,* when Satan and his legions are hurled out of heaven, and they consider among themselves what response they should make to their peculiar challenge, the Prince of Devils declares: "I give not heaven for lost." He calls then upon his counselors for advice on how to proceed. Moloch counsels fight, "armed with hell-flames and fury." Belial counsels "ignoble ease and peaceful sloth": accept, resign to fate. Mammon urges privatization: "Live to ourselves . . . dismissing quite all thoughts of war." Beelzebub, the last of the counselors to speak, rejects all previous suggestions, and quite devilishly (for he is inspired by Satan) directs attention to "some new race, called Man . . . Seduce them to our party," he urges, "that their God may prove their foe, and with repenting hand/ Abolish his own works." The bold design pleases all; and their matchless chief himself volunteers for the task, and sets out in search of the new world, to begin his seductive cell-firing. Satan was the first critic.

CHAPTER EIGHT

Show-Biz, Politics, and Dissent

The journalist can realize the ideal of the modern universalized man . . . He deliberately interweaves his destiny with that of the epoch. He takes alarm, he suffers, and he balks when he encounters Nothingness. He becomes insincere when he is content with that which brings satisfaction to the majority.

KARL JASPERS

IN AN EARLIER CHAPTER, I quoted with approbation Jaspers' idealization of the journalist, and accepted its prescribed code of conduct for the critic. It expressed well my own notion of the proper function of the critic, operating from a ground of ethical value. To the prescribed behavior must be added, however, a most important critical characteristic—namely, the capacity for taking into account the negation of one's own values, for representing the opposition fairly in the inner debates which go on in the critic's mind, and for giving outer expression to the opposing point of view when the critic formulates and sends out his cell-firing messages.

The necessity for taking one's opponent into account does not stop with fairness to him; it extends to the demand for the fullest possible knowledge of an object under critical observation. Expertness is a requisite for criticism—familiarity with the history, the literature, the *dramatis personae* of the field in which a critic operates. I have used the word "sophistication" earlier to epitomize the necessary bundle of qualities. Sophistication may have to be learned.

In my previous analyses of critical pieces (the Toynbee–Chicago television series and the hearings–investigations–United Nations group), I noted how this lack of sophistication faulted the early critiques because I was, during that early period in my development as a critic, not sufficiently aware of the market-place realities of the commercial broadcasting system. I was not entirely unfamiliar with them; my career in broadcasting as "creative talent" had brought me face to face with the dominance of the economic factor in programing: but the interface was largely on a personal level, that of my own programs, my particular production problems. It was not until I had been writing criticism for five years that I did a piece on the Federal Communications Commission.

The institutional framework of broadcasting did not loom large in my critical consciousness in the early years. My pieces show concern for the technical aspects of the creative process in broadcasting, for large social issues, for the development of educational broadcasting. I occasionally looked across the Atlantic and envied the British their BBC. The promise of technological innovations attracted my attention—color television, phonevision (pay TV), transistors, the possibilities inherent in the development of FM and of the UHF channels. The internal business aspects of broadcasting seemed to hold little interest for me, but they became eventually the most important lessons that I had to learn: the creator's view had to be broadened to include the market-place complex in which the creator is the least important element. Talent, however publicized and misrepresented as the *sine qua non* of the game, is really the pawn, disposable, dispensable, and easily replaceable. The man who can choose the winners in the program race has the talent that is truly treasured by the managers behind the scenes.

To know the real rules of the game is to be able to challenge one's own critical faiths and hopes with their counter-dialectic, which compels the critic to try to fight his way out of dialectical collisions to a higher level of insight. One can be faulted for not having mastered lessons in expertise which already exist, which are in the possession of other observers who have studied the game; one hurries to catch up: but what is the critic to do when he faces the inscrutable teacher whose lessons no one can know in advance—history. He must master such lessons as they unfold, he along with all others (unless, like a Marxist or some other ultimate knower, he possesses the certain key to the future and can predict it or adapt it to his theorizing). Mastering those lessons, growing in his own awareness of the dynamic web of experience and consciousness, he perforce, in keeping with his particular theories of being and of value, must seek to change the world in accordance with his beliefs.

This is his Kantian categorical imperative; his morality becomes his duty: but the critic, above all others (although it would be well if all others—politicians, artists, businessmen, just plain human beings—adhered to the prescription), must be dialectically responsible, and must take into account what Clio teaches. History will change the critic (he is no critic if he does not change), and the critic must transmit the changes into his criticism; he must recycle change in his cell-firing, for the higher the level of consciousness in the total critical mass, the higher is the energy potential of the critic, for whom the total living, growing system is not only the receptor of his critical effluvia but also the ineradicable source of its regeneration. The critic must expect to be surprised by history, but he must be ready to deal with the surprises dialectically, responsibly, taking novelty into account, whether it be in accord with his own prejudices or opposed to them.

In reviewing my criticism, I found no surprise more striking than the one tendered by the future at the interface where politics meets television—campaigns, conventions, and the relationships of network news departments to government administrations. The record reveals an early cavalier attitude of "a plague on both your houses" (politicians' and networks'), an irreverent, often cynical sense of detached amusement, an ambiguous tension between hope for the democratic process and ironic despair. Then this attitude sobers, as the icy atmosphere of the unrelenting, global cold war intensifies the polarization of the political currents in the United States. A forthright, partisan posture is slowly articulated; but with a determined, dialectical taking-into-account of virtues and faults in friend and foe—a posture at once detached and committed, biased and yet intent on reflecting rather than distorting; a posture loyal to the critic's own position only to the extent that that position is loyal to a dialectical whole in which the total organism is both challenged by and responsive to each cell of the system.

For a hit-and-run type of criticism, strong on prophecy but weak on analysis and dialectic, the politicians confronted by television were an easy target ("Campaigning Before the Cameras," sr, October 6, 1951). Noting that 1952 would see "America's first national political campaign conducted in significant measure on television," I commented on some early examples—in that year's New York State campaign for governor—of experiments in visualization and movement on camera, as opposed to the old fireside chat technique, inherited from radio, with its protagonist reading from a script. ". . . the crust of custom has been broken," I wrote:

> Candidates for public office, national or local, will in the future be constrained, each according to the funds and facilities available, by the mere pressure of comparison and competition, to pursue this new path of tv political debate. Television will make it insufficient henceforth for candidates to be laudable. They will have to be viewable. This means daring exploitation of new political communication techniques—the discussion, the documentary, perhaps even the variety show. Why not? In striving to hold the audience, the candidate could well utilize the satiric sketch, the song, even the ballet. The ultimate would be the relegation of the argument to the status of the commercial—in jingle form. It would certainly make for livelier campaigns: the results could hardly be worse than they have been; they might even be better. As for sober reasoning— that would scarcely be missed. When has it been present, in politics or on television?

A light touch, solemnity avoided: why not? No reader can mistake the critic's slight bitterness: of course the critic values "sober reasoning," and he would like to see it both in politics and on television, but the implication is that its presence in either is not altogether vital; the republic will endure. A year later, a heightened sense of the same playful approach—intensified by an esthetic relish for a tragicomic piece of political theater—signified that the critic still regarded televised politics as entertainment to be filed with old play folios rather than as meaningful history.

"IT SAYS HERE WE SHOULD TALK"   *August 9, 1952*

TELEVISION'S IMAGE of the Democratic or (as the Republican orators
are so cunningly calling it this year) the "Democrat" party's convention will be yesterday's show when this column is in print. The
nominations will have been witnessed, the demonstrations endured
—and all the audiovisual details of the political circus, serious, trivial,
antic, dull, or disturbing, will be history. "Politics in the public eye,"
says an NBC ad, "makes for a show you'll tell your grandchildren
about."

I don't know what the reader will tell his grandchildren about;
but civil rights, filibuster, Governor Adlai Stevenson, President
Truman, or any dark horse running to or from the nomination
notwithstanding, I do not believe the second exposé from Chicago of
the nation's chief game for adults will produce anything to rival the
spectacle when Mr. (then General of the Army) Dwight D.
Eisenhower broke convention tradition and called on Senator
Robert A. Taft at the defeated candidate's headquarters in the
Conrad Hilton Hotel for a closing-of-the-ranks posture and a joint
harmony statement.

The Puerto Rico delegate demanding a roll-call of three was
amusing; Representative Dirksen's pointing of the accusatory
finger at Governor Dewey was a study in hate; General MacArthur's
keynote address was a lesson in anticlimax; Minnesota's change of
vote, which climactically threw the victory to Ike, was a brilliant
riposte in the unexpected, etc. But for a scene "coming up like
thunder," a Roman-candle scene of words, pictures, and silences, of
Elizabethan fustian, Mack Sennett gaiety, biblical bitterness, and
Homeric irony and pity— the denouement at the Conrad Hilton
goes into my permanent memory vault as Exhibit A.

The reader may have missed it: it happened—like death and
triumph in a comparable arena—in the afternoon. The sudden
nomination after the first ballot caught everyone by surprise,
particularly the television networks. In a later column, when TV's
coverage of both conventions is available for appraisal, the writer
hopes to comment on it. Meanwhile, whatever one may think of the
conventions themselves, it is obvious beyond the largest cavil that

TV, the eye that talks, did a magnificent reporting job, rich in distributional success and generous with consequences for our now fluid political mores.

At the Conrad Hilton, though, immediately after the nomination, it appeared to this viewer that the TV production masterminds were caught with their cables and cameras kaput. Perhaps they had reckoned on Taft calling on Eisenhower at the winner's headquarters; perhaps the sudden excitement unhinged all precision. Whatever happened, events took the ball away from the Republican party convention organizers and network staffs alike. The marvelous moments that followed found television the unplanned, unwilling, and unmatched star of the show it was covering.

As the master-control panels cut to Taft's headquarters, the viewer faced a small, uncertain line of reporters facing their own cameras. Microphones in hand, earphones on head, cables snaking to perspiring technicians, the newsmen stood like Horatius, or as Greeks at Thermopylae, their backs resistant to the undulating surges of an anonymous, shirt-sleeved chorus behind them. Hectic, frantic, frenetic, they burbled and gurgled in their ad-libs, trying to find out what was happening, striving to be interesting, and above all, heroically struggling not to be hipped out of the camera and away from the spot where they guessed the Taft-Eisenhower romance would be played.

The suavity of the TV-radio newsman, cool, dispassionate, detached, was gone. It was every man for his network and the guilt of the damned to pay if he allowed himself to be strong-armed away from this pooled morsel. Antagonistic cooperators, the reporters jollied each other but their chins were out. Someone handed Clifton Utley, usually a brilliant analyst, a piece of paper. He glanced at it, fingered it, glanced at it again, and then said rather hysterically to two colleagues: "It says here we should talk to each other."

Well, talk they did—the tapes have the record. It will never get into a textbook of model newscaster behavior under fire, but it was splendid, hilarious fun, fun at the newsmen's predicament, fun with them at the monkey-wrench in the show's unctuous machine. It was the suffering-with-laughter mood that audiences enjoy most.

Then came a squad of cops boomeranging through the Chaplinesque world. They disappeared stage right, they boomeranged back.

It was Taft and Eisenhower. The laughter curiously enveloped the protagonists. Literally pushed and shoved into the choked iron ring of the camera's eye, the Senator and the General tried valiantly to maintain their mutual dignities. It was no go. The viewer felt for them, but the deflation of political pomposity made a delicious, hissing sound.

The General suffered it with an amateur's amiability, but the Senator, more seasoned mufti campaigner (with little to lose now that he had lost), finally had enough. Like an irascible teacher he took control of the situation and braved the brief ceremony. And here came the bitterness, the irony, and the pity. For, as with set smiles the victor and the vanquished rendered unto political expediency and the sportsman's code their perfunctory obeisance, tides of emotional conflict, via sympathetic identification, tugged at the viewer before his screen.

Beneath the General's mask lay the clear realization of the humiliating burden of brass-knuckle politics on the human psyche; beneath the Senator's the galling savor of defeat at the hands of a political novice. It was a moving tableau—and in an ambulatory sense it moved as hurriedly off stage as it had moved on. "That's all," said Senator Taft. The General grimly echoed him, and as the burly cops opened a hole in the chorus, the tragic actors disappeared and the clowns took the stage again.

Out of a magnificent, unstaged bedlam montage of shoulders, hands, backs, ear-lobes, and haircuts passing in close-up before the hot-breathing cameras, emerged the still-mumbling figures of the newsmen. Hair askew, eyes displaced, deservers of TV's purple heart, they stagged on defiantly, wearily, until merciful fadeout. It was an uproarious finish to an unforgettable scene played in concentric circles of high drama, small comedy, and epic background.

This piece has always been a special favorite of mine. Observed under the spectroscope of our three-beat critical formula, it does not make it. Essentially the piece says: "Wow! It was some scene. Let me tell you about it." True, in the two paragraphs before the last, it probes the deeper human emotions underlying the episode; but in the end it merely reiterates the opening note of unforgettable comic drama, without kicking off some novel insight which transcends the episode itself by relating it to something other than itself. Nevertheless, I have never been a dogmatist or a purist, especially in the case of my own formula. I like that part of Nietzsche's thinking which permits contradictions and dramatic paradox. I do not go all the way with him to an apparent chaos of utterance; but I am sympathetic to the opinion put forward by the Nietzschean scholar, George Allen Morgan, who observed in *What Nietzsche Means*:

> His [Nietzsche's] thought on any topic is not a simple-minded opinion but a significant strife of ideas through which he works toward some complex synthesis. Whether successful or not, that effort electrifies the mind to wrestle in turn with issues of ineluctable importance . . . Nietzsche gives one a new conception of depth. The objects he describes take on half a dozen dimensions instead of two or three.

The Eisenhower-Taft piece may have, arbitrarily, one beat and a half—but in my opinion the piece works; and that may be due to the fact that the thinness of the architecture is compensated by the richness of the texture. The observed scene itself is so vivid, with so many internal dimensions, that it may be said to contain its own significance as well as its sign. The event speaks a critical proposition, a novel togetherness which is not verbalized but which we feel, nevertheless. There is, in criticism, a dialectic of feeling, perhaps, as clear as that of knowing; wiser thinkers or feelers may someday translate it into the verbal code.

Two weeks after the Eisenhower-Taft piece, in "Time on My Eyes" (SR, August 23, 1952), the critic moved from cynicism to sentiment about conventions on television. He wrote about the nominating conventions of both parties, which had recently been televised:

> Despite various predictions, the fact is that all the frontier accoutrements and tin cans of political cut-up, horseplay, and wind-baggery that we have come to identify with conventions were regrettably and offensively present. [He predicted that]

lacking a creative renaissance in the strategy committees that plan the conventions, the 1956 nominating sessions will be substantially the same in tone and *mise-en-scene* as the 1952 'deliberations.' Conventions are business meetings, [after all,] and not dramatic creations; they cannot, worse luck, be firmly 'staged' by the talented hand of a bold, imaginative *regisseur*.

It may well be that TV's great social modification potential has been overrated. All television has never known a more compelling show than the 1951 Senate Crime Committee hearings chaired by the erstwhile candidate from Tennessee, Estes Kefauver. The potential dynamite was atomic (or so it seemed in the heyday of Hill, Halley, and Frank Costello):

Nevertheless, the writer has not heard or read of any gambling laws passed by the Congress to deal with a patently revealed national situation. As for local laws, my radio informed me recently that this year only a handful of New York's bookies renewed their operating licenses. The white-slip boys are chesting again in their contempt for the law.

Looking ahead to 1956, and advising viewers who planned to buy television sets how to conduct themselves while witnessing the quadrennial political ritual of the nominating conventions, he wrote in the same piece:

The blunderbuss rhetoric of the keynote, nominating, and guest speeches may disgust you; the synthetic snake-walk demonstrations appall you; the doubtfully motivated polling of the individual state delegations drive you to tune off. On the other hand, there will be moments when you sharply search candidates' faces and voices, gestures and ideas. The speaking camera will reinforce many of your impressions about individual politicians, completely reverse others . . .

There will come the blue-chip moments when out of the earthquake, wind, and fire of your emotions the still small voice of meaning will emerge. And that will be when the delegates vote. And when the roll-call begins you should get a thrill. For these men and women are free, and this is democracy with a small "d." You may except as you will that the delegates are people in politics serving their own ends and that these ends are not always consistent with what we vaguely call "the public good." You may talk of machines and bosses, and of the cynical realities of how government really operates—and you may be right.

Notwithstanding all, however, there is still the undeniable truth of choice. In the same delegation the delegates splinter. One man is Eisenhower, another Taft; one Harriman, the other Russell. And the provincial fervor of their announcements as they call out their votes for the chairman, the convention, the folks back home, and the nation to hear is a drum-beat for spirits depressed by the signs of the times.

It was not always so in the long record of governments and men. It is not everywhere so today. Barely several years ago it was not so in Europe and Asia—how quickly we forget!

Television also covers the elections in November and we see and hear the reporters as the votes roll in. But in November the voice of the people is silent, invisible. Only in July every four years, via TV, is the voice in the open, identified with a face, touched with diverse accents of a sectional heterogeneity. Listen to that voice; look at that face closely. They should be familiar. They are, after all, the voice and face of our free institutions.

Thus far, then, the critic exposes his ambiguity: politics on television are pomposity, wind-baggery, fustian; but in flashing moments underneath the bitter nonsense pulsates the elusive prom-ise of democracy with a small "d," a *fata morgana* that may really be there. Four years later the critic ignores the 1956 campaign; he writes nothing at all about it; presumably his attitudes toward politics on television have remained the same. In the next four years, from 1960 to 1964, a slight change is discernible. Three individual pieces written in 1960, 1962, and 1964 reflect a sobering of his views. He begins to evaluate television's impact on politics seriously and to apportion responsibility among politicians and networks.

"Who," he asks ("Pavlov and Politics," SR, January 23, 1960), "is going to discuss the *issues* of the [1960] presidential campaign?" His question has been triggered by a speech made by Mr. Sig

Mickelson, president of CBS News. The network executive, in that speech, claims for the electronic medium that it has "increased the degree of independent thinking . . . It has resulted in balloting more on reason than emotion. Television, I believe, has made enormous contributions toward creating a more knowledgeable and more sophisticated voter." But then, in the light of the foregoing, the CBS executive makes a surprising segue. He advises political candidates to avoid preempting regular entertainment programs for paid political talks. Better get on regular newscasts, he recommends. People who tune in the news are not put off by candidates when they appear on their tubes; but if the candidate takes the place of a viewer's favorite Western, the result is irritation at the intrusion. The critic observes that: "The picture of an audience 'knowledgeable, sophisticated, thinking independently, and balloting more on reason than emotion' is out of synch with the soundtrack of an audience prepared to take politics as news but not as an unwelcome intrusion on 'Dennis the Menace.' "

The critic indulges, in this piece, in a favorite exercise—confronting network philosophers with cracks in their syllogisms. Pavlov is the bi-sociation element which he unites, in this piece, with politics on television. The critical proposition is stated in the opening paragraph:

> A favorite argument of the advocates of sponsored broadcasting
> is that you have to feed mass audiences regularly with bread
> so that when cake time comes around they will be there,
> available for the feast. You must hold them with escape
> entertainment, in other words, so that when presidential
> elections arrive you'll have a ready-made rostrum built, from
> which the candidates can communicate to voters who will make
> the wiser choice. The theory encounters a Pavlovian difficulty,
> however. If you condition a dog to salivate and feed at
> prescribed stimuli, the Russian scientist showed, you will only
> irritate and confuse him if you disarrange the sequence of
> the signals . . .

The Pavlov beat, which integrates the total piece, is threaded in again, briefly, in the middle:

All media, generally, share with TV the credit for conditioning the escape-oriented citizen-voter. At election times, our national plebiscites, which should be matters of dialectics, must accommodate themselves to the prevailing winds of rhetoric which please and persuade.

The network executive's advice to candidates is: "get yourself an advertising agency—an indispensable requirement to a successful political campaign." Be natural, informal; have human interest. And the campaign, the critic anticipates, "will be conducted on TV in precisely this adjusted manner. It will be good business for the news departments of the networks; it will give minimum disturbance to the basic pattern of TV entertainment which must continue when the elections are over." Now the critic splits the hitherto indiscriminate double image of the politician and broadcaster and points a finger singularly at the networks:

The real challenge of the 1960 campaign on TV, it would seem, lies not at the feet of the politicians but at the door of the news departments of the networks. If it makes sense to them to shepherd the debaters into their tidy, TV news and human interest corners and off the rougher highways-for-the-confronta-tion-of-ideas, then the newsmen must take up the slack and illuminate candidates and issues searchingly and with editorial coverage.

And, in a commendable effort to button up his third beat, with a return to the critical proposition, which attempts to push it yet further—beyond the end of the piece—hopefully in the *reader's* mind, the critic concludes:

I can name a few newscasters who I am sure will attempt to do this, but looking at television's conditioned reflexes generally, I am afraid the dilemma would be too much even for Pavlov.

1960 was the year of the great Kennedy-Nixon debates; but the critic ignored them. He was then—and remains still—among the minority of observers of the television scene who were never impressed with the value of the debates for voters interested in issues rather than in personalities, nor with the allegedly decisive impact of the debates on the 1960 presidential election. He held to this view in spite of the impressive array of polls and scholarly studies of the debates which contributed to the general impression that they were extraordinarily effective in modifying voter behavior. He could produce no comparable evidence for his own view of the matter; and this in itself may have been evidence of a rather blind stubbornness in the face of "fact;" but the whole field of verbal responses to questionnaires is mined with so many semantic and psychological booby-traps, that he regarded his suspicion of the methods which measure behavior change in terms of verbal description as reasonable if not justifiable. Voters do change their minds midstream during campaigns, and television must have an effect on the dynamic pattern of choice; but to attribute singular and decisive weight to the images emanating from the tube at election time, and to ignore the complex web of factors, personal and social, within which television operates, is to take too simple-minded a position.

Two years later ("Little League Great Debate," SR, September 22, 1962), the critic referred, in an offhand, negative way, to the Kennedy-Nixon confrontations on television. The occasion was a piece commenting on the Massachusetts Democratic primary contest for Senator between Edward "Ted" Kennedy and Edward M. McCormack:

> The Kennedy-McCormack debates on television demonstrated again the uselessness (for the public) of the format which calls for opening statements, panel questions, candidate answers, rebuttals, and summaries. The devices permit a candidate complete self-service without his ever being seriously challenged on anything.

Again ("The Making of a Documentary," SR, January 18, 1964), reviewing the ABC network program that Theodore H. White fashioned from *The Making of the President 1960,* the critic made this negative comment, as if to justify his bias against television debates:

Videotapes of the studio preparations that preceded the first of
the "great debates" on television between Kennedy and Nixon
were especially interesting. The atmosphere in the studio was
clearly that of a prize fight: the referee (producer) instructing
the champ and the challenger (the candidates); the seconds
(advisers) milling around; and the "come out fighting"
handshake. The impression of a boxing match was heightened
by a narrator's reference to the gray suit worn unfortunately
by Vice President Nixon: it didn't photograph as well as
Senator Kennedy's black suit.

In commenting on the 1962 Kennedy-McCormack "Little League
Great Debate," the critic concluded:

If television is to serve politics wisely; if it is to help and not
hinder the democratic process, it must move—and require the
candidates to move—away from the nonsense of the hit-and-run
panel.

The concluding comment on the major subject of the piece, "The
Making of the President 1960," was that the documentary film
should be shown often:

Aficionados of gut-politics, like Mr. White, will find in it an
affirmation of the virtues of our democracy. Other viewers may
see it as a brilliant fulfillment of some of de Tocqueville's
more gloomy predictions.

History, it seems, was moving the critic. Politics on television
were being commented on more often; he was taking a more serious
view of the marriage of the media of persuasion to nondialectical
manipulation. Faithful, after his fashion, to his notions of ethics
involving the views of others, he was taking into account views different from his own: but he was not reluctant to assert that the
shadows were growing longer. A broadcasting system in the United
States which was dominated by and submissive to a government of
the extreme right—this was the fear that, for the critic, loomed

largest in the shadows: communications without a critic at the heart of the public life of the nation.

To a liberal-minded critic, the worst possibility, naturally, would be broadcasting subservient to a right-wing political administration. The question immediately arises dialectically: would the critic fear as much the subservience of the media to a left-of-center government? His convictions have not yet been tested in the fires of history, but his ethical system demands that he reply at once and strongly: Yes. A nondialectical situation—a political organism without a built-in critical faculty—would be unacceptable, whatever the shade of the politics involved. It would be a necessary violation of the theory that negentropy depends on dynamic modification, which can be achieved only by applying to the established system fresh stimuli which strive for novel togetherness—the esemplastic drive.

In 1964, the critic was compelled to adjust his position to the unexpected phenomenon of a break in the *entente cordiale* which had hitherto existed between the broadcasters and the politicians. He could no longer expediently say "a plague on both your houses" when the occasion arose, or thrust at one and then the other with a sense that his targets were qualitatively identical. The rupture occurred at the GOP nominating convention which selected Senator Barry Goldwater as its candidate for president. Commenting on it ("The Candidate and the Broadcasters," SR, August 8, 1964), the critic noted the "torrent of hostility on the networks and the press at the instigation of General Dwight D. Eisenhower, when, in his address to the convention, he expressed disdain of 'sensation-seeking columnists and commentators.'" By a number of unfriendly actions, the Goldwater forces who were managing the convention showed "their scorn for the theory that the radio and television image of a candidate for the presidency may be the decisive factor in his victory or defeat." They said, in effect, to the electronic media: "We don't need you; we don't want you; we can win without you, whatever treatment you give our nominee."

The right-wingers had long felt that the networks had treated them unfairly with news and documentary programs; and the critic went on to say that, at the convention: ". . . with leaders like General Eisenhower and Senator Goldwater opening the door for

the expression of their resentment, it poured out in mass emotion
and with undisguised contempt":

> The Republican party will probably return to a policy of
> cooperation with the networks if Goldwater loses in November.
> But if he wins, the networks will face an unpredictable
> situation. He will have demonstrated that a candidate can
> affront the broadcasters and become President. The situation
> might then become disturbing. The networks could move to
> the right to stay in the mainstream of the national political
> majority, or they could become critics of a Goldwater
> administration. In either case, the country would be in for
> something new and possibly dangerous in the interlaced
> worlds of broadcasting and politics. The idea of an extreme
> right-wing administration summons up frightening specters
> of mass-communications control.

The critic's sympathies were with the network commentators
in this historic break. He noted that they had "reacted on the whole
with restraint and dignity":

> David Brinkley (NBC), probably expressing the thoughts of
> all his colleagues in the industry, said on the morning after
> Goldwater's acceptance speech that the reporters would
> continue to report as objectively as they could, while reserving
> their right to dissent. Historically, the major television and
> radio organizations have been middle of the road in their
> political attitudes on the air . . .

But the almost instinctive act of taking sides with the newsmen did not entirely overwhelm the critic's sense of horror at what
he considered to be an unforgivable departure from the ethics of
reporting conventions:

> A serious error that all three networks made in the convention
> coverage suggests how television could subtly shape attitudes.
> In the volatile moments after Goldwater finished his acceptance
> speech, the network camera pool director chose to super-

impose a giant American flag over the Goldwater image. It was a "go-for-broke" director's climax, the roaring finale of a musical comedy. Pro-Goldwater viewers surely loved it; and anti-Goldwater watchers may not have noticed; but neutrals, swept along by the show, were having their chauvinistic impulses played upon. Supering one camera image over another is a technical contrivance; it is not straight reporting. When its message is a loaded, emotional symbol—in this case the flag—it becomes an esthetic act, a commentary that focuses subjective values. As used at the Cow Palace, it tended to enhance the Goldwater image with the aura of devotion and authority given exclusively to the symbol. Whatever the motives of the director, it was an indefensible touch of electronic demagoguery that should send shivers down the back of every responsible broadcaster.

The critic proved a good prophet in this instance: the Republican party did not continue its hostility to the networks while out of office. Indeed, Richard M. Nixon went to the opposite extreme: having come to respect the influence of the televised image on the success or failure of candidates, he and his image-builders for the 1968 contest became, in effect, the *regisseurs* of network coverage of their convention and campaign. They took over control of the image from the networks; the latter became merely accommodating technicians, brokerage firms for their dual clients, the politicians and the sponsors. But the "frightening specters of mass-communications control" now showed their lack of respect for party labels. It was 1966: the administration of President Johnson seemed bent on fulfilling the promises that Barry Goldwater, his defeated opponent in the last election, had made for escalating the war in Vietnam. The critic, on the side of criticism itself no matter which party occupies the White House, attempted to nerve the network news departments to their dialectical duty. "There is little doubt," he wrote ("Giving the Doves a Break," SR, March 5, 1966), "that an administration, once it arrives at a considered policy, uses every propaganda weapon to advance that policy."

The thrust of this piece was that the networks ought deliberately to "give more attention to the arguments of the critics of the administration than to the President and his team." "The proposal may seem unfair," the critic self-countered. "Why not give an evenly balanced picture?" He then developed his argument along two lines:

> [The administration] has the advantage over its critics by creating the news when it has majority opinion behind it. The President's hastily arranged Honolulu trip in the face of mounting Senate pressure for testimony of the "hawks" is evidence of that.
>
> For fallible television news editors who must make quick judgments, the policy of favoring the administration critics would . . . seem a reasonable one. There's no danger of cheating the administration of its fair share of coverage; it cannot fail to get the lion's share anyway.

In support of the second argument, the critic noted that the networks' evening news broadcasts on one occasion had ignored a statement by Senator Wayne Morse (D-Oregon), made at a tele-vised hearing of the Senate Foreign Relations Committee, in which the outspoken critic of administration policy on Vietnam had made "an impressive attack on secrecy in government." Taking into ac-count other viewpoints, the critic attempted to simulate the role of news editor:

> How could a responsible editor miss the most important part of the proceedings? Was it "manipulation" or an error in judgment? The editor could undoubtedly justify his selection. It could probably be attributed to a mere difference of opinion, an editor's choice. But how can the viewer be sure that an editor is objective? For that matter, how can the editor himself be sure? The question is vital if we are to sustain the proposition that the thinking voter in our democracy is sovereign.

The debate on Vietnam is growing fast, the critic observed; in the weeks ahead it would be "hotting up." Eric Sevareid, in a "CBS Special Report," had spoken of "the formal and official raising of doubts by responsible men, probing into the conduct and legality of the war and its ultimate outcome." The critic then urged the net-works to play their dialectical role:

It is the sharpest attacks of the critics that we must seek out and broadcast. I cannot remember which of the CBS correspondents said it . . . but it was well said, quoting President John F. Kennedy: "The men who question power contribute as much as the men who use power."

The full fury of the struggle between men who use power and men who question power was not to manifest itself until the Chicago Democratic party convention in the summer of 1968; but shortly before that event, the critic, traveling in Europe, found ominous echoes there of the dialectical tension, in the United States, between communications media and the governments of the day. In Rome, the unhappy specter of mass-communications control by the Italian government seemed fully realized ("Reflected Image," SR, July 27, 1968):

> The paternal, authoritarian tenor of Italian life has fashioned radio-TV news into a bureaucratic, submissive, manipulated arm of the political parties that dominate the government. The basic structure of Italian broadcasting, fixed under Mussolini's dictatorship, has not been changed despite World War II and the brief Allied occupation of Italy. The facade of democracy was built and in it resounds the liturgy of a free press, objective and fair; but the men who work at the press desks will tell you that it's a depressing farce.
>
> The directors of RAI (Radiotelevisione Italiana) are all political appointees; they can be removed at will if they do not serve their appointers. Parties that share in the government have their representative quotas of appointments and staff positions. RAI has 550 journalists (200 in Rome alone); most of them are not professional newsmen, but "ambassadors" for their sponsors—they watch to see that their politicians get a share of the broadcast pie. Government officials actually count the amount of words in newscasts and quarrel over the division of the time. A change of government always sees new jobs added to an already over-feather-bedded payroll, and the firing of civil servants is a virtual impossibility.
>
> Down this chain of political command runs the heavy hand

of censorship, shielding the Italian viewers from things that
"they ought not know." Strikes and youth demonstrations are
reported verbally, but films of the events, shot by RAI
cameramen, are rarely shown (except to the police). The
official explanation for this "caution" is that Italians are
"volatile" and it is better not to "alarm" the people . . . Violence
in other countries, particularly in the United States, is shown
on Italian TV with alacrity and completeness. A guild of
Italian newscasters recently issued a protest against this
authoritarian pattern, but informed observers predict that it is
merely a "symbolic gesture." When the chips are down, the
majority of radio-TV newsmen will talk but not strike.

In Germany that year, the critic filed a piece from West Berlin
("West German Broadcasting: House of Cards," SR, August 17,
1968):

Perhaps a moment of truth has arrived for . . . the hitherto
independent West German broadcasters. The next year may
tell Americans whether the house of broadcasting that they
built after World War II in West Germany can stand the
strains of political controversy and uphold the tradition of an
open system of independent journalism that scrutinizes all
political parties—right or left.

Student dissent, which was exploding at that time in the United
States, had exploded earlier in the Federal Republic of Germany.
The critic termed it "a unique amalgam of social criticism of the
technological society combined with grievances in the field of education that are generally acknowledged to be just." Newscasters,
commentators, and documentary producers in West Germany had
been giving attention to student demonstrations, and politicians
were complaining that the attention was too much and too favorable. The pressure was on:

One request recently passed down to the professionals (from
the politicians) was that they cease referring to the students'

activities as "extra-parliamentary" and label them "anti-parliamentary." Several outspoken commentators have been shifted from their jobs (they are civil servants and cannot be fired easily). One nationally respected commentator was told to "take a holiday for a while . . ." A commentator who is told to desist in his criticism must think of where he can go if he refuses and resigns. There are not many openings for outspoken liberal journalists in the West German press.

History had opened her hand in 1968: the television-politics scene had come a long way in sixteen years from the carefree, un-portentous alliance between the media and the political parties that the critic remembered in 1952. His tone had turned solemn, polemical: he was taking alarm. If he now understood that the chief danger in the unfolding story lay in the loss of independence at the media end of the new misalliance, he was not blind to the symbiotic nature of the network-government relationship. However dedicated to the safety of the republic the news departments might be, however professionally committed to critical autonomy for no other sake than pride of profession, they were still essentially, in the jargon of the marketplace, "loss leaders" for the primary business of peddling audiences to advertisers.

To outsiders, the fear on the part of the networks, which own and operate a limited number of licensed stations (the networks themselves are not licensed)—that the government of the day, through its control of the Federal Communications Commission, can punish them for misbehavior by taking away a license—seems a bit paranoid. To some network executives, however, the fear is very real and tangible. Moreover, in many respects, as will be touched upon later, the interests of the government, the advertisers, and the networks all merge profitably in areas beyond partisan politics. The critic, like a Victorian mother, vigilant over the premarital purity of her daughter, is forever hovering over the virginity of the newscasters (when he is not castigating them), warning them against temptation and seduction. This mother instinct is very clear in the piece which the critic wrote just after the notorious Chicago Democratic convention.

CHICAGO: KUDOS AND CONFLICT   *September 21, 1968*

MOST VIEWERS who followed the NBC and CBS television gavel-to-gavel coverage of the Chicago convention of the Democratic party would probably agree that these two networks did outstanding jobs reflecting accurately the drama and the truth of the most ghastly week in the history of American politics. The consortium of convention autocrats did everything in their power to use TV as a mirror of a political party resplendent with unity, confidence, and justice for all.

The CBS and NBC news crews of reporters, commentators, and technicians battered persistently at Mayor Daley's ugly fortress and breached it often enough to reveal in full the true picture of the steamroller that pushed Vice President Humphrey to a tarnished nomination for the presidency. The newsmen had a personal as well as a professional stake in this battle of Chicago. Mayor Daley's police and strong-arm guards inside and outside the convention amphitheater included the news crews in their clubbings and beatings. "Faceless, unidentified men," David Brinkley called the "people clogging the aisles, following our reporters wherever they go, listening to every word they say." The physical rough stuff, the harassment, and the restrictions that the Mayor imposed on the mobility of the newsmen angered them and gave them an extra incentive to get the story that the managers of the convention were trying desperately to hide. But to the credit of the reporters and the commentators, they generally kept their cool— expressing at times uncontainable emotions of shock and dismay but separating them scrupulously from the reporting of the facts as they saw them, and genuinely trying to give a fair shake to every position in the hostile, chaotic melee.

Only in two instances did this viewer notice any confusion of the roles of reporter and commentator. In one case, Jim Burnes, an ABC reporter, burst out, overwhelmed, as he watched the Chicago police savagely wield their nightsticks on the demonstrators outside the Conrad Hilton Hotel. "The police have gone mad!" he cried. "Gone is all restraint. Could there not have been a more reasonable way?" This was an understandable remark, an unguarded, human response.

The other case was more serious, involving Walter Cronkite and Mayor Daley. Placed in perspective, in the total context of the CBS anchorman's wearying task of filling his team's key spot alone, it does not mar the overall performance, but it does have disturbing implications for future confrontations between network news departments and political parties—in which the public has a great stake. Early Thursday morning, the CBS newsmen were having their quiet chat in the empty amphitheater after the convention had adjourned. Inside, the Vice President had won the nomination; outside there had been "the cold ferocity by policemen on young men and young women," as Roger Mudd commented. "Never," he added, "have I been so shaken in a long time." Cronkite concluded: "We have been so angry at times that we have wanted to pack up our typewriters and get out of town. But the people who want managed news want us to do just that. We will stay on the job and report the news as we see it."

Next day, before the convention convened, Mayor Daley appeared with Walter Cronkite to tell his side of the story, in what turned out to be an amiable interview that began with personal compliments by the Mayor to Cronkite and ended with a friendly handshake. Nothing was wrong with giving the Mayor his say; civility is always desirable. But to the dismay of many viewers, Cronkite was guilty of a most unfortunate confusion of roles, and it resulted in an unchallenged snow job by the Mayor on the viewing public.

Daley called the reporter by his first name, assured him that he was not complaining about him, but about all those "other" reporters. He read a prepared statement and then defended in conversation the actions of his police as justifiable behavior in the face of a "Communist" conspiracy of intended assassination of himself and the candidates. Cronkite at the time conceded that the Mayor had a point—or he countered very feebly. There was not the slightest trace of the anger and defiance he and his CBS colleagues had displayed only hours before. Perhaps he was tired or flustered. The worst suspicion was that someone had ordered this strategy to appease the Mayor. CBS, if it wanted to give Daley a fair shake, had other alternatives. Cronkite could have heard the Mayor's statement and let it go at that. Daley, indeed, had made the same statement earlier to the press and had walked out without subjecting himself to questions. Here he had a single, very congenial questioner.

CBS could have presented a delegate who differed with the Mayor immediately before or after his remarks. Cronkite himself could have represented the challenging viewpoint. Daley made one spurious attack that Cronkite didn't field at all. The Mayor charged that the networks failed to show the demonstrators provoking the police in the early stages of the march before it reached the Hilton hotel. When NBC's David Brinkley heard this charge, he refuted it by noting that it was Daley's restrictions on the networks' mobility that had prevented them from having cameras at locations early in the march. NBC and CBS had to put their cameras in the windows of the hotel, and they could report only what happened within their range. The CBS anchorman, interviewing Daley, failed to make this appropriate comment.

When David Hoeh, chairman of the New Hampshire delegation, was arrested, roughed up, and jailed for proving that the Mayor's "computerized credentials machines" could be fooled, by inserting a Dartmouth University identification card, NBC played it right—they put Mr. Hoeh on to tell his story, and then they put on the two police officers who had arrested him to tell their story.

American politics appears to be hardening at the extreme ends: the right and the left will grow stronger as repressive, generalized, institutional violence breeds specific, physical counter-violence in a reciprocal crescendo. As this polarization process goes on, great numbers of fair-minded people in the center, who want the democratic process to work, will be struggling to make intelligent decisions. They will need accurate information to help them decide how to act and vote.

The lengths to which a political party can go to preserve or to win power have been frighteningly demonstrated in Chicago. The press, particularly radio and TV news, is a strong hope; but to warrant trust it must be above suspicion. Broadcast journalism must not become the instrument for anybody's unchallenged view of the truth.

The piece as a whole invites several retrospective comments. First, it lacks a transcendent insight. Essentially, it is a report of and a judgment upon the network's handling of the convention, with a concluding commentary on that judgment. The dialectic could usefully be continued by raising a question beyond the ethical appeal: "What if the critic's worst suspicions and fears are correct? What if broadcasting should become the instrument for some particular, unchallenged view of the truth?" The fruit of a dialectic triggered by such questions is impossible to predict: one must, we repeat, enter the labyrinth and pray for luck. The trail might lead to an insight that would restructure the whole piece. The problem lies in the gravitational pull of the matter at hand. It is the convention per se, the networks' handling of it, and the Cronkite-Daley episode, which the critic wishes to talk about. He must not stray so far off the subject that he loses touch with his specific content.

One can easily begin a trail of generalizations and abstractions that will lead always to larger universals, unmanageable and so general as to be utterly without interest—trite. This is somewhat akin to doing research in the social sciences: the unmanageable problems are usually the most interesting; the manageable ones are the least intriguing. In criticism, the dialectic comes to rest somewhere between the absolute and the meaningless concrete. The critic's quest is to find the ideal combination in each specific instance. By his own criteria, he missed it in the Chicago convention piece, but ethically, reportorially, and dialectically it covers quite a bit of ground. Of particular interest is the judgment of Cronkite's alleged lapse in the total context of his admirable handling of the convention chore. Most important is the critic's willingness to explore alternatives to the action for which he faults the newscaster. It is the point about "the confusion of roles" that is the heart of the critique: for all of us, in whatever pursuits, tend to forget that one man or one woman, privately or professionally, is called upon to play many roles, to move concurrently along several tracks; and it is useful therapy occasionally to step back to try to untangle and mark the different tracks for their separate and unique functions.

Walter Cronkite, in a letter to sr's Editor, gallantly agreed with the critic's final admonition, and tried to put at rest the suspicion "that someone had ordered this strategy to appease the Mayor." The newscaster said that the responsibility for the interview with Daley was entirely his own.

"The republic will endure." The reader will find that conviction expressed earlier in this chapter, in a sentence which explained the critic's "playful approach" in his first pieces on politics and television, written in 1951 and 1952. The thesis he has been developing in the pages that followed those early pieces is that he was an *ingenu*, so far as history is concerned. He had to wait for events to unfold and to temper his sense that politics on television were relatively unimportant, with the realization that the serious question of the openness of democratic institutions was at stake in the dangerous conflicts and tensions that developed between the broadcasters and the politicians from 1952 to 1964. It may come as a surprise to the reader, therefore, as it does to me, that in 1968, at the conclusion of the campaign for the presidency, the critic makes a full turn and is once again, ironically, dancing the playful attitude. The unexpected regression occurs in a piece commenting on the wind-up election eve telecasts that were mounted by both Hubert Humphrey and Richard Nixon.

THE SHOW-BIZ–POLITICS SCENE   *December 7, 1968*

OF ALL the paid political telecasts in the 1968 presidential election campaign, the most persistent image in my memory bank is that of Hubert Humphrey playing straight man to Buddy Hackett, the comedian, on the telethon that climaxed the Vice President's drive for the White House, the evening of November 4, on the ABC television network. Mr. Hackett is a superb comic, and I have no reason to doubt that, as a citizen, he has serious political convictions. They may have impelled him to join many other show-biz celebrities who did their bit for Humphrey-Muskie that night, but there was something fiercely incongruous, even alarming, in the sight of Hackett bouncing gags off a desperately ebullient Horatio as the Democratic aspirant for the presidency made his final pitch to the American electorate.

The comic and the candidate, mixing fun and issues in a sort of *Hellzapoppin'*, symbolized the leading edge of the love affair between TV and politics that steadily grows hotter every four years. Where are we heading? To sense the possibilities, one has to recall the final razzmatazz radio show that the Democrats put on coast to coast in 1944 (over the CBS network) ending President Franklin D. Roosevelt's campaign for a fourth term. The program was, I believe, the first election spectacular that joined show biz, broadcasting, and politics. It was produced by Norman Corwin and originated largely in Hollywood. A parade of stars of stage, screen, and radio, plus "names" from other fields, sang songs, played in skits, and made speeches for FDR. I had a hand in the New York pickup and remember a line of celebrities who walked to the microphones to voice short endorsements, including Milton Berle, the philosopher John Dewey, and Frank Sinatra. But it was only at the very end of the program that an announcer, in rather awed tones, pronounced: "And now, the President of the United States." At which point, the show switched to the White House and President Roosevelt delivered a brief talk. That was the courtship stage; politics and show biz romantically inclined but politely distant as befits a relationship between court and jester. Twenty-four years later, Sinatra was still in the picture, but now he sat at the head table solemnly interviewing Muskie. No ceremonial gulf separated the candidates and the players; indeed, Humphrey and Muskie were buddy-buddy, arm in arm with Sinatra's daughter, Nancy; Johnny Carson; a member of The Mamas and the Papas recording group; Herb Alpert; Bill Cosby; and more than forty other entertainers.

Meanwhile at another studio in Hollywood (NBC) another contender, Richard Nixon, was deep in his own telethon spectacular, *sans* show people but with pretty all-American girls, including his two daughters, answering phoned-in questions in a more sedate but far duller show. Nixon, of course, played the part of the lone, responsible statesman, maintaining the image that had won him his commanding lead in the polls. Humphrey's intent was to catch the young McCarthy holdouts, the undecided swing vote; therefore the vibrant, mobile, openhearted appeal. He probably offended many McCarthy supporters with his obvious tactics, but he may have also picked up a whale of a lot of would-have-been Wallace votes. TV stars, the fun people of the affluent society, may be the culture heroes of such viewers: they probably made Humphrey more attractive.

Certainly we have not yet attained the apogee of the show-biz–politics orbit. Some people worry about demagogues with huge budgets and Madison Avenue savvy winning presidential power in the future. The worriers suggest voluntary advertising agency–network–party guidelines for a more honest pattern of TV campaigning. But as TV pulls the candidates nearer to voters, the candidates tend to draw back from close scrutiny, and to place symbols of themselves between the voters and the real men. The sad prospect is more manipulation and less restraint.

One actor (Ronald Reagan) has already been in the running for his party's nomination; another (Dick Gregory) actually was a candidate. For any future candidates, the wind blows in the direction of heavier role-playing. Let's ride with the tide if we cannot block it. Don't abolish the Electoral College; transform it into an award jury. Every four years let it hand out, not Oscars or Emmys, but Prexys for the best quadrennial election makeup man, writer, producer, scene designer, lighting man, composer, best supporting player (Agnew?), and, of course, the best performance. Which, in the end, will be the most cherished goal to the man who makes the White House—the presidency or the Prexy?

What becomes—in the light of the foregoing piece—of the critic's theory that the years had worked upon him the transformation from jester to preacher? Either the critic's alleged growth is false or the original hypothesis of his early ingenuousness must be corrected. Thinking it out as I write, I share with the reader what I believe to be the explanation of the sudden incongruity. The key to the puzzle lies in the final sentence of the paragraph before the last: "The sad prospect is more manipulation and less restraint." Note the word "sad." The critic draws back, in weariness and disgust, from the spectacle of the *Hellzapoppin'* love affair between TV and politics, growing steadily hotter every four years and not yet attaining the apogee of its orbit.

The sight of the "ebullient" Horatio playing "straight man" to Buddy Hackett, the sight of the man who would be chosen President of the United States, drawing back from close scrutiny and placing a symbol of himself between the voters and the real candidate, has not foreshortened the critic's historical perspective: it has lengthened it. The regrettable fawning upon entertainers, by men who ought to comport themselves as statesmen, in order to win the electorate's favor, now brings to his mind the comparatively seemly distance that Franklin D. Roosevelt maintained, in his restrained exploitation of show biz names and personalities, even though he enjoyed mingling heartily with the people of the worlds of arts and letters.

Once again, as in the 1952 Eisenhower-Taft piece, the spectacular *mise en scène* of a political event on television dwarfs any intellectual content that ought to be considered by the critic. He describes what he saw, he assigns it a place in a deteriorating value scale, and then suddenly he recoils from it with the word "sad." He was not aware, when he wrote it, that the word is aptly chosen; for the root of the word "sad" is *sa,* the same root for the word "satire," which is the code for a literary work "in which irony, derision or wit is used to expose and to attack folly or wickedness." The cognate words "satisfy" and "saturate" are also derived from the identical root, *sa.*

Immediately after expressing his sadness at what he has been describing, the critic, in the final paragraph of "The Show-Biz–Politics Scene," launches into projective, satirical fantasy—just as he did in 1951, when he counseled candidates to "utilize the satiric sketch, the song, even the ballet" in their television campaigning, even to relegate "the argument to the status of the commercial—in jingle form." He notes the trend to actors standing for public office, the wind blowing in the direction of heavier role-playing: and he presents his own candidate for the orbit's apogee—namely, the reconstitution of the Electoral College into an award jury, handing out not Oscars or Emmys but Prexys for the best performance as President of the United States.

The satire is an attack: in primitive magic rituals, from which all art is said to have sprung, the words are incantatory weapons directed at hostile environments, designed to kill, to ward off, to curse, so that rebirth, control, and a healthy environment can reappear, as a result of words which bless—the other pole of the magical verbalization. The critic discharges his aggression; he "saturates" his target, and "satisfies" himself in the act, "cooling" himself, so that he can thereafter take up again the painful task of reforming mankind—aware at all times of the presumption of his missionary zeal. It was Swift who, in a letter to Pope, wrote with a plain touch of self-mockery:

> I will never have peace of mind till all honest men are of my
> Opinion: by Consequence you are to embrace it immediately
> and procure that all who deserve my Esteem may do so too.
> The matter is so clear that it will admit little dispute.

The critic is akin to Gulliver, who, after his travels, and after the publication of his book which related his voyages, gave his countrymen six months, surely more than sufficient, to improve—*and they moved not a bit*. The preacher had preached and the congregation had not listened. Had the critic moved, then, like Gulliver (perhaps like Swift himself?) from the *ingenu* to the misanthrope? It is a dangerous possibility; but it can be avoided, as Swift avoided it, by satirizing his own satire: and that is the ultimate, crucial difference between satire as magic and satire as art. I am indebted for these insights to Robert C. Elliott's study, *The Power of Satire*, and to Kenneth Burke, who directed my attention to it. Elliott, commenting on the ultimate rejection by three great satirists of the primitive satirists that they created in their literary works, writes:

> That is not to say that the works are thereby softened.
> Shakespeare, Molière, Swift—each, it seems clear, looked full
> into the abyss of despair. What that meant in biographical
> terms we can only surmise. But we have the literary evidence
> that somehow in the act of creating the image of despair, each
> artist transcended the abyss. The primitive satirists of their
> work, are, in the total literary sense, satirized. Their creators,
> rejecting the irresponsibility of the primitive mode, assume
> the plenary responsibilities of art.

It is a felicitous statement. I like especially the use of the word "transcendence" and the phrase "the plenary responsibilities of art," which responsibilities I extend to the creative art of criticism. This critic, in his Show-Biz–Politics piece of 1968 has not at all regressed; nor has he contradicted himself. He has merely discovered that he has grown since 1951 and yet is essentially still the same man. Bergson poses the paradox brilliantly when he writes in *Creative Evolution:*

> Duration is the continuous progress of the past which gnaws into the future and which swells as it advances.
> Our past remains present to us.
> In reality . . . it follows us at every instant; all that we have felt, thought and willed from our earliest infancy is there, leaning over the present which is about to join it, pressing against the portals of consciousness that would fain leave it outside . . . Doubtless we think with only a small part of our past, but it is with our entire past, including the original bent of our soul, that we desire, will and act.

What the critic considered a playful approach to politics and television, derogating their importance in the life of the republic, was, even at the time of writing, a satirical response to a prospect difficult for him to face, the corruption of the democratic ideal. The response had a double identity—the preaching and the satire. If the second was muted as the first emerged more strongly, it did not vanish: it was there all the time but shooting up slowly, growing, ripening under the surface. When it suddenly broke above ground at the sight of buddy-buddy Hubert Humphrey and Frank Sinatra, and of Richard Nixon with pretty all-American girls, it was right on the same button of the fate of the republic, but the finger pressed more firmly: for the jest now was not in general terms of satiric sketches, songs, ballets, and commercial jingles. It juxtaposed, in its final sentence, the two irreconcilable opposites that, in collision, could shatter the republic—the presidency and the Prexy.

To the critical, creatively dialectic spirit, nothingness, negentropy, is the absence of dissent. To withhold consent, to oppose, negate, refuse, demur is to practice contradiction, to feel differently about something so that, in the apartness, the thing itself may be challenged to transform itself into an entity minutely less susceptible of contradiction. Like the sign for infinity in mathematics, it is theoretically possible but it eludes capture as quantitative measures shrink into quarters, eighths, sixteenths, and so on, eventually vanishing across the submicroscopic frontiers to probable immateriality.

At the heart of the conflict between politics, television, and government is the survival and character of dissent in a democratic system. Where mass governments and mass publics exist, consent and dissent are massively formulated and managed at the level of mass communications. For citizens concerned with keeping alive the possibilities for novel togetherness and for fresh insights into society, the openness of opportunity for dissent at collective communications levels is crucial. To the critic—watching the evolving struggle among networks, elected officials, and candidates—the two horns of the dissent dilemma are equally threatening.

By 1968 the networks and the politicians, in and out of office, had demonstrated that they were capable of voluntary alliances in the management of public opinion. They had also given witness to the fact that the alliances could, at times, be sundered acrimoniously, creating the danger that in the sundering, the networks' handling of news and public affairs would be involuntarily subject to government preferences. Society's critics, the great refusers, were substantially disfranchised in either event. With the networks acting as exclusive gatekeepers along the major highways of the formation of public opinion, forces for dissent were entirely dependent for their public images upon the selective judgments of the network news editors.

Technological and consequent institutional changes in mass communications—cable television, satellites, pay television, the development of the home communications center with its consumer-controlled rather than producer-controlled message power—might conceivably, when fully developed, bring about changes in the movement of dissent; but for the immediate future the citizen addicted to criticism was largely in the hands of the manipulating giants.

In a piece commenting on television's coverage of the first moon landing, the critic, amid a universal chorus of excitement and approval, registered his own small dissent over what impressed him as an unseemly lack of detachment on the part of the networks that covered the historic event.

COSMIC NIELSENS   *August 9, 1969*

UP THERE at Tranquility Base, *Eagle*'s television camera could afford us, from its fixed position, only a limited view of the astronauts' activities as they danced man's first lunar choreography. No one could quarrel with that particular barrier to our vision: to creatures on spaceship Earth it was manna from the moon. Down here at the TV receivers' end, network reporters and commentators deployed their cameras along a rather narrow intellectual range; their rigidity was a matter of institutional policy—and disappointing. The moon landing was fraught with deep currents of ambivalence— rip-tides of incredible and even thrilling technological achievements crossing sluggish drifts and backwaters of Earth's poisoned psychic as well as physical environment. Television's encoding of that multidimensional event was depressingly one dimensional.

It was all sunshine and public relations and hurrah for our side. From the Sea of Tranquility, where the flag was planted and the plaque enshrined (nationalist prestige in a collectively explosive world), to the White House, Disneyland, the Vatican, and the man in the street, there was no area of darkness or even earth-shine—just progress, mechanistically defined, laden with the attitude that today is no time for critics and cynics. Walter Cronkite, for CBS, who seemed unflaggingly exhilarated despite his wearying task, illustrated the dominant mood when he exclaimed, shortly after the *Eagle* had touched down on the surface of the moon: "People have the audacity to say nothing new is going on these days. I'd like to know what those kids are saying who pooh-poohed this. How can one turn off from a world like this?" Later he held up a copy of the next morning's *New York Times* to show the camera the historic record-sized headline: MEN WALK ON THE MOON. It was the same edition that ran two full pages of comments from public figures under the heading: REACTIONS TO MAN'S LANDING ON THE MOON SHOW BROAD VARIATIONS IN OPINIONS.

In some of the press handling of the moon landing there was context, and a search for meaning, for a sense of relatedness. On the networks there were tension, suspense, bits of information, marvelous pictures, impressive simulations, and artful animations—but one would be pressed hard to say the coverage was not a full-blown commercial for the government, NASA, the space industry, and the broadcasters.

Wherever explorers go in the future accompanied by television cameras, they will be actors, making their nebulous exits and entrances for the benefit of multi-planetary audiences. Nowhere will there again be pure events (if ever there were); everything hereafter will be stage managed for cosmic Nielsens, in the interests of national or universal establishments. Vision-filters, however, ought to be more than one-focus affairs. One of the sharpest contrasts in television's coverage of the moon landing was that which distinguished the language of numbers—used almost exclusively by the astronauts and their earth command—from the inadequate verbalizations of the network commentators. The spacemen, making computer talk, spoke a kind of quantitative poetry—eloquent, pellucid, terse.

The reporters, at moments of highest tension, were admittedly speechless, or remarkably colloquial. One, when the lunar module successfully fired the engine that lifted it from the moon's surface, cried out, "Oh boy! Hot diggety dog! Yes sir!" The emotion was genuine and understandable, but one can spin an implication off his remark: Man talking in numbers and commanding things is master of sophisticated communications; man relating to other men is sadly tongue-tied. This is the state of the world and this is television, alas! But is despair in order?

Perhaps when space ships are shuttling between Earth and moon and crews in controlled environments will be readying for farther reaches into space, television will have winged its way over its public relations barrier and will give us a deeper representation of such events, as well as a poetry of qualitative experience to match the brilliance of the quantitative mode in the realm of science and technology.

The double image of dissent and "cosmic Nielsens," stage-managed "in the interests of national or universal establishments," appeared again in the critic's very next piece. It commented on a book which had been published by a small firm in New York and was designed for scholarly circulation. Not a single review of it had appeared anywhere, either in the general or the scholarly press. The author of the book, a colleague, an economist, was concerned with the value aspects of communications study; and I felt that his book was important enough to warrant a wide readership. Following SR's publication of the piece in which I commented on the book, reviews of the work appeared in a variety of other publications; the publisher received purchase orders; and even a staff reporter for *Broadcasting* magazine telephoned me to learn where he might buy the book: subsequently he gave it a brief review in the magazine.

The piece illustrates how a fragment of a structure at which the critic directs his attention can become his discovery, his third beat. The disconnecting of the "alarm system," a phrase used by the author and quoted in the first paragraph of the review, becomes, by a dialectical twist, the motivating energy of the entire piece when it is transformed into the critic's own impulse to sound the alarm, in order to make the warning system work again. The critic's deepening doubt of the networks' willingness or ability to commit themselves authentically to the work of sounding the alarm is reflected in the last paragraph—where he accepts the proposition that the best hope for switching on the alarm is for "dynamic subgroups in American society" to acquire "access to the massive consciousness of the general public."

SOUNDING THE ALARM   *August 16, 1969*

A NEW BOOK by Herbert I. Schiller, *Mass Communications and American Empire,* is must reading for people who want to switch on the alarm signal that warns against the dangers of the military-industrial complex in the field of communications. In 1961, President Eisenhower said in his much-quoted farewell address: "Only an alert and knowledgeable citizenry can compel the proper meshing of the huge industrial and military machinery of defense with our peaceful methods and goals, so that security and libery may prosper together." Professor Schiller, of the University of Illinois, and editor of the *Quarterly Review of Economics and Business,* notes that citizens need true information to be alert to potential threats against their liberties. But then he asks: "What happens, however, if the military-industrial power enclave has grown up strongest in the information apparatus itself? What may be expected, if the alarm system, so to speak, has been disconnected by those very elements it was designed to signal against?"

Schiller's independent, scholarly work is the first comprehensive examination of domestic and international mass communications structure and policy in the United States. The book documents the facts—drawing on industrial and government sources—about "the emerging imperial network of American economics and finance," and how it "utilizes the communications media for its defense and entrenchment . . . and for its expansion."

Most fascinating is the explanation of how the informational alarm system, implicit in President Eisenhower's warning against the military-industrial complex, came to be switched off. The military establishment first gains command of the nation's telecommunications policy. This is done under the necessities of the cold war emergency. Eventually "control over governmental users of the spectrum has been concentrated in the Office of the Secretary of Defense and in the Office of the Director of Telecommunications . . . a mobilization agency . . . administered by a former general officer in the Armed Services.

The military then becomes the insatiable customer of the nation's electronic industry. "The industry sold well over 60 per cent ($12.2 billion) of its output of approximately $23 billion in 1967 to the national government, the overwhelming share of which went to the Armed Forces."

In turn, the giant electronics producers are interlocked, informally and structurally, with the broadcast networks, whose business is the international cultivation of "consumerism," and the penetration, globally, of television, radio, and film markets.

While the media are busy with their global sell of the good, American life—directed mainly at the rich nations in the northern latitudes of our planet—the military maintains its own "crisis-management" and "counter-insurgency" global communications network, ready to put down protests against hunger, poverty, and illiteracy in the southern latitudes, where the have-not nations are located.

The Defense Department spends annually an estimated $2 billion for telecommunications, while the role of communications in the enlightenment of the developing world limps along in pitiful proportions. "Communications," Schiller comments, "are being developed as the supporting instrumentation for the global enforcement of the status quo."

Meanwhile, at home, a 1967 Associated Press survey reported "that the biggest domestic publicity network is maintained by the military." (Annual budget $32.3 million; 3,000 employees.) "NASA is next with 300 employees and a tab of $11.5 million." Defense and space contractors charge the government for public relations. "One estimate is that the taxpayers directly pay at least $200 million a year for such press-agentry on behalf of private companies."

Military communications preparedness, harnessed to commercial media that overwhelm weak nations incapable of defending their cultures from a far more subtle form of imperialism than the old colonial diplomacy—that's the picture drawn by *Mass Communications and American Empire*. The author's prescription for switching on the alarm system again is the acquisition, by dynamic subgroups in American society, of access to the massive consciousness of the general public. It is a hope and a faith. If it is ever to be achieved, a giant first step would be for alarm-menders to study this indispensable blueprint, and to discover how the warning system has been disconnected in the past twenty years.

From the concept of Prexy—awarded on television for the best performance every four years by a candidate for president—to the notion of the Man in the White House as the Man from Glad is a small step. The critic took it in a book review written, by invitation, for the Sunday "Book Week" section of the *Chicago Sun-Times*. The Man from Glad (readers who have never met him on television should be told) is an Apollo-like figure in a commercial for a transparent plastic sandwich wrap. He appears, like some *deus ex machina*, at the scene of a kitchen crisis involving hamburgers and onions for picnic or party, and smilingly restores matronly equanimity by miraculously producing his ultimate wrap.

The piece itself is a light one, designed to be informative in a key that is suited to the book under review. Aside from the notion of the Man from Glad, which represents its try for a dimension beyond the book—a third beat—it has three points of retrospective interest for me. First, it plays between the two poles of fun and solemnity: at the latter pole, the critic envisions readers "urging the book upon their friends" in a fight against the ethos of political hucksterism, as a breaker of hypnotic spells. He considers it a weapon and wants to fire cells with it.

The second point of interest lies in the critic's questioning the motives of the author, who gives no hint in the book to indicate whether or not he acted as a "spy" in the unsuspecting Nixon camp. The implication is that the critic disapproves of such a deception, even if it is committed in the name of useful muck-raking. That it *was* a deception was revealed by the author in many television appearances after the publication of the book. It is an ethical question of ends and means, a difficult one; the critic might have made it the focal point of his effort.

The third point is that the book's revelations provide concrete evidence that the critic's generalization in his piece "The Show-Biz–Politics Scene" was accurate when he wrote: "But as TV pulls the candidates nearer to the voters, the candidates tend to draw back from close scrutiny and to place symbols of themselves between the voters and the real men." The anecdotal ending is a sign that the Man from Glad cornerstone was weak and never carried through; but again, sometimes an event, all by itself, can be so pregnant with complex implications that one is tempted to make it serve climactic purposes. The critic in this case succumbed. It reveals a great deal about the men who sold the Man from Glad to a majority of the American electorate for service in the nation's number one establishment.

JUST LIKE THE MAN FROM GLAD   *October 5, 1969*

FIRST THEODORE H. WHITE wrote *The Making of the President 1968.* Now Joe McGinniss has written *The Selling of the President 1968.* Soon, surely, another author will write *The Consumption of the President.* Manufacturing, selling and consuming: the American gestalt. Why should we be surprised that the Man in the White House is packaged in exactly the same manner as the Man from Glad? Or that Madison Avenue, on television, pushes Happy Presidents for Happy People?

For readers who believe that the nation, every four years, can switch harmlessly from one brand of president to another, this will be a titillating exposé.

It takes them behind the scenes, to where the 1968 Nixon presidential campaign was created for the mass media, chiefly for television. There they'll witness the candidate being shaped, like Pinocchio for the marionette show, so that he in turn, can manipulate the "basically lazy, basically uninterested" American voters, who love to be seduced in the quadrennial con game of televised politics. They'll hear Mr. Nixon say, during the taping of a commercial: ". . . it's all about law and order and the damn Negro–Puerto Rican groups out there." They'll thrill to the four-letter words of the candidate's staff of image-makers, to their cynicism about themselves as well as about their candidate, their amorality, and their hopelessly befuddled McLuhanesque hucksterism.

They'll chuckle at Mr. Nixon's aversion to psychiatrists (especially a Jewish one); at Pat Nixon's horror-struck expression when she was caught on camera, applauding herself; at the Nixon staff's estimate of Agnew ("mush meets tapioca, a marriage of meringue"); and at their estimate of Mr. Nixon himself: "Nixon has not only developed the use of the platitude, he's raised it to an art form. It's mashed potatoes. It appeals to the lowest common denominator of American taste. It's a farce, a delicious farce; self-deception carried to the nth degree."

Readers who take a more somber view of the unholy alliance of television, Madison Avenue, and the choosing of a president will find their biases enormously supported. They will not wish to settle for the soothing slogan that the voters are "peasants who think Camelot fun, as long as it is televised to their huts." They will insist on calling the game rape and not seduction. And they will probably want to fight—by urging the book upon their friends as a hypnotic spell-breaker.

Joe McGinniss doesn't give them much direct help. Though he dedicates the book to his parents "who care," he provides no clues to what they care about; in fact, he implies that the villains of his piece are not the politicians and their image-mercenaries, but the voters whose appetite for illusion provides the basis for their consumption of "marketable human models . . . mass-produced to satisfy the market . . . a new category of human emptiness."

The author plays his own game of Hide Joe McGinniss.
A lively, admired columnist for the *Philadelphia Inquirer*, he joined
the Nixon campaign to write a book about it. Either he was a
master of shorthand or adept at hiding a tape recorder, for the
result is largely a journal of verbatim conversations and remarks
that no honest journalist would quote unless they were accurate.
He recounts what happened at taping sessions and in conferences,
and he appends the texts of memoranda written by Mr. Nixon's
image-makers before and during the primaries and the presidential
campaign.

His blunt portraits of the candidate and his staff are
unflattering, often sickening. But he damns them with words from
their own mouths or by his own commentary; he never records
anything significant that he himself must have said in
conversations.

One wonders whether he went along with the Nixon imagery,
spoke his piece honestly, or was merely a tight-lipped spy in the
camp of all the king's horses and all the king's men that put
Humpty Dumpty together again. No one, of course, can prove
that the televised images that Mr. Nixon's staff fashioned were,
on election day, actually translated into votes.

McGinniss notes that the staff rode cool, calm, and confident
in the early phases of the campaign, but that Mr. Nixon seemed
to turn away from them at the end, when the Humphrey image
started moving up in the polls. They finished in the running, but
they were embittered by the fact that Mr. Nixon finally sought
guidance from old cronies, the professional politicians.

For the television mercenary that dominated the staff—
Frank Shakespeare—there was a payoff: the directorship of the
U. S. Information Agency. The man who now runs our official
propaganda mill all over the world is quoted as saying of the
Russians: "They're out to get us, Len. They always have been
and they always will be. They're ruthless bastards and they're
trying to conquer the world. We have to stand up to them at every
turn." When the Russians invaded Czechoslovakia during the
campaign, Shakespeare was exuberant. "What a break! This
Czech thing is just perfect. It puts the soft-liners in a hell of a box!"

A month later, the critic, in a piece commenting on the net-works' handling of a day of national demonstrations against the war in Vietnam, again directed attention to the fact that television newsmen tend to shy away, in non-consensus situations, from as-suming their role as social critics. A year had passed since President Nixon's election: the probationary time granted him to set his own executive machinery in motion was fast expiring. Dissatisfaction with the continuous engagement of the nation in Vietnam and the slowness of highly touted efforts at disengagement were enlisting growing numbers of adults as well as students who were willing to express their protests in public.

COOL MEDIUM   *November 8, 1969*

FURTHER NATIONAL DEMONSTRATIONS against the Vietnam war are scheduled for November and December, and on into next year, and television and radio naturally will cover each of them. Although press accounts of the broadcasters' handling of the October 15 moratorium were generally favorable, my own view is that television, particularly, failed to communicate the essential spirit of a day that searched the nation's conscience.

The failure illustrates the proposition that the degree to which reporters and commentators feel themselves to be personally involved in an event is the crucial factor in their reporting and interpreting of that event. Doing justice to an event, therefore, means taking into account the variable of involvement and consciously making an effort to balance reportage and commentary to compensate for hostility, indifference, or unrepressed sympathy.

In this sense, television collectively did not appear to be involved in Vietnam Moratorium Day: it reported and interpreted it, but made no real attempt to get under V-M Day's skin. Television played it cool, objectively, dispassionately, which, as many people feel, is proper for networks to do when they are communicating events that are politically controversial. However, this wasn't the way television treated the moon landing, for example (I make the comparison conscious of the larger order of magnitude of the space event). There, the reporters and commentators were personally involved all the way, not inhibiting their own feelings in the slightest. They were clearly on the side of the space program; they had no qualms about joining the almost universal chorus of support, excitement, and suspense.

In national political campaigns and elections, the networks' staffs also allow themselves to become personally involved; overtly they do not back any candidates, but they leave no doubt about their enthusiasm for the political game. In covering the 1968 Democratic convention in Chicago, reporters and commentators quickly developed a posture that was clearly hostile to the convention managers, although they avoided outright displays of sympathy for the demonstrators in the streets. People may quarrel about what television mirrored in Chicago, but the reflection was vivid.

The October 15 moratorium represented the kind of event upon which networks do not take positions. In backing off from any show of personal involvement, reporters and interpreters permitted the wine of the event to drain away.

V-M Day had a central stillness about it, nonviolent, unsensational, yet dynamic. People felt deeply, their experiences were intimate; yet there was an open sense of sharing. Participants assembled, talked, listened to speakers, voted resolutions, marched, lighted candles. Crowds—of old and of young—behaved as individuals: that was the uniqueness.

Moments of revelation flashed on the TV screen, as when in Duluth, Minnesota, high school students demonstrating against the war in a city that had never known such a phenomenon sang "America, the Beautiful." Young war protesters on the Capitol steps in Washington contributed a mix-up of political symbols when they sang "Up With People," the theme song of a traveling musical show sponsored by members of the radical Right. Georgia's Governor Lester Maddox, at an anti-protest rally in his state, led legionnaires in the singing of "God Bless America"; close-ups of the faces of the singers were grim portraits of super-patriots.

Viewers had to wait until the prime-time, business-as-usual shows were out of the way, before the CBS and NBC late evening specials came along. The CBS staff triumphed over logistics in assembling film clips from various cities and in lining up important persons; but although the commentators searched for the day's significance, their interpretations lacked both spirit and eloquence. Why, on the other hand, could they exult with the spacemen, show excitement with election watchers, and express spontaneous revulsion at convention tyrants? The answer is national consensus—or at least the presumption of it.

The problem, then, is how to catch the true spirit of an event if no consensus exists. One answer is for the network interpreters to stay cool if they refuse personal involvement, but to invite panels of involved demonstrators to do their own interpreting.

If the networks, however, do choose to be involved and to show it, let them allow panels of the non-involved to express their opinions. More of the spirit of V-M Day, pro and con, could have been communicated had the networks allowed panels of blacks, poor people, students, and John Birchers to express their thoughts about the meaning of the day, not merely in edited excerpts but in sustained conversations, just as the network newsmen did.

As it was, a single viewpoint, which reflected only white, middle-class, corporate America, had the exclusive privilege of selecting and organizing the image of a significant event. In a nation divided, it takes more than one viewpoint to articulate the meaning of social revolution.

"Cool Medium" is of interest in that it does not rest with making a negative judgment on the manner in which the networks covered V-M Day: it goes on to examine the reasons underlying that coverage. It offers the proposition that the element of involvement or non-involvement of the newscasters, overt or repressed, is the key to a dialectical position. The critic is still guilty of a residual degree of naivete—when he suggests that the networks should present panels of dissenting voices, from the political left and right, black and white, to offer their own interpretations of national events. Nevertheless, he hammers away at the essence of the matter—participation for others besides the controllers of the media in the vital game of dialectical clash. If the critic is taking alarm circumspectly, and in accord with his own theories of taking others into account, he is beginning to call the game by what he believes to be its correct name—social revolution.

A fortnight later, the administration, speaking through its second in command, launched its notorious, outright frontal attack on the news departments of the networks. To the astonishment of television observers who were impressed with the muted or non-existent dialectics of the networks in their handling of the government, the Vice-President charged them with prejudiced hostility in their criticism of the administration's policies. Hindsight suggests that the new "fit" thrown by the administration at the broadcasters was not a deep, structural fissure but a manifestation of a chronic fault. "Man from Glad! Man from Glad!" is the Twenty-third Psalm of the consumption society. Unlike the Scriptural Shepherd, however, the savior in the refrigerator is non-dialectical: there are no valleys or shadows in his plastic pastures. He cannot admit, any more than any other commercial sophist can, the possibility that another product can be superior to the one he celebrates. It should not have come as a shock, then, that the Man from Glad, once in the White House, should be sensitive to political criticism.

The critic, hurrying into print at the request of his editor, with an editorial, reflected long enough to make sure that he would not be trapped by the schizophrenic swings of the politics-television pendulum. The moment had to be seized to enlarge the public's vision of the much bigger game being played.

THE TIP OF THE ICEBERG   *November 22, 1969*

VICE PRESIDENT AGNEW'S recent attack on network newsmen for their television commentary immediately following President Nixon's November 3 speech on Vietnam presents both a danger and an opportunity. The danger lies in confining the issues that Agnew raised to a debate between the White House and the networks over government intimidation and freedom of the press. The opportunity inherent in Agnew's polemic is the opening for public examination of the larger questions brought to light in this debate.

What were the Vice President's objections? The newsmen were critical and querulous; they contradicted and challenged the President. Agnew objected chiefly to their "instant analysis," claiming that their minds were made up in advance. Actually, the newsmen read the President's speech shortly before he spoke. The Vice President was irked that the newsmen characterized— through their prejudices—the President's words and thoughts before his audience had a chance to digest them. The criticism of the press, he implied, should be defused, controlled, and delayed.

Even to verbalize these notions is to make explicit their untenability in democratic theory. As for instant feedback, Agnew has apparently forgotten the McLuhanisms with which the Republican party's image-makers fashioned their mythical candidates. The instant quality of the TV message, according to the Canadian theorist of communications, is the very medium itself. Shall it regress into slow-plodding print? Commentators seek to get at the truth behind the facts. Personal journalism has its pitfalls, but its essence is sticking one's neck out—and the opposite of ignorance and prejudice is being resolute, inquiring, bold. Intentional slanting of the news cannot be defended; but the vigor of personal belief in opinion should be supported.

The trouble with broadcast journalism is that there is hardly enough personal opinion. It is true, as the Vice President argues, that the network news teams constitute small groups of men who have great power in their selection and treatment of what they judge to be the news. Concentration of control, however, in the hands of fewer and fewer gatekeepers is a fact of life not limited to the networks. There are fewer decision-makers in all media. Agnew's proposed strictures on the networks, made with the obvious accord of the White House, would tend to concentrate control more narrowly.

The networks give too much time, he complained, to minority spokesmen, to marchers and demonstrators. The Vice President confused genuine controversy in the news with the emphasis that networks place on the search for excitement.

Encounter and conflict are the staples of mass journalism, of course. But the ideologies that the newsmen evolve are notoriously middle-of-the-road and hardly representative of the full political spectrum. The force of the Vice President's attack pushes them to still narrower centers rather than to broader reflections of diverse viewpoints.

Beyond news, television hugs the bland and the neutral in the much more significant areas of repetitive entertainment and advertising. It is in such domains that our culture is mostly shaped, its agenda set, and in these areas the networks are part of a pattern involving industry and government. Agnew chose to fight in one small corner of the battlefield; his fight is a family feud—the people are not broadly involved.

Agnew's speech-writers were shrewd. They had read the record and they allied the Vice President with many who have been criticizing television on other counts. But their case is poor, and it should be separated from the larger issues. The Vice President's writers made one important error. They included, as ritual, the late Judge Learned Hand's celebrated view that right conclusions are more likely to be gathered from a multitude of tongues than through authoritative selection. They also noted the Supreme Court's *Red Lion* decision, delivered six months ago, in which the right of the public in broadcasting is placed higher than that of the broadcasters. But they neglected to add exactly what the court said the public has a right to hear and see—namely, the very thing that the Vice President decried: "the presentation of vigorous debate of controversial issues of importance and concern to the public . . ."

The court unanimously held that "it is the right of the public to receive suitable access to social, political, esthetic, moral, and other experiences. . . ." The Vice President charged that the newsmen are provincial and that they distort the news. He is open to the same criticism. The network journalist gets only five per cent of TV's prime time schedule; the average station devotes barely ten per cent of an eighteen-hour day to the news. Agnew's parochial finger touched but the tip of the iceberg; the probe should be directed at the underlying mass. He has begun a debate that should go on. The public interest rests neither in a maintenance of the status quo nor in a contraction of it. It rests in a multiplication of the voices that have access to the medium, and in an escalation of the quality of all the messages.

If the battle were to be fought between a government of the day, allergic to dialectic, and the networks, and if one network, for whatever motives, chose to dissent, the critic's sympathies naturally led him to support the latter. This he did in a piece commenting on the unprecedented sight of a network news department, defending itself on the air, against a charge of "fakery" directed at it by a spongy package of government public relations maneuvering. This piece is offered to the reader as an excellent example, in the critic's judgment, of his third beat fulfilled.

There is an element in the event that is commented upon—a photographic blow-up—which the critic bi-sociates in the dialectical, combinatory play, with Antonioni's film, *Blow-up*. This collision, unexpected but fruitful, delivers the dominating notion of fantasy versus reality which is the source of psychic energy in the piece. On this carrier wave, so to speak, the episode is delineated, commented upon and judged; and the fantasy-reality theme is returned to in the end with a provocative twist which produces a satisfactory round of cell-firing.

BLOW-UP   *June 6, 1970*

WHEN "CBS EVENING NEWS," in a recent broadcast, defended itself against charges that a filmed atrocity incident filed from Vietnam had been faked, one of the devices its news staff employed to substantiate the report was the blowing up of single frames of the film. Two blow-ups proved that a combat helicopter on the scene had been American and not Australian, as was suggested by Pentagon experts. Another blow-up established that it had not been an Australian but an American adviser with a South Vietnamese outfit who observed the cold-blooded stabbing of a wounded North Vietnamese prisoner by a South Vietnamese sergeant.

In Antonioni's film *Blow-up*, the photographic enlargement was the basic metaphor of a story that dealt with fantasy and reality. In the CBS/Pentagon (and White House) episode, fantasy and reality are also the essential ingredients; so, to get to the truth of the matter, let's blow up one phase of the six-months-old story.

After CBS News first reported the stabbing early last November, a Pentagon official asked the network to cooperate in an investigation of what might be a war crime by furnishing the

Pentagon with film outtakes (discarded footage) of the incident, and with the name of the Vietnamese photographer who had filmed the episode for CBS. The network refused, claiming freedom to protect its news sources and asserting that the life of the photographer would be endangered if his identity were made known.

If (and here is fantasy) the Pentagon had respected the traditional rights of a free press, it would never have made such requests in the first place; it would have conducted its own investigation. After all, the military spend large sums for the activities of an army of intelligence-gatherers in Indochina, whereas CBS, like other broadcast organizations, has only a handful of correspondents there. Had the Pentagon conducted its own investigation properly (it had videotapes of the CBS film and could have made its own blow-ups), it would have been able to ascertain the report's authenticity.

Then (continuing our fantasy), it ought to have condemned the stabbing and subsequent mutilation of the corpse as a violation of the Geneva convention.

In reality, the Pentagon chose to explain the report as a "cut and paste job" by CBS. This explanation was not made publicly, or even directly to the network, but instead, according to CBS, was disseminated by way of an "undercover campaign" in which a purported White House memo on the affair was first leaked to the Des Moines *Register-Tribune,* and then to syndicated columnists Richard Wilson (whose column appears in sixty newspapers) and Jack Anderson (in 620 papers). Somewhere along the line, as the campaign to discredit CBS News developed, Clark Mollenhoff, Special Counsel to the President, became involved. He is a former Pulitzer Prize reporter for the *Register-Tribune.*

When CBS News broadcaster Walter Cronkite presented the unprecedented rebuttal on the air, he refuted the Pentagon's suggestion that the stabbing had occurred during a training exercise rather than in a battle, and that the prisoner was already dead when the South Vietnamese sergeant (on camera) removed the knife from the prisoner's back, turned him over, and deliberately plunged the knife into the belly of the helpless victim. CBS reporter Don Webster interviewed the sergeant who did the stabbing; the sergeant admitted his act, asserting that the captive might have reached for a nearby rifle (a patent absurdity, as the camera's eye indisputably revealed). He also stated that the Vietcong had murdered one of his children. Subsequent to the incident, the sergeant was chosen Soldier of the Year by the South Vietnamese military.

In a brief press flurry following the Cronkite broadcast, administration forces neatly side-stepped all responsibility. The White House stated that it had never investigated CBS News: Mr. Mollenhoff admitted that he had received a Pentagon report, but had not leaked it selectively to the press. The Defense Department said that it had never questioned the integrity of CBS News.

Is this a case of men acting under orders, or of men looking at fantasy and believing that it is reality because that may be what they wish to see?

As long as the grim reality in Washington is a government of the day apparently intent on bending all media to its own selective fantasies, it behooves all supporters of a free press to commend CBS News for its willingness to blow up the truth.

A month, almost to the day, before the appearance in print of the "Blow-up" piece, National Guardsmen at Kent State University, in Ohio, fired pointblank into a small cluster of students and shot to death four of them. One was a nineteen-year-old girl, Allison Krause, a freshman. The following night, the NBC Huntley-Brinkley evening newscast carried a moving statement on the death of his daughter by Allison's father, Arthur Krause. Viewers who witnessed it will never forget it: it was shown only once, and the critic, deeply stirred, wrote the following piece.

UNTITLED, *undated*

A MAN ASKED QUESTIONS on television recently: his name is Arthur Krause. He came out of his house in Churchill Borough, a Pittsburgh suburb, and faced the network film cameras and read a statement. He wept as he read and he fought back his tears.

The text of his statement, as I heard it on the NBC Huntley-Brinkley news program, May 5th, follows:

> She was deeply interested in helping people. She truly cared about people. On Saturday evening she called home to tell me there was some trouble in the business section of Kent. She said there was some property damage and she was against that. She was not involved in that; but she felt they had to do this because there was no other way to express themselves. She resented being called a bum because she disagreed with someone else's opinion. She felt that the war in Cambodia was wrong. Is this dissent a crime? Is this a reason for killing her? Have we come to such a state in this country that a young girl has to be shot because she disagrees deeply with the actions of her government? *I want something to be done.* What I would like to see happen is that my daughter's death, and those of the other three children as well as the wounded, not be in vain. I would like to see Congress investigate the situation to determine who authorized live ammunition to be brought against children by a tired and frightened National Guard. Also, who approved such an action. Can Congress find out why our children can't express themselves?

The subject of Mr. Krause's threnody was Allison, his daughter, age nineteen, a freshman at Kent State University, one of the immediate victims of that ghastly moment on May 4th, when National Guardsmen knelt quickly on the campus and fired into clusters of students who were protesting (some just watching) against President Nixon's order that sent American troops into an escalated Indochina war. The anguished father's words have haunted me ever since I heard them. They have haunted others who were deeply moved. I cannot understand why leading newspapers, including *The New York Times,* failed to mention Mr. Krause's statement. Cross-media competition is surely no justifiable explanation for ignoring so cogent a statement that is of interest and importance to all fathers and mothers.

Mr. Krause's questions demand answers; and they inspire a question that is addressed to the television and radio networks and individual stations. Why not rebroadcast the statement, again and again, until the questions are answered? Repeat broadcasts are a regular practice of TV and radio stations. Commercials are repeated *ad nauseam*. When a jockey fell off his horse in the last Kentucky Derby, there were instant replays, in slow motion, so viewers could see as clearly as possible what had happened. I have seen fatal accidents in motor-car races, which were repeated so that viewers could relish the gruesome details. Entertainment programs are rerun now not only during summer months but during the regular season as well. More, much more is involved in a repetition of Mr. Krause's questions about our college youth than the stakes encompassed by amortizing costs of production and by profitable residuals—which loom large in decisions to repeat television programs and commercials.

At stake is the erosion of our democracy. Our college students are presumed to be the inheritors of the chief responsibility for preserving that democracy. Anyone in touch with campus life today knows that American higher education is fundamentally irrelevant to the most aware and sensitive of our students until the war in Asia is liquidated.

The American people as a whole, including Mr. Agnew's silent majority, must be made to understand that they share this stake, too. The repetitions of the questions posed by Arthur Krause, and the dialogues that must arise are the only vehicles by which this understanding can be widely shared; and there is no more powerful distributor of such understanding than the television networks. Implicit in President Nixon's personal decision to send our troops across the Cambodian frontier was his desperate gamble to win a second term in the White House.

Arthur and Doris Krause, Allison's parents, gambled on American democracy when they sent their daughter to Kent State— and they lost. For thousands of other fathers and mothers with children on campuses, the dice are still rolling. When American soldiers at home fire deadly volleys into crowds of American college students, it is not only Cambodia that is now being "Vietnamized," it is America itself that is being Nixonized. "Can Congress find out why our children can't express themselves?" The answers can come only from the deepest roots of our nation, its character, ideals, and goals. They cannot be equivocated or temporized. In this gamble there are no objective reporters and commentators. The dice roll for all. Repeat, repeat: "Is this dissent a crime? Is this a reason for killing her?"

The piece above is untitled and undated because it was never printed. *Saturday Review* editors declared it "too editorial." The critic was surprised: he was under the impression that he had been writing editorials for twenty years. Tempering his surprise was the secure recollection that, in two decades of writing for SR, this was one of only four occasions when his column was "dropped" for reasons that were persuasive to his editors. No one ever told him what to write, although, as befits a healthy relationship between a working critic and his editors, his attention was occasionally directed to possibilities for timely copy. In selection of subject matter, in freedom of expression, his autonomy and permitted independence —in a world of diminishing individuality in professional journalism—has been something of a miracle for which his appreciation is immense.

As for the emotional tone of the Kent State piece—the critic had moved a long way from his amused approach to politics on television. At the murder of Allison Krause, he had "taken alarm," he had "suffered," and he had "balked" when he had encountered Nothingness.

"The basic problem of our time," Karl Jaspers wrote, "is whether an independent human being in his self-comprehended destiny is still possible." The nightmare of the critic, in the summer of 1970, the summer of "Blow-up" and the Kent State murders, was that the answer to the philosopher's problem could very well— for the future of the United States—be negative. He drew some dialectical comfort, a few months later, from a CBS News television broadcast which demonstrated that, even in the shadow of that repressive negative, men still "solidarize themselves against the possibility of Nothingness." That television program, which the critic commented upon in the following piece, was about the genesis of open dissent in the Soviet Union.

THE OPEN CONSPIRACY   August 22, 1970

CBS NEWS put an inaccurate title on its recent notable broadcast in which dissident Soviet intellectuals courageously presented themselves, in filmed interviews, to American television viewers and forthrightly condemned their government for using repressive, terroristic methods to silence political criticism of the regime. The program was called "Voices from the Russian Underground"—a title that suggests secrecy and conspiracy.

The remarkable characteristic of the statements by Pioris Yakir, Andre Amalrik, Vladimir Bukovsky—all writers—was their complete openness and lack of secrecy. These men are known to the Soviet police. They have been arrested for speaking freely before (Amalrik was rearrested as a direct consequence of the CBS filming), and they expect to be arrested and sent to labor camps or mental hospitals (essentially political prisons).

Bill Cole, former CBS News bureau chief in Moscow (who was expelled for filming the interviews), several times asked Yakir, Amalrik, and Bukovsky to reconsider their action, to withdraw their requests that the films be shown in the United States—but they insisted. "There's no going back," Yakir said. "We're trying to publicize every arrest, every dismissal . . . They'll beat us, and they'll kill us. All the same, people will go on thinking differently."

The writers elaborated on the picture of a spreading dissident "democratic movement" among young, well-educated Soviet citizens. Information is passed along through a system of hand-typed "chronicles." The authorities, the dissidents assert, can no longer control it; furthermore, the police are afraid to repress it with more brutal terror, for if they revive Stalinist methods the repressors, too, may be caught up in the terror. Also, authorities fear such measures might produce worker apathy at a time when the government is seeking to provide incentives for increases in production.

Also heard on the CBS News program was a voice recording of Alexander Ginzburg that was smuggled out of a labor camp where the celebrated writer was imprisoned in 1967 for protesting political trials of other writers. He spoke of the recent deaths of sixteen political prisoners. "Nevertheless, we hope to hold out," his voice declared. "We are sustained . . . by the wrath, protest, and solidarity of all honest people, of all who hold dear the dignity of man, democracy, and peace. In decisive resistance to modern barbarism I see the only real guarantee that the rights of man will be observed, here and throughout the world." It was a distinguished, moving broadcast, and it has displeased the Soviet government, which, through its Washington representatives, tried to persuade CBS News to cancel its promised presentation. The network had invited a Soviet spokesman to appear on the program along with the two American Kremlinologists, Patricia Blake and Abraham Brumberg, but the Soviets declined.

The American government will probably exploit the journalistic coup by making copies of the program and distributing it widely here and abroad to score points in the cold war. CBS News people say they can't help this: Bill Cole was doing a journalist's job; the network chose to pay the price of indefinite exile from Moscow in order to get this important journalistic "first." The *realpolitik* aspects of the event, though, should not obscure its deeper human dimensions. What is so profoundly significant about the program is that fifty years of Soviet education, designed to produce the new Soviet man, utterly loyal to his government, should have produced a modern version of the Christian martyr among the Communist elite.

It was Toynbee who observed that communism is a Christian heresy, Marxism an emotional and intellectual substitute for Christian orthodoxy. The early Christian martyrs, too, were no secret conspirators. As John Henry Newman wrote, believers "were seen equally to defy the powers of darkness to do their worst . . . They cheered and ran forward to meet [the enemy's] attack." The comparison may send shivers of revulsion down the spines of Communists and Christians alike; and yet here are rational, twentieth-century atheists behaving exactly like the fervent theists that toppled Rome in seven or eight generations. Newman postulated the power that did it as "a sense of the unseen." Maybe in all ages, in all circumstances, it is a human virtue that always arises as a direct consequence of terror.

Planetary Pollution and the Cowboy Economy

> *"But what happens when you come to the beginning again?"*
> *Alice ventured to ask.*
> *"Suppose we change the subject," the March Hare interrupted,*
> *yawning. "I'm getting tired of this."*
>
> LEWIS CARROLL

ALICE, unlike Satan, was no critic. In the modern vernacular she
was a critical cop-out. In Chapter Seven (the mystical chapter?)
of her Carrollian adventures, she comes upon a "table set out under
a tree in front of the house." The March Hare and the Hatter were
having tea at it, and a Dormouse was sitting between them, fast
asleep. In this seventh chapter we find the three again: it is all a
sort of anti-matter of the authentic critical trio—the Mariner, the
Hermit, the Wedding Guest. For here, too, we find a dialectic going on, but a marvelously topsy-turvy one.

Alice intrudes upon the scene and the contradictions begin.
The sleepy Dormouse is fitfully roused from his doze; riddles and
paradoxes are bantered back and forth. Alice is confused, and when
rudely spoken to by the Hatter, "she got up in great disgust and
walked off." The Dormouse fell asleep instantly, and the Hatter
and the March Hare took no notice of her going. True, "she looked
back once or twice, half hoping that they would call after her: the
last time she saw them, they were trying to put the Dormouse into

the teapot." The teapot could be *The Rime of the Ancient Mariner's* Wedding Feast; and the Dormouse qualifies as the Wedding Guest, waiting to be "stunned," as opposed to being "stoned" in the teapot.

Had Alice *stayed* she would have been a Mariner-critic. The fact that she left suggests that her cells had never been adequately fired by a Hermit. Or that she had never had the Mariner's profound experience; there was no "woeful agony" compelling her to preach to the congregation, to unburden herself of "a ghastly tale." Someday, perhaps; but until then, she was not a member of Jaspers' "solidarity of the best," of the messianic critical community. Alice, when she awakened, told her sister all the strange adventures that she had had in her curious dream; and her sister kissed her and told her to "run in to your tea; it's getting late." Alice merely thought, as she ran, "what a wonderful dream it had been." It was her sister, though, who was the critic of the day—a young lady much ignored by that great multitude in time and space who have been stirred to dreamings of their own by Lewis Carroll's gentle satire. For it is the sister, and not Alice, who signifies for the reader the *meaning* of Alice's adventures—just as it is the Hermit who clarifies for the Mariner the third beat or critical proposition of the latter's voyage.

The tales of both Coleridge and Carroll are half fantasy, half real: one cannot choose the reality without being haunted by the dream, and so in reverse. Alice's sister sits, with closed eyes as the sun sets, and half believes herself to be in Wonderland, re-dreaming for herself Alice's own dream:

> Lastly, she pictured to herself how this same little sister of hers would, in the after-time, be herself a grown woman; and how she would keep, through all her riper years, the simple and loving heart of her childhood; and how she would gather about her other little children, and make *their* eyes bright and eager with many a strange tale, perhaps even with the dream of Wonderland of long ago: and how she would feel with all their simple sorrows, and find a pleasure in all their simple joys, remembering her own child-life, and the happy summer days.

The collapse of the fore- and aft-dimensions of time, the thrust into the distant future, the preservation of the passing moment for minds yet to be born—what are these but the exercise of the critic's widening vision as he reaches for relationships that the superficial glance has missed? As for uncritical Alice—the best that may be said for her, without condescension, is that she was merely a Dormouse with her eyes open. She, too, bemused by facts, had her head in a teapot. As a creature of Carroll's imagination, she is without fault; her creator willed that she should leave the tea party. As a symbol excised from the story for our own purposes, she stands admirably for the failure of the dialectical nerve, the most dangerous sin of which the critic is capable.

Let us attempt to illustrate this danger by reference to two pieces written approximately ten years apart. The reader is invited to read them in sequence, in their entireties, before we undertake some significations.

TELEVISION'S MAD HATTERS   *December 23, 1961*

YEAR'S END is when television takes the world seriously, looking behind and ahead. It is also the time when it is impossible to take television seriously: one is ambivalently charmed and appalled by it, as Alice was—in Wonderland—at the Mad Hatter's tea party. The March Hare had murdered time, remember; it was always tea time, six o'clock—no time to wash the things between whiles— so the Hatter, the Hare, and the Dormouse kept moving round the tea table as things got used up. The 1961–1962 television season is still in its spring; but TV's Mad Hatters are already moving things around again for the season of 1962–1963. The house is full of promise and improvement. There's a new "mood" and "climate." Oases will bloom in that bad-man-from-Washington's metaphorical wasteland. "Originality" is the key word; "quality," "creativity," "freshness," "difference" are its bold, refreshing variations.

Broadcasting, the trade weekly, reports the major changes coming in regularly scheduled TV program fare—fewer Westerns and private eyes, more "meaningful drama," family situation comedies, a resurgence of games and quiz shows, live variety, and children's programs. The report deals exclusively with entertainment; the number of public affairs programs is expected to "remain about the same or increase slightly." Half-hour shows, the survey predicts, will return in force; the hour program, so grandly bugled just before the coming of this current season, will be considerably less fashionable. Hour shows, it seems, are harder to replace when they fail; and yesterday's widely rejected thirty-minute format has now become the key to unlock the gates of program diversity. The cartoon trend has been blunted and "violence for the sake of violence" is allegedly in disrepute. "Experimentation" will govern the efforts of "new things by top-flight people." Let us hope that all this new tea will really be served. Yet it is difficult to forget that in television, as in Wonderland, time has been murdered and it is always six o'clock. We have been here before.

Last summer *Telefilm* magazine looked ahead to the present season before the new film programs were unveiled on the network. Twenty Hollywood producers explained what was "different" about their upcoming shows. Few were able to resist hyperbole. "Adult, honest, serious, and authentic stories about people in medicine . . ." one producer promised. Another promised "maturity of theme and treatment . . . a welcome change from programming which excites the emotions but overlooks the mind and soul." A third said his crime series would have "the ring of truth, perform public service, and break new television ground." Then, as now, the "different and unusual" were coming 'round next season's bend. Hour and half-hour—we have tasted the tea and the producers have our sympathy. The now familiar and pedestrian programs range from the inanities of "The Hathaways," in which a man and wife seriously play house with three chimpanzees who are their "children"—to the offensiveness of "Bus Stop," which recently presented a story of "a cocky and arrogant eighteen-year-old who murders in cold blood for the fun of it."

The producer of "Bus Stop" said last summer that his series would deal with "important, contemporary ideas and people," and win back, with good theater, television's "lost" audience. The series, he continued, "is directed toward a mature audience and will reflect those aspects of maturity which have been so long neglected by a medium which has only to speak to the intelligent to become a greater part of the increasingly sophisticated life of America." In one "Bus Stop" I caught, a homosexual murdered a seven-year-old girl. This is all solemn and serious, as was the essential satire of Lewis Carroll; and yet it is delightfully mad. Are these Mad Hatters in television masters of cynicism or are they insensitive to the absurdities of what they say and what they do?

The point is that in television, as at the Hatter's tea party, we're back at the beginning again; and at that point, the March Hare interrupted Alice, yawning, and said: "Suppose we change the subject. I'm getting tired of this." Like every good jest, there's some sadness in it. The fourth member of Alice's adventure in the wood was the Dormouse. He was always asleep, poor creature, and the last time Alice saw him as she left the wood, the March Hare and the Mad Hatter were trying to put the sleepy Dormouse into the teapot. Any resemblance between the Dormouse and 49,000,000 American television homes . . .

SEEING AND BELIEVING   June 27, 1970

METROMEDIA BROADCASTING GROUP's two-hour-long television special on the ecology crisis, "1985," was presented the same day recently on the group's five stations in New York, San Francisco, Los Angeles, Kansas City, and Washington, D. C. It represented a fascinating study in what Samuel Taylor Coleridge, in his *Biographia Literaria,* termed "the willing suspension of disbelief." The program simulated an actual Metromedia newscast in the year 1985, in which the group's newscasters, speaking from their respective cities, reported and editorialized on a global disaster involving the complex effects of overpopulation and environmental pollution. Viewers were asked to accept the proposition that Los Angeles was enveloped in deadly smog; New York was blacked out, with mass transportation broken down and food supplies dwindling; Chicago couldn't be reached by television contact; Kansas City was deprived of produce that had been destroyed by pesticides; the nation's capital stank from festering vegetation in the dead Potomac.

In India, China, and Japan there were food riots; Africa experienced mass starvation; death, epidemic, and hunger bestrode all the continents. Governments were taking Draconian measures to save mankind. Guilt, recrimination, despair, and hope for some miracle were expressed for all sufferers by the Metromedia newscasters, who asked: "How did we get here?" and "Shall we be saved?" In the end, the fictionalized newscast implied, everything would prove too little and too late. One by one the cities lost contact with Metromedia's station in the capital, where presumably the program was originating, and finally the circuitry from Washington fizzed out in a white dot on a black screen.

It was a reasonably grim ending, in keeping with the commendable intention of the Metromedia producers "to blast through the modern-day facade of ignoring a problem in the belief that it will disappear." "Belief" is the operative word. Metromedia wanted us to believe its fantasy Dystopia of 1985. Yet throughout the program, at regular intervals, a voice accompanied by a visual slide announced: "This is a dramatization of a news program in the year 1985. The events described here are not actually occurring at this time." Similar disclaimers were also "crawled" from right to left at the bottom of the screen. The precautions, of course, were taken with historical retrospect, harking back to the nationwide panic set off by Orson Welles's "War of the Worlds" (which employed simulated newscast techniques).

Either the disclaimers worked or modern TV audiences are more sophisticated than radio listeners were when broadcast news was young. No one, apparently, panicked over "1985," although Metromedia telephone operators reported a flurry of calls from viewers who were eager to comment on the suitability and propriety of fictionalized news as a device for attacking the ecology problem.

People generally are sufficiently impressed with the seriousness of the environmental crisis to accept the plausibility of fantasized disasters in 1985. The program's content was competently researched and often eloquently written by Don Bresnahan and Vernon Hixson, although the newscasters themselves were not quite up to playing the "roles" of newsmen convincingly. They were a bit too rigid and did not successfully execute some of the emotional directions given to them by the script.

Belief, however, is a matter of duration as well as intensity.

Did the audience (including myself) *really* believe the program?
The answer, I think sadly, must be no. For if we really believed
that doom is coming—and within the next two decades—we would
certainly do something about it. True, the hour-long, follow-up
program presented by WNEW, the Metromedia station in New
York, did address itself to what the individual citizen could do.
It encouraged, among other responses, a revolt in the supermarkets
against consumer convenience packages—don't buy nonreturnable
bottles; bring your own shopping bags; etc. These are small
evidences of earnestness, but we all know that averting impending
worldwide famine will require the massive political, economic,
and technical cooperation of every nation, particularly the
United States and the Soviet Union.

To be successful such an effort would necessitate a
redirection of the economic resources of the two super-powers on the
order of up to 20 per cent of their GNP for at least ten to fifteen
years (a mutual estimate made by C. P. Snow and Soviet
Academician Andrei Sakharov). May we reasonably question
whether we, as a nation, and our leaders are psychologically,
intellectually, or financially prepared for such a radical convulsion
of belief and behavior?

As for Metromedia, if it really believed its own message, the
group would either abandon the television medium or convert into
a missionary enterprise. What is the good of even an admirably
mounted two-hour ecology special, in five cities, extensively
promoted and offered without charge to other stations for
replaying—if the stations return to business as usual, running
endless commercials (without disclaimers) that entice viewers, in
the words of the 1985 script, into "excessive consumption and the
consequent rape of the Earth's resources . . ."?

"If we are to survive," prognosticated Metromedia
correspondent Glenn Hanson toward the end of the program, "a
massive educational program is imperative . . . We need to institute
a no-growth national economy, and perhaps we need to legislate
and enforce a zero-population-growth plan freezing all families
at a maximum of two children. And then, and perhaps most
importantly, we must prepare for a far simpler life." This is clearly
a call for what Kenneth Boulding has termed "the space man

economy"—a cyclical ecological system, without unlimited reservoirs of anything either for extraction or pollution. The call for a simpler space man economy has a special irony when it issues from commercial television, which is dedicated to education for "the cowboy economy," illimitable, reckless, exploitative, romantic, and violent, where consumption and production are regarded as good things in a context of infinite reservoirs from which material can be obtained and into which effluvia can be deposited.

The conclusion must be that most of us who saw the program didn't believe it—because we're still excessively eating, drinking, procreating, wasting, and polluting—and spending $2,000 for military hardware and personnel for every dollar spent to control human fertility. And so, not believing, we will go on toward 1985, over the edge of extinction promised by the program. (Note: This is a fictionalized critique of Metromedia's splendid ecology program "1985." Do not believe it. No such events will actually occur. Do not believe . . . do not . . . do. . . .)

For me, the major chord struck by a comparative scrutiny of the two pieces is the feeling of what the French call *déjà vu*, the illusion of having been there already when one experiences something for the first time. In "Television's Mad Hatters," the critic, having been at the game for eleven years, is already experiencing an exhaustion of the critical spirit. His early lack of sophistication has been redeemed: the passage of time has taught him valuable lessons; and history has discovered to him her capacity for surprise. His technical abilities have matured with unremitting exercise: but the more that things in television seem to change or not to change, the more the landscape remains familiar. The failure of the Mad Hatters piece is the critic's failure to put *himself* into the picture. He documents briefly the case for the delightful madness of television's "here we go again—back to the top"; but he doesn't note, or at least he does not comment on, the fact that the repetitive monotony in programming must produce some echo in his own emotional responses. He sees a jest in the March Hare's yawning commentary, "Suppose we change the subject. I'm getting tired of this"—and he sees sadness in it. But the jest is also on him.

The sleepy Dormouse stands for 49,000,000 American television homes, the public whose critical mass the critic has been arduously attempting to fire for eleven years: he, too, is back at the beginning again. If the American public is bemused by drowsiness, isn't he, the critic, somnolent with the delusion that he can *wake* the Dormouse? He accuses television's Mad Hatters of being insensitive to the absurdities of what they say and do. What about his own insensitivity to the absurdity of his de-hypnotizing efforts? It took another nine years for the opportunity to present itself, in which this absurdity could be articulated clearly. The critic in "Seeing and Believing" is once again "sad." The Mad Hatter's tea party has grown to universal proportions. The "things" that couldn't be washed between whiles, that kept piling up as the guests kept moving 'round the table, are now piling up all over planet Earth. The crisis has grown to global proportions, the crisis of the " 'cowboy economy,' illimitable, reckless, exploitative, romantic, and violent, where consumption and production are regarded as good things in a context of infinite reservoirs from which material can be obtained and into which effluvia can be deposited." As in the mad tea party, so in Metromedia's "1985," it is always six o'clock; time has been murdered.

If, in the earlier piece, the critic's response was sad amusement, with a mixing up of fantasy and truth, so too in the later piece, the response is essentially the same—neither flight nor confrontation but a joke tinged with bitterness. For the critic who has "been here before," what other response is possible? The polemical mood, the prophetic, the hortatory, are responses that can be mounted successfully only when they need not be sustained for long periods of time. It is not only the March Hare who is impelled to remark: "Suppose we change the subject . . . I'm getting tired of this." The critic also is afflicted with the temptation. Remember, after the Mariner, on his voyage, has shot the Albatross, it is a "silent sea" into which the ship bursts:

'Twas sad as sad could be;
And we did speak only to break
The silence of the sea!

Again, when monotony besets the idle ship upon the painted ocean:

> . . . every tongue, through utter drought,
> Was withered at the root;
> We could not speak, no more than if
> We had been choked with soot.

Whitehead writes:

> We have seen that there can be no real halt of civilization in
> the indefinite repetition of a perfected ideal. Staleness sets in.
> And this fatigue is nothing other than the creeping growth
> of anaesthesia, whereby that social group is gradually sinking
> towards nothingness. The defining characteristics are losing
> their importance. There may be no pain or conscious loss.
> There is merely a slow paralysis of surprise. And apart from
> surprise, intensity of feeling collapses.

It is not only the "indefinite repetition of a perfected ideal" that
produces staleness; the same result is brought about by an imper-
fected ideal. But here is the sticking point at which the Alices are
separated from their sisters, the March Hares from the Ancient
Mariners, and the Mad Hatters from the Hermits. The critic *has*
to stay at that tea table: his compulsion is not external, as in the
Mariner's situation; it is internal. As with Socrates, the demon that
bids him play midwife for wisdom is a command implanted in him
by "an oracle." He has no choice; he cannot, like the affronted
Alice, get up and leave in disgust the mad tea party of the world
that he criticizes.

 This is a hard thing to say. There have been critics, particularly in television, who have thrown in the sponge because they
could no longer endure the murder of time and the dishes piling up
absurdly. Occasionally, one such returns after having left. When
the retirement is permanent, susceptible of compassionate understanding, the genuine critic is then distinguished by the continuing
exercise of his critical faculties in whatever other areas of experience he chooses. The critic who stays must face the possibility
that he is rationalizing about the practical circumstances of his life

which hold him to the job when he indulges in self-serving notions of internal compulsions that arise out of some alleged nobility of character. The essential point, however, is that the critic who is tired of the subject and yet stays, *knows* that he is tired of it, knows that he would like to change the subject, and knows that it is only spontaneity, novel togetherness, which refreshes surprise and keeps him locked into that mad course of movement around the table with the Hares and the Hatters. For just as the compulsion to stay comes from within, so does the surprise.

The "spring of love," which made the Mariner bless the water snakes and suddenly uncover his liberty, gushed from his "heart." It was a psychic spring, an ingression from beyond the Mariner's own reserves. "Sure," the Mariner tells the Wedding Guest, "my kind saint took pity on me." So, from "Television's Mad Hatters" in 1961, to "Seeing and Believing" in 1970, there are no exterior surprises in the mad television scene, which both charms and appalls. The stakes grow bigger, that's all: the crisis deepens. No assurance is given of salvation, nor even of significant change; yet the critic persists. He threads his weary way along his chain of Wedding Guests, searching for and occasionally finding the springs of surprise and spontaneity in his third beats, drawn from the rock in the desert where time was murdered at six o'clock. It is not only the readiness, but the awareness that is all.

CHAPTER TEN

Consumers, Commercials, and Men About Town

—"By thy long gray beard and glittering eye,
Now wherefore stopp'st thou me? . . ."

THE "STOPPING" in *The Rime of the Ancient Mariner* presumably is designed to deliver the Wedding Guest to the Mariner, as another in the latter's long line of unwilling but receptive hearers of his tale: that, traditionally, has been the understanding and interpretation of the arrest. If we take the long leap, however, from the first verse of the poem to the penultimate and final verses, another explanation becomes possible:

The Mariner, whose eye is bright,
Whose beard with age is hoar,
Is gone: and now the Wedding Guest
Turned from the bridegroom's door.

To turn the Wedding Guest away from the Wedding Feast—that is the ultimate motive of the Mariner; the telling of the tale, with its traumatic impact, is merely the method by which the Mariner accomplishes his true aim:

He went like one that hath been stunned,
And is of sense forlorn . . .

I have already alluded to the "stunning" effect of the Mariner's tale, in its application to the ends of critical signification, discovery, and transformation. I should like now to direct the reader's attention to the fact that the Wedding Guest was "forlorn" of sense—which may be interpreted to mean that he has "forsaken" sense. The word "sense" also takes on a special meaning. "The Bridegroom's doors are opened wide," the Wedding Guest remonstrates, when the Mariner accosts him:

> And I am next of kin;
> The guests are met, the feast is set:
> May'st hear the merry din.

A wedding is a joyous occasion: beneath the conventional ceremonial artifice, the ritual, the often shallow conviviality, lies an undeniable stratum of profound human experience susceptible of being properly sanctified with secular or religious approbation. But neither can anyone deny that usually the free food and drink, generously provided by the hosts, for their invited guests' unlimited indulgence, are an attractive concomitant of the more solemn aspects of the event. Physical gratification and worldly pleasure, from their innocent, diverting, and useful modes to their more dubious measures, may be subsumed under the meaning of "sense," as we find it in Coleridge's poem. At an even deeper level, we may attribute to it an allegedly more negative materialism, which is at the opposite pole from presumably more "ethereal" values.

The transient as opposed to the lasting, the appearance versus the reality—these are other terms by which we can try to capture the sense of "sense" that we are entertaining here. That the Wedding Guest misses the actual wedding, by virtue of his being "held" by the Mariner, is not so important for him as the fact that he turns away from the Wedding Feast that follows. The feast may have been what he really came for—with all due respect to the bride and groom. But the Wedding Feast is our important symbol. The Mariner "hath his will" in order to turn the Wedding Guest from the inferior forms to their superior ideas. In Nietzschean terms, it is the familiar struggle between the Dionysian and the Apollonian ways of life, the way of the instincts versus the way of the mind, of reason. "Socratic ethics, dialectics," wrote Nietzsche, "the temperance and cheerfulness of the pure scholar—couldn't these, rather than their opposites, be viewed as symptoms of decline, fatigue, distemper, or instincts caught in anarchic dissolution?"

The German Dionysian was contemptuous of the Greek ironist. He would have scorned and laughed at the Ancient Mariner's final message to the Wedding Guest:

> O sweeter than the marriage feast,
> 'Tis sweeter far to me,
> To walk together to the kirk
> With a goodly company!

For Nietzsche, disorder, chaos, and mystery were part of "the true being of things"; community lay not in amalgamation with the herd, the multitude, but in the separation, the individuation, of men with an urge to power from the men with slave morality who constituted most of mankind. Appearances, shifting, changing, were the closest approximations to truth; reality is bottomless. Nietzsche rejected transcendental consolations, and he doomed man, in striking affinity to the Mariner's experience, to "the loneliest of all sea voyages."

"Follow me," the Mariner says to the Wedding Guest, "after I am gone. Walk in my footsteps: that is the best way to go." Socrates spoke similarly to all whom he taught. Plato, in his dialogue *Gorgias*, confronts his mouthpiece philosopher with "the three wisest Greeks of our day," Gorgias, Polus, and Callicles. They are Sophists, rhetoricians, the professional dispensers of knowledge, with whom Socrates contended all the days of his teaching. Since the dialogue is Plato's play—and Socrates is his man—the three are vanquished in the end for their lack of dialectical skill. Socrates proves to them that it is a higher form of statesmanship to make men better than to flatter them. Gorgias is a venerable, celebrated persuader; Polus is an impetuous youth; but it is the figure of Callicles that dominates the trio.

"In Callicles," B. Jowett wrote, in his Introduction to the dialogue, "far more than in any other sophist or rhetorician, is concentrated the spirit of evil against which Socrates is contending, the spirit of the world . . ." Callicles is a "man about town," an Athenian gentleman, who anticipates Nietzsche. He despises mankind and deprecates philosophers. Philosophy, he asserts, is fine for effeminate, immature men; but maturity ought to make one wise and show him that the pursuit of wealth and power and the satisfaction of the passions are the only desirable ends for men of honor, ability and courage. Might is right, not virtue. Stop splitting words and surrounding yourself, he tells Socrates, with a few admiring youths who know nothing, and use your talents in the marketplace, among real men who are ambitious, unscrupulous when necessary, cynical, materialistic, and shrewd in assessing the main chance. Callicles, as we have seen in the exploits of the Mad Hatters of television, is very much a figure of the contemporary television scene.

To him Socrates, at the conclusion of the dialectical combat, delivers one of his most earnest exhortations:

> Follow me, then, and I will lead you where you will be happy
> in life and after death . . . And never mind if some one
> despises you as a fool, and insults you if he has a mind . . .
> When we have practised virtue together, we will apply
> ourselves to politics, if that seems desirable, or we will advise
> about whatever else may seem good to us, for we shall be better
> able to judge then. In our present condition we ought not to
> give ourselves airs, for even on the most important subjects we
> are always changing our minds; so utterly stupid are we!
> . . . the best way of life is to practise justice and every good
> virtue in life and death. This way let us go; and in this exhort
> all men to follow, not in the way to which you trust and in
> which you exhort me to follow you; for that way, Callicles, is
> nothing worth.

It is the "nothing worth" from which the Mariner wishes to save the Wedding Guest, as he stops him at the Bridegroom's door. It is the "nothing worth" of contemporary television and radio against which the critic of broadcasting inveighs. "Stop!" he says to the people of television and to their vast audiences; not from using and enjoying this remarkable medium of human communication, but from using it badly, immorally, for inferior purposes. The Wedding Feast is the "sense" world, the world of "common sense"; make of it a medium for uncommon sense. It is only a distorted vision that would condemn television utterly; but it is also a distorted vision that would debase it to degraded ends.

For "Wedding Feast" read the acquisitive-consumption orientation of commercial broadcasting, and you will have the touchstone with which to encounter the eleven pieces which follow. Their major theme is the tragic waste of the potential of broadcasting in this country. Would that the water served at this feast, as at another wedding in a certain Mediterranean scene, could be turned into wine—the wine of community as opposed to collectivity! The reader may note that the critic offers no formula for accomplishing the miracle. In later chapters, some suggestions may come into view; however, if a critic is to play philosopher-king, as well he might, it were better that he lean more heavily on the side of philosophy than of kingship. It is more necessary for a critic to maintain detachment than to become altogether involved; for in total involvement lies the danger of dogma, whereas the very essence of the critical spirit is that it be ever ready to negate its own negation, should that become desirable in order to reach a higher affirmation, and so on.

The question of choice ought to be answered: why this particular combination of pieces of all the possibilities? The answer, candidly, is—I think these are among the best. Probably my judgment is colored by the fact that they express my special biases. When a critic has freedom of choice concerning the objects to which he will give his attention, he generally tends to be guided by his own selective perception—that is, he more often than not chooses to attend to those objects which afford him the richest opportunities to express his own prejudices. By prejudices, I do not necessarily impute to him a negative attitude; rather, I mean that he seeks constantly to allow his rivers of conviction to run in expedient channels. The pieces that I have selected cannot, of course, adequately represent the whole range of subjects that I have covered in two decades: they represent some of the high points.

In reading and rereading them, in sifting, combining, rearranging, in order to discover integral coherences, I have been struck with a number of things which the reader might reflect upon. The first is the push, in most pieces, for universals, large universals, which exist, before their connection, at great distances from the objects of critical attention. In his Introduction to Plato's *Republic,* Jowett wrote of Book VII:

> All things in which there is opposition or proportion are suggestive of reflection. The mere impression of sense evokes no power of thought or of mind, but when sensible objects ask to be compared and distinguished, then philosophy [read criticism] begins.

Earlier in the same Introduction, Jowett also makes a comment, on the search for universals, which we apply to criticism:

> There seem to be two great aims in the philosophy of Plato,— first, to realize abstractions; secondly, to connect them. According to him, the true education is that which draws men from becoming to being, and to a comprehensive survey of all beings. He desires to develop in the human mind the faculty of seeing the universal in all things; until at last the particulars of sense drop away and the universal alone remains. He then seeks to combine the universals which he has disengaged from sense . . .

The critic finds a strain of irony in these pieces, an attempt to see television whole, to warn the reader, to wake him up to the institutional arrangements which are the hard, tough underbelly of television and radio. There is an ineradicable hope, a yearning for escape, for freedom from the oppressive misuses of the medium; but one cannot overlook the deepening note of anxiety and frustration—as irrationality and grotesque absurdity intrude—and ultimately the fear of complete loss of identity. "Stop!" the critic calls to the readers, as he meets them at television's door. "Turn from the Wedding Feast and its appearances. Follow the Mariner—to reality."

Of the eleven pieces that follow, all but the first require no accompanying note. They appear to be self-explanatory, even for readers who may never have seen the programs mentioned and who are not aware of the contexts of the subject matters that are treated. The first piece, "The Tragedy of $64,000," invites the following . . .

COMMENTARY

"The $64,000 Question" was an early luminary in the television trend, during the 1950's, to high-money-stake quiz programs. It was inspired by a radio show called "Take It or Leave It," in which contestants, answering questions that were put to them by a quiz-master, could elect to play for higher and higher stakes, leading to the ultimate win—$64.

"The $64,000 Question," a dramatic escalation of the original formula, spectacularly heated up the acquisitive gambling instincts of the nation's television audience. Its contestants, generally ob-scure individuals, rocketed almost overnight to great reputations. The answers to the questions asked of the contestants were guarded between programs by personnel of the Manufacturers Trust Com-pany, to assure secrecy. The contestants offered themselves as ex-perts in particular fields—baseball, opera, history, etc. The cameras peered at them through the glass windows of "isolation booths" where, hearing only the voice of the quizmaster, they agonized over their suspenseful answers, as described in the piece; the cameras also caught remarkable portraits of empathic suspense in the faces of even more agonized individuals in the studio audience.

The "plateaus" referred to in the piece were the increasing amounts of money that they became eligible to win, as, week after victorious week, surviving all challengers, the winners successfully mounted the ladder of encyclopedic glory, rich financial rewards, and international notoriety. Eventually, the bubble of the quiz programs burst with shuddering impact on a cheated nation's of-fended resentment at being "suckered." It was revealed that many winners, including a celebrated academic, were given knowledge of the answers before they went on the air. Their nail-biting mo-ments of breathless suspense, while the audience waited to hear whether or not they would be demoted as champions of wisdom were, after all, mere masquerades, executed at the instructions of program directors. The cheating came to light on one particular high-stake program, "Twenty-One": but in the subsequent furor, which even prompted the Congress of the United States to investigate, other programs were involved, and rather widespread collusion was revealed among the networks, advertising agencies, sponsors, and program producers. Careers were ruined and reputations tarnished in the debacle.

This critic shared neither the ignorance of this deception nor the sense of outrage at its discovery. In a column written before the storm broke ("What Would You Do?" sr, June 8, 1957), he had written:

> "Twenty-One" is not even an honest test of a man's hoard of facts . . . any contestant . . . could be stopped the first week . . . as any quiz writer will tell you—if the mass media masquerade were ever to be played in earnest. (To wit: "Name the Pharaohs of the Third, Ninth, and Sixteenth Dynasties, according to Manetho.") The technique of the Big Quiz is simple: get an interesting personality and keep him on from week to week till the public gets bored.

The critic had taken exception, in that same piece, to the adulation, as a national hero, of a certain professor who was a champion of the program "Twenty-One." The critic had decried the "confusion between wide reading plus a retentive memory and the far more subtle complex of philosophic attitudes and values which are loosely described by the word 'intellectual' . . ." He had observed that the professor had "poorly served the better intellectual qualities of mind and spirit by encouraging the public's mistaken identification of the intellectual as a grown-up quiz-kid."

In harmony with the critic's bias toward universals, when the scandal became public he went on, in a later piece ("Havoc Up One Sleeve," sr, October 31, 1959), to inveigh against the "evident evils of inadequate self-regulation by the industry." "Is there no indignation left in the house," he asked, "for that sponsor-dominated morality the end of which is to hold audiences by whatever means it can get away with?"

Quiz shows subsequently returned to television, after a period of circumspect absence. Many advertisers and broadcasting professionals never could understand why such a storm had been blown up over what they considered to be merely a traditional, innocent expression of the spirit of theater, in which actors play "let's pretend" roles for the entertainment of willing audiences. There are more modest quiz shows on television today: they still trade largely on the acquisitive instincts, but the accent now is on winning expensive consumer products rather than the old cupidity-cell-firing windfalls of cool cash.

THE TRAGEDY OF $64,000   *September 24, 1955*

THE GREEKS had a word for "The $64,000 Question": tragedy. Sophocles' audience, the whole population, came early, prepared to spend the day in the bleachers (Frances Ferguson tells us in the brilliant work *The Idea of a Theatre*); "the actors were not professionals in our sense, but citizens selected for a religious office, and Sophocles himself had trained them and the chorus." The bold, imaginative Louis G. Cowan, who created the Revlon international episode (Tuesday nights, CBS–TV), would blush, I am sure, to be joined to such august company as the author of *Oedipus Rex*, and yet the analogue is accurate. Gino Prato, Gloria Lockerman, Captain McCutchen, *et al.*, are citizens, not actors in the professional sense. But "religious office"?

The point is: there on the Revlon stage, as on the platform in Sophocles' time, a modern scapegoat is to be offered who will purify us of our baser lusts for certified checks, harmonize our obscurities and frustrations, and render our unpublicized, individual lots palatable till "the next plateau." Gino Prato a scapegoat? But $32,000, four press agents, a $10,000-a-year job, reunion with Papa on a mountain in Statale, Italy, after thirty-three years? Alas, scapegoat, indeed.

One has merely to follow Gino Prato's itinerary, from standing ovation at La Scala, in Milan, to sidewalk cafe in Rome with Madame Ambassador Claire Luce and ex-outfielder Joe DiMaggio, to appreciate the parallel. From the time of Oedipus' exile from Thebes (according to the play's sequel, *Oedipus at Colonos*) he became a sort of sacred relic, like the bones of a saint; perilous, but "good medicine" for the community that possessed him. Antigone, his daughter, went with him on his blind wanderings.

Of Gino recently the Associated Press reported that he "climbed a mule trail on foot to reach his birthplace in the north Italian mountains. Church bells rang and nearly every resident gathered in the town square to welcome him." Riding beside him on a mule was—his daughter.

But what of the scapegoat theory? Struggle, dismemberment, death, and renewal—this was the passion, the pathos of the perennial winter-spring conflict which underlay the Greek theater. Now, consider the Revlon isolation booth, into which the tragic heroes of "The $64,000 Question" must enter when they approach the ultimate mystery of pumpernickel bread and antidisestablish-mentarianism. Regard the agonizing loneliness of the spotlighted figure in the soundproofed booth. He is face to face with the very meaning of his life, with the most desperate crisis of his aspiration. And the community, the audience, the 50,000,000 who pity and fear, who echo the unutterable prayer of a Mammon-culture—observe (courtesy of the clever, naked, searching camera's eye) how they are dismembered by the trial, the suspense, the unendurable torment of the hero who is expiating publicly their private, unacknowledged sin of greed.

Aristotle, who set forth on the basis of the Greek plays spread out before him some still-viable insights into the art and value of the tragic drama, would have appreciated the cunning of "The $64,000 Question." Even as the television public appreciates and commends and enjoys its success. Aristotle was no old, moralizing fogey like Plato. Aristotle opined that the end of poetry (or literature or TV) was—simply and unashamedly—"delight."

Nevertheless, this program, passing a phenomenon as it may be, has struck so big a note precisely because it is an unconscious communal ritual. We, the people, imitate here not rites of fertility. The womb of "The $64,000 Question" glitters with the appearance of life. Still, it is sterile. Oedipus was an essentially noble human being, innocent, affectionate, of uncalculating benevolence and public spirit. At Colonos he died, redeemed from the consequences of his errors (patricide and incest) and at peace. Mr. Prato, kindly man, is but the instrument, in these paragraphs, of a literary device. We wish him the fulness of his innocent good fortune—and all the other conquerors of the golden plateaus.

But their roles in the Revlon rites suggest sobering afterthoughts. Let us hope that another and perhaps greater Sophocles will arise to purge the Thebes of our national conscience of the sinister corruption that lives behind the window where no sound comes save the riddle of the Manufacturers Trust Company.

THE MISSING DIMENSION   *April 27, 1968*

MARTIN LUTHER KING, JR., had planned to lead a march in Memphis, Tennessee, on behalf of the city's striking garbage collectors. The day after King was buried in Atlanta a statement was expected from the mayor's office in Memphis that the strike had been settled. The striking city employees, it was anticipated, would win at least three of the eleven issues involved in the labor dispute: 1) union recognition and a written contract; 2) a payroll check-off for union dues; and 3) an hourly wage increase. The average pre-strike wage had been $1.75 per hour. The garbage collectors had demanded $2.35 to $3 per hour; the mayor had offered an immediate increase of 8 cents an hour; the city council offered 10 cents; indefinite further increases had been promised for July.

In order to get this information, I had to call the city desk of *The Commercial Appeal* in Memphis. In the five traumatic days and nights of close, continuous attending to TV and radio, from the moment Martin Luther King's murder was reported to the final memorial services, I never once heard mention of the specific demands of the striking city employees. I participated emotionally in a historically unique national ceremonial catharsis, but the experience afforded me not the smallest understanding of the immediate goal for which the martyred black American hero offered himself as an easy target for an assassin's bullet.

Therein lies a commentary on the role that broadcasting can play—and does play—in our national life. The facts about the garbage collectors' strike were specific. The TV and radio coverage provided a setting for anguish and dignity, compelling mass response but diverting attention from the bargaining that was going on beyond the national spotlight, in negotiations involving inequalities of wealth, concrete benefits, and allocation of public resources. The ritual undoubtedly "cooled" the nation. It gave us all images of heroism, greatness, and nobility. But in quieting resentments and allaying doubts, it probably dulled needed critical faculties.

The fact that black men and white participated as actors and spectators merely underscores the panic felt by both races at the tragic events which shook the tree of American beliefs and loosened the underpinnings of social order. Their joining of hands and aspirations in the throngs that marched in Atlanta reflected, in part, their mutual efforts to persuade each other of the usefulness of the experience.

Since many Americans accept the proposition that all share the guilt for Martin Luther King's murder, let us look at the media's performance. The images of the Negro that TV and radio have delivered in the past, it may be plausibly argued, have contributed to the black stereotype—a servant who helps white America live the good life, if he keeps his place, but who becomes a violent threat when he makes demands, justifying counterviolence. The stereotype is blurred by contradictions aroused by Martin Luther King's Christian love and nonviolent behavior, which stir guilt in persons educated in the Judeo-Christian belief system. The ambivalence exists on both sides, black and white—a tension of compassion and threat, love and violence. It becomes unbearable. After the shooting there is a mass outpouring of emotions. Television, particularly, resonates and magnifies it with enormous power.

Bills are accelerated through legislatures as evidence of good faith—bills which alter basic patterns much too slowly. All the while, the cameras continue to offer images of tenderness, brotherhood, idealism. Negative images are screened out: Black militants are nowhere to be heard or seen on the air. Perhaps by pure coincidence, black men and women suddenly appear in greater numbers than ever before on TV commercials. In panel discussions interspersed in the long memorial services, the talk is always about power and equality in broad terms, never in specific details—such as the particular issues in the garbage collectors' dispute. Pictures of lootings and burnings in other cities also seem to exude the general symbolic imagery. It is all useful magic: it restores law and order and moves the race problem, hopefully, another painful inch toward justice.

What the public really needs, if the democratic reality and not the symbol is to prevail, is more attention by the media to the hard economic dimensions of the problem, as exemplified by the off-camera details of the garbage collectors' negotiations. The key to Martin Luther King's kingdom on earth is not in the moving account of his apotheosis offered by TV, but in the medium's more scrupulous reporting of private and public acts of government in everyday life.

THE ART OF BAMBOOZLEMENT   *July 29, 1967*

IN HIS NEW BOOK *The New Industrial State,* John Kenneth Galbraith has a number of references in the index to television, radio, and advertising. *The Affluent Society,* by the Harvard professor of economics, published in 1958, contained not a single index reference to any of these subjects, although both works scrutinize the impact of the corporate economy on the quality of modern life. It may be counted as a sign of progress that an outstanding economist, who writes against the grain of the conventional wisdom in his discipline, should be reaching out to a recognition of the advertising-broadcasting dimensions of changing economic theory.

Mr. Galbraith, in fact, chides "solemn social scientists" who tend to think of "any institution which features rhymed and singing commercials, intense and lachrymose voices urging highly improbable enjoyments . . . and which hints implausibly at opportunities for antiseptic seduction, as inherently trivial." "The industrial system," asserts the author, "is profoundly dependent on commercial television and could not exist in its present form without it. Economists who eschew discussion of its economic significance, or dismiss it as a wicked waste, are protecting their reputation and that of their subject for Calvinist austerity. But they are not adding to their reputation for relevance."

Galbraith is very relevant in the serious attention he has paid to the world of show biz and hard sell, although he still has nothing to say about the actual programs which, presumably, are the modern equivalent of the old free lunches in the saloons which drew the customers to the counters where they bought the beer. His next book, hopefully, will remedy that defect, for, just as the economist alone cannot construct the comprehensive theory of the consumption society—without the help of law, psychology, sociology, etc.—so the subtle and complex description of the author's "technostructure" must include the relationship between commercials and entertainment, as well as the connections between corporate growth, planning, production of goods, and managed consumer demand. Galbraith's main thesis is that the consumer is not "sovereign," as the textbook economists hold. He does not tell product-makers what he wants; he does not "vote" by his purchases in a "free" market.

The truth is, says the Harvard economist, that the product-makers cannot risk random choice in the buying of products. They manage demand through mass persuasion: The consumer has the illusion of freedom; actually he is in the "benign servitude of a household retainer who is taught to love her mistress." Granted this explanation is adequate to explain buying for psychic gratification, but the question arises: Is the demand for programs similarly "managed"? Evidence to support Galbraith's theories about the commercials may be found abundantly in the broadcasting trade journals every day. A radio-TV vice president for a Hollywood advertising agency recently stated: "I am convinced the right kind of radio commercials can make a teen-ager do your bidding in most any direction."

A "TV commercial experimental laboratory" opened recently in New York. It announced that it would bring "new, unique effects in film to television by use of abstract forms, color, and music . . . which call the viewer's emotions into play, eliminate the 'debate' on his part, and allow the essential meaning of the message to come through with deeper penetration." Mr. Galbraith, in his new book, however, might be guilty of some self-deception of his own. This is suggested by the unsatisfactory explanation he gives for the effectiveness of television commercials in motivating people to buy the products that they advertise. He accuses the producers of commercials of "well-considered mendacity." They do not, he says, believe their own lies, but take some professional pride in "workmanlike bamboozlement."

Consumers, also, don't really believe the commercials. They make a "nearly total discount for all forms of advertising." Yet, he maintains, they respond "automatically," where the purchase does not merit a great deal of thought, despite the fact that they dismiss the claims of the commercial messages on television.

The psychology of this explanation is ambiguous. People act on lies, knowing that they are lies, because of some cumulative, fantasy image. It needs refining. Galbraith himself has a possible answer in another part of his book, where he writes: "It is possible that people need to believe that they are unmanaged, if they are to be managed effectively."

To believe that some intangible, imprecise mechanism makes us do the buying is a serviceable myth that protects the ego. Galbraith may be committing a common elitist error in assuming that, because he is on to the bamboozlers, everyone else is. He may actually be perpetuating the dangerous illusion by telling people that they don't believe the commercials—the people who produce them as well as those who act on them at the market. Better to face the possibility that the new industrial state, for its inevitable but limited social purposes, has brought most of us to the condition where we take as truth the daily small lies in the vast mass media apparatus for the management of demand. In that recognition may lie the first step toward freedom.

THE LOLLIPOP TRAP   *January 1, 1966*

THE MOUNTAIN behind which the Pied Piper led all the children of medieval Hamelin Town has exploded and poured its moppets into Hollywood and Madison Avenue to be sorted interminably through television's programs and commercial messages. This is the foremost impression left by the first half of the 1965–1966 television season. It is the year of the child actor in the world of the small screen. The phenomenon is so pervasive that one is tempted to view it as a historic turning point, a moment of truth. The shape of advertiser-supported television—so long evolving, so long anticipated with mixed feelings—has finally been made clear. It is not education's panacea: it is not entertainment's apotheosis. It is merely a lollipop trap—a pattern of prime-time entertainment programing planned, produced, and directed primarily at the twelve- to seventeen-year-old viewer. Under this teenage umbrella it is assumed that subteens can also be attracted, along with older viewers, particularly young adults.

Certain sponsors who manufacture geriatric products do aim at viewers over thirty-five; and all sponsors do not mind having all age groups represented in their audiences. The main thrust of television's programing, however, is delivered at the crucial teenage center because it is the teenager who has the headiest love affair with the TV set, who starts its electricity flowing most frequently, and who sets the pace for the nation's viewing habits. Younger children generally like to watch what their teenage brothers and sisters enjoy. Parents in one-set homes often face the triple choice of overruling their children's program preferences, of watching along with them, or of abdicating the TV set to them. Generally, in the permissive American manner, they abdicate. Television's descent into the lollipop trap began with an original, historic marriage between radio and children. In the early 1920's— when radio broke upon the American scene—it was the teenagers who built the first "crystal sets" in their workshops. When receivers became standardized and expensive, adults purchased them: radio listening, as an early novelty, was primarily a family affair in American homes.

The novelty of television, after World War II, brought a fresh cycle of family viewing. There were popular kiddie shows ("Howdy Doody," "Kukla, Fran, & Ollie"), but prime-time evening programing was adult oriented. Then a number of things combined to spring the lollipop trap. Television's novelty faded and adults cut their viewing time. Television also began to feel the impact of the rapidly growing "youth market." Consumer research, developing sophistication after the war, had already discovered it in other media. Movies had nurtured their own teenage cinema subculture, ranging from macabre horror to sex, sand, surfing, and how to stuff a bikini. Teenagers had become the darlings of the record industry; and their music tastes had captured radio.

In the field of magazines, the editors of *Seventeen,* an outstanding success, boasted that "teenagers are the most powerful, influential, affluential chunk of the population today." Kids have always been the most important factor in entertainment; and adults have indulgently looked over their shoulders—but today's youth binge is headier, hipper, and commercially harder.

Teens experiment with tastes; and exploiters carefully scan fan clubs for new trends; but they also shrewdly feed back stimuli into the young groups and help to develop marketable fads. Matthew S. McLaughlin, assistant general manager of the Ford Division, told members of the New York Advertising Club recently: "We live in a youth-oriented society. The young people of this country are the pace-setters, not only in society but in our economy as well. So far we have experienced only the leading edge of the youth explosion in our population. The crest of the wave is yet to come." When Leonard H. Goldenson took control of the American Broadcasting Company in 1953, his network was Number Three to CBS and NBC. As he added affiliate stations he pursued an aggressive "counter-programing" policy, predicated on action-adventure programs aimed at the "young adult" market. They relied, to an unprecedented degree in broadcasting history, on sex and violence ("The Untouchables," "Maverick," "Cheyenne," "77 Sunset Strip").

ABC was so successful that CBS and NBC had to follow its lead. All three networks programed on the same "flow of audience" principle—children were served in the early evening hours: progressively, they went to bed and the programs served adults; until, presumably, in the late time-periods, there were few children left. Many parents began to express concern over the possibly harmful effects of TV's programming on children. Congressional committees hailed network executives to Capitol Hill and made headlines with negative images. Network heads rolled; and program suppliers, in an effort to mute the criticism, turned to the situation comedy as an inoffensive, staple brand of programing. This was the penultimate trap to the lollipop trap. While all this was happening, the Beatles came along. Ed Sullivan, the dean of variety programers, found that whenever he featured the long-haired thumpers and screamers, his ratings shot up spectacularly. In radio, advertising agencies producing commercials for clients, discovered that whenever they introduced the rock-'n'-roll beat into their sponsors' messages, and used teenage music combos, retail shelves were swept clean of the advertised products.

ABC put "Shindig" on the air—the first regularly scheduled night-time teenage show. Its success prompted NBC to schedule "Hullabaloo." The climactic event which, by then, had pushed television utterly into the lollipop trap, was the publication of the 1960 U. S. Census Bureau figures. The census projections predicted that by 1970 roughly half the nation's population (111,000,000) would be under twenty-five years of age. Fifty per cent of today's brides are under twenty years of age. Young adults, accumulating income and possessions, constitute the "acquisitive" heartland of America's rich consumer market. "Get your brand in the pot early," is a key Madison Avenue maxim. It means that children must be taught at a tender age to recognize and accept standard brands.

You furnish them with a model of their own world in its most general, superficial, and childishly captivating aspects. You give them other children with whom to identify; you picture the child as the center of the universe, with the adult revolving in secondary orbits around the youthful hub. Programs that fit these specifications can offend few viewers. You are successfully and harmlessly ensconced in the lollipop trap. Paul L. Klein, director of research for NBC, rejects the proposition that teenagers dominate TV. "Since there are three networks," he said in a conversation, "to have a solid hit, you must win at least a one-third share of the audience. How can the teens dominate TV viewing when only 30 per cent of TV homes have teenagers in them?" Edgar Sherrick, vice president, ABC–TV network programs, said: "Of course we're interested in the teenage market. Anyone in the entertainment world would be an ostrich to ignore the population breaks."

John A. Schneider, president of the CBS Television Network, asserted that his comedy shows are not consciously aimed at teenagers. "We have to have broad-based family shows," he said. "But if the teens are having a greater impact on our culture, our responsibility is to reflect it. This is cultural democracy." At Young

& Rubicam, Warren Bahr, director of media, was philosophical. "National sales," he said, "reflect a powerful lot of committed baby-sitter money. The electronic media are basically for entertainment. It's a matter of filling time. The Romans had circuses: we've got mass leisure and television." At another advertising agency, an executive, too cautious to be quoted, said candidly: "At this shop, if a program is not for kids, forget it." David Levy, executive producer for "The Addams Family" (ABC) admitted that his show's "greatest strength lies with kids and young housewives." The most impressive evidence for the lollipop trap thesis, however, can be found in the new television programs presented this season on all three networks. Half of the thirty-three new shows feature children as members of the cast—moppets to teenagers.

"Please Don't Eat the Daisies" has kids: "My Mother the Car" has kids: so has "Lost in Space," "O.K. Crackerby," and "The John Forsythe Show." "Gidget" is a teenager: so is "Tammy." "Hank" is Horatio Alger working his way, unregistered, through college—but he has a kid sister. "Camp Runamuck" opened the season with a shot of probably one hundred boy campers tramping along a country road in charge of allegedly adult counselors. Halfway through the season recently, "The Man from UNCLE" raised the kiddie ante to a new high with "Children's Day Affair," an episode in which THRUSH trained little boys in a European school to be sinister, deadly assassins. A few of the new shows have fared poorly in the ratings race and will be cancelled; but juvenilia marches on night after night. Sad testimony to the power of the teenage market is the capitulation of the variety programs. Red Skelton, Danny Kaye, Perry Como, and Steve Lawrence have followed Ed Sullivan in paying profitable obeisance with guest spots for teenage music combos. Sammy Davis, Jr., was the only adult performer on a Thanksgiving Day special. The upward teen trend may also be detected in daytime television, particularly on ABC. "Where the Action Is," a remake of the Dick Clark "Bandstand" program, is scheduled afternoons on the presumption that teenagers hurry home from school to "come alive." ABC has also given a more youthful treatment to its soap opera schedule, switching from the emotional problems of the middle-aged woman

to those of "the young marrieds." In the commercials day and
night, the young in heart and in pocketbook march across the
American television consciousness in unremitting hosts. Children
badger mothers about Teflon pots, teenagers weep at unkempt
hair until witches sparkle their tresses into loveliness with shots of
magic spray, older daughters compare watchbands with young-
looking mothers, and young housewives, only twenty-four, shudder
at the first appearance of dry skin.

And what of the future? The key to tomorrow's television
success, many Hollywood producers believe, is the pop music act
which is a teen-age favorite. Dick Friedberg, of Premier Talent
Associates, a New York talent agency which handles Herman's
Hermits and Freddy and The Dreamers, said in an interview that
he had been "inundated" with offers from west coast television
studios. "Screen Gems, Warner Brothers, MGM and others want us
to provide the acts, and they'll build pilots around them for
situation comedies. The trouble is, our acts are making so much
money in public appearances that they can't afford to commit their
time to a television series. Herman's Hermits earns $25,000 a day
in personal appearances. MGM Pictures paid the group $50,000 and
a Cadillac limousine for singing two songs in the film *Where the
Boys Meet the Girls*. Freddy and The Dreamers were guaranteed
a sum of money in the seven figures to do Coke commercials on
the radio. They were such a hit that they used up the guarantee
in five and a half weeks and are now in the higher rates for
residuals. How can we afford to spend six months doing a
twenty-six-week TV series? But the studios say they'll shoot around
us—do four or five shows a week. We're considering it."

The networks seem to have found the level they want to
perform on. The lollipop trap will diminish further television's
standing among the better educated; but the industry does not
seem to mind its own arrested development. In a culture which
worships the myth of perpetual youth, the realities of aging must
inevitably clash with desperate attempts to obey the culture's
mandate to stay young. Older people are robbed in such a neurotic
situation of the expansive, integrating experience of maturity.
Children want and need adults to set the reasonable limits of their
innovating, exploring, and rebelling. Youth and maturity are

necessary partners. We upset the sensitive balance if we give more weight to one than the other. Today, television is playing back to children nothing more than a distorted, market-substitute of their own natural, adolescent exuberance. There are no models of maturity for youth to admire in television.

Parents think too lightly about television. They believe that if it is ever proved that their children are being harmed by the medium, they can take command. What is seen, heard, absorbed, and done in childhood will be there in the adult. The young— denied their heritage of maturity; the aging—rejected in their traditional role of guide and mentor. These are the present fruits of the lollipop trap. The biblical judgment—Paul's wise summary to the Corinthians: "When I was a child I spake as a child, I understood as a child, I thought as a child; but when I became a man I put away childish things"—cannot be spoken of contemporary American television.

DANIEL (BUBBLEGUM) BOONE   *September 5, 1964*

A NEW television series, "Daniel Boone," makes its debut on the NBC network September 24. Whatever its quality, its "merchandising" potential must have contributed greatly to its success in winning a place in the network's prime-time evening schedule. In merchandising a program "property," the owners grant licenses to retailers who pay for the privilege of "tying in" their products with the program (for instance, a clothing manufacturer might sell Buck Rogers sweatshirts). The tie-in television industry, according to one estimate, "now grosses some $200 million a year (compared with total TV broadcast time sales of $1,318 million and with time sales of $591 million for AM and FM radio in 1961)." The impressive figure reflects the thickening blur in the line between broadcasting's advertising context and its non-advertising content.

The first legendary hero of the American frontier enjoys great stature with the kids. Fess Parker plays him in the new television series, and he did pretty well with "Davy Crockett" on TV, as parents with long memories will recall. The real Daniel Boone was a man of extraordinary courage and considerable simple dignity, which even the coolest of modern historians have not denied him. He was not averse to publicity in his later years, and he even tried unsuccessfully to make some money out of his memoirs. But the clash of this American legend with television's cash-nexus tie-ins has its ironic overtones. An NBC publicity release indicates that even before "Daniel Boone" hits the air, the merchandising market will exceed the bullish expectations of its promoters.

The first meeting devoted to merchandise tied in with the series was "an overwhelming success," reports NBC's manager of merchandising enterprises. "It attracted an overflow crowd of ninety-five buyers, whose enthusiasm indicates an even greater selling response than the 'Davy Crockett' campaign of 1954. Forty licenses have been signed to date: T-shirts, pajamas, sweat shirts, frontier jackets and trousers, bubblegum with frontier trading cards, toy wagons and canoes, and toy forts with soldiers." Other tie-ins include a Daniel Boone–Fess Parker look-alike doll, a special frontier-style lunch kit, and a comic book that will contain application blanks for membership in Trail Blazer Clubs (monthly distribution: 5,000,000). "A special plaque is being designed . . . in conjunction with logos, identification patches, hang tags, and labels . . . Many variations are available . . . covered-wagon displays, Log Cabin syrup containers, powder horn packages . . . etc."

An Indian tepee, a pioneer cabin (suitable as a Trail Blazer Clubhouse), a Fess Parker–Daniel Boone knapsack, and a birch-bark canoe—"self-liquidating premiums"—somehow don't harmonize with the hardships, cruelty, and death that attended the savage Indian wars on "old Kaintuck's dark and bloody ground." The feeling persists that the kids are being exploited. They are trading their childish credulity and admiration for a culture hero for a mess of Log Cabin syrup and comic books. "Nonsense!" counters the acquisitive spirit. "You're being much too solemn; it's all perfectly harmless, and useful to the national economy."

Boone himself might not have frowned upon the tie-in. His whole life was "a great speck" (speculation), to borrow one of his favorite phrases. He loved wilderness hunting and scouting, but they also had a purpose. He traded in furs, surveyed land for real estate developers, and dreamed of owning his own vast acres as the payoff for his opening of the Wilderness Road and establishing the first settlement beyond the Appalachians. He was actually rich for a time. But he was a poor businessman and ran into bad luck; and in the end he had but a few paltry acres in Missouri to show for his service to his country. Kentucky sold ten thousand acres of his property for back taxes the very same year it honored Boone by naming a county after him. He was an exploiter, it may be fairly said also, along with the rest of the nation as it pushed its early eighteenth-century Manifest Destiny. He persuaded the Cherokees, in 1775, to sell 20,000,000 acres to a land company for 10,000 pounds of "Indian goods." When the "merchandise" was parceled out, "one disgusted brave complained that his share was only a shirt that he could easily have earned in a day's hunting on the land they had given away."

The deal with the Cherokees probably seemed reasonable and harmless to Boone and his associates. The universal myth of superabundance in land and game was abroad. Having exploited Indians and having been exploited himself, he might see no harm in his exploitation by television. He might even find in Fess Parker, the actor who plays him, the embodiment of the American dream. "Although Fess Parker is the personification of pioneer America before the cameras," relates an NBC biography, "away from TV he is a far-sighted fellow with diverse interests. He is a sportsman, investor, businessman, and developer. In Santa Barbara, California, he is part owner of Rancho Santa Barbara, a $1,500,000 mobile-home park."

HOW NOT TO MAKE A DECISION   *October 31, 1964*

IN THE SPRING of 1963 Jackie Cooper, an actor, proposed to James T. Aubrey, Jr., of CBS Television, that he play the part of a Peace Corps volunteer in a new television series. Merle Miller and Evan Rhodes describe the scene in their new and nervously hilarious book, *Only You, Dick Daring! or How to Write One Television Script and Make $50,000,000* (William Sloane Associates). "He [Aubrey] said, 'I don't like snoopers' . . . Then he leaned back in his chair . . . 'I see a man in a dusty pickup in the Southwest . . . wearing a Stetson and khaki pants. I don't know exactly what he is, but he's not a cop; he doesn't carry a gun. I don't want him to be a policeman or a law enforcement officer.' "

It was an expensive vision. Seven months later it had cost
$346,000, written off in some financial report as "corporate
development" for a fifty-two-minute pilot program on film at $7,000
per minute. "After the conference . . . Cooper went to Washington
to find out what kind of a guy wore a Stetson, khaki pants, and
drove a dusty pickup. Somebody told him about county agents."
Merle Miller (collaborating later with Evan Rhodes) was called in
and invited to write the plot of "Calhoun," a television series based
on the life of a county agent. CBS Television offered no objection,
and Miller and Rhodes commenced a saga of television pilot writing
that lasted five months and eight days. "The script for 'Calhoun,' "
writes Miller, "was totally rewritten at least nineteen times by me;
it was partially rewritten by me and Evan 782,946.17 times. It was
tampered with unnumbered times by people I have never seen
and by people I have seen."

A film was finally shot from the endlessly tortured script, but
it failed to find a place in the CBS Television schedule. "Later,
James T. Aubrey, Jr.—'I see a man in a dusty pickup in the
Southwest'—said that he had never liked the county agent idea
much anyway." On the final product Miller and Rhodes say:
"There was not . . . any indication of who a county agent was or
what he did . . . There was also nothing to move, enlighten, arouse,
enlarge, or entertain anyone."

Why an experienced television executive should have believed
that a series about a county agent could be sold for prime-time TV
is a mystery. Typically, the real county agent is an amiable
agronomist whose daily activities offer small prospect of violence,
sex, melodrama, or physical action. "In the first thirty seconds a pilot
should go like this," lectures another program executive in the book.
"Fifty thousand murderous Berbers are headed toward Cairo, and
only you, Dick Daring, can stop them . . . You have to keep
everything moving at all times, moving, moving, moving. Fast, fast.
Action. No studying of the navel, no introspection." Mr. Miller
naively made the intellectual's mistake of challenging television's
Berber mystique by doing intensive research among live county
agents, reading books, compiling cartons of notes, and hoping
eventually to do a story about "a dedicated man who believes
that the human being comes first."

Out of the incredible fantasy of their experience (to which Mr. Miller clung for economic and psychological reasons, not to mention the obvious chance for a writer's-revenge book after it was all over), the authors have fashioned a "fast, fast" exposé of decision-making in television, a record with flashes of the navel and some introspection. Other writers in the industry have lived through similar macabre jests but have kept their lips sealed, preferring to hold onto their employment opportunities. Mr. Miller, who has written seven novels and two nonfiction books, has not feared to burn his bridges. Executives, agents, producers, directors, writers are all revealed in the full scale of their professional value systems. The authors are gentle with their cast, describing them as "picaresque—lovable rogues and vagabonds." The implications, nevertheless, are oppressive. Not all pilots are failures. Those that succeed rarely face demands of the no-navel school of television programs.

Mr. Miller and Mr. Rhodes have rendered the public a genuine service with their chronicle of the times in television. It is easy to split one's sides over the absurd antics and egocentric posturings of the prime pillar of our popular culture. But underneath the laughter is the tragic waste of human potential. The authors underscore the point that one of the principals in the story is a product of Phillips Exeter Academy and a graduate of Princeton, cum laude. His associates generally are talented, intelligent men. Someday someone may write a book, illuminating the mystery of how the best education our society can give comes out looking like fifty thousand murderous Berbers.

THE RELEVANT QUESTION   *December 14, 1963*

IT WAS Sunday morning, November 24. For almost forty-eight hours the nation's television and radio audiences had been following broadcasting's greatest, saddest drama. The epic events in Dallas and Washington had unfolded with a cruel, bewildering mesmerism. Television viewers had shared with great public figures and anonymous spectators a numbing sense of shock, bewilderment, and grief. The collective solemnity with which the participants and reporters strove to overcome the heavy weight of the irrational tragedy had been transmitted with full force. The protagonists and artifacts of the crisis had been delivered to the nation with instant immediacy—the poignant, heroic President's widow, the uncomprehending children, the flag-draped casket, the riderless horse, the arrest of a suspect, Lee H. Oswald. The experience had begun in anarchy and ended in ritual, and through it all the sound and sight media had triumphantly demonstrated the healing catharsis of broadcasting in which practically nothing is allowed to stand in the way of events as they are.

By this bright and chilly Sunday morning, only one thing was missing. It was as if this story, too, had to have the obligatory ending—the visible lesson that crime does not pay. Though the mind may utterly reject the notion, there is a contagion in public violence; our learned disciplines have far from plumbed the obscure connections between individual deed and collective thought. And on that Sunday, television provided the missing murder in full view of an estimated 15,000,000 viewers.

As this is written, therefore, we may never know, beyond doubt, who assassinated President Kennedy. We have been told in press and pulpit that political and racial extremists bear a measure of indirect guilt. In the mood of self-examination that often follows sorrowful events of great moment, we must ask what share television played in the killing of Lee Oswald by Jack Ruby. The networks and stations rendered a great service to the nation in its three-day ordeal. Broadcasters not only responded to the general mood of sad unity—they helped to create that mood. The industry suffered severe financial loss and displayed resourcefulness and taste in the job of improvising, directing, and sustaining the coverage.

Yet the question persists: Should Oswald have been moved from the Dallas city jail in the presence of cameras, microphones, and the attendant clutter of onlookers? It was, of course, the Dallas police who permitted the coverage. They may have sincerely thought that the people had a right to see the man they had publicly accused. But whatever their motive, they overlooked the fact that our government is founded on law that seeks to protect the individual in the long perspective against the immediate clamor of well-meaning or evil forces. The broadcasters, in the same manner, gave this point no consideration if they thought of it at all. May they properly lay the responsibility at the door of Dallas and claim that if the police chose to do it, they had the moral right to cover it? Is it true that the media are only brokers, serving the needs of the public, and that the public insisted on seeing the alleged assassin at that particular moment?

There is the long and the short of the public—the public of the now and its immediate thrusts of attention, and the public of our religious and secular heritage and our future. The immediate public has a right to know—but not at the price of violation of the great tradition that embraces all publics, past and present. Should the broadcasters have exercised restraint and refused to cover the transfer of Oswald in so volatile a situation? If some had refused, would the competition have scored a beat? The problem is ethical. Where does one draw the line between the drive to get the story and the discipline that respects the long perspective of justice?

Nor is this an idle query. Assassinations of great men may be rare, but television's handling of accused individuals is common. Answers are not easy; but at least we can ask the relevant question. And the relevant question is not always "Will it succeed?" Sometimes it may be "Is it right?"

THE HISTORY GAME   *October 30, 1965*

EDUCATION ON TELEVISION is not exclusively the domain of educational television stations. Commercial television can be educational, too. Take history. Any day or evening you can probably find an old movie that tells a World War II story. *Action in the North Atlantic,* for example, was recently available, starring Humphrey Bogart in a merchant marine convoy adventure. *Tomorrow the World* was another Nazi story, with Frederic March. There was a movie about smuggling rubber out of Japanese-occupied Malaya. *Heroes Die Young* told the story of the daring American air raid on the Ploesti oil fields in Europe. *All Through the Night* dealt with Nazi spies.

This educational matter is not limited to old movies. Television series like "Combat," which deals with American infantrymen in Europe, and "12 o'Clock High" episodes recalling the sacrifice and gallantry of our fliers, reinforce the heroic image of our soldiers and the abominable portrait of the enemy. Nor does fiction exhaust television's teaching about World War II. The documentaries, in series and in special programs, unfold around the great central figures (Roosevelt, Churchill, Stalin, Truman, Hitler, Mussolini) and give the factual outlines of the cataclysmic seven-year conflict. On this side the angels; on that the devils, clear and unmistakable. They invite—nay, they command—strong, polarized emotions of hate and admiration.

Now comes the new television season, and several programs add another educational dimension to the World War II image of the enemy. The new picture of the Nazis and Japanese clashes sharply with the images perpetuated by the old war movies and their small-screen derivatives. There's "Hogan's Heroes" on CBS, a fast-moving, rowdy farce about Allied prisoners of war in a Nazi POW camp. They suffer no deprivation, cruelty, or psychological isolation. They run a successful escape center for Allied soldiers streaming out of Germany. They are resourceful and have constructed an underground pleasure palace with all the comforts of home. And, in doing this, they outfox, blackmail, and make utter fools of the Nazi commanders and guards. The terrible Teuton is played for laughs. He has become a vain nitwit or a fat, bumbling clown—in either case, utterly harmless. The fangs were also pulled from the sibilant, hissing Japanese in an incident on the first episode of NBC's World War II comedy, "The Wackiest Ship in the Army." The USS *Kiwi*, a wooden sailing ship, is really a secret espionage vessel. It encounters a two-man Japanese sub on a shakedown cruise. Inside the sub, we encounter two ragged, bewildered Japanese sailors who disagree about whether to surrender or die in a suicide attack. The winner of the debate conks the loser over the head with a wrench, and submits happily to being taken in tow.

The enemy in an early episode of "Convoy," NBC's new series about the North Atlantic run, turned out to be a beautiful lady physicist kidnapped by British commandos from a heavy-water project in Norway. Hardly the world-conquering Aryan, she professed scientific neutrality to politics and war. Our hero, skipper of a destroyer, battled not only for the safety of his ship in getting away from the Nazi hunters, but also for the soul of the sexy enemy. Home, at dockside, he won. "I want to join your world," she said. "This is a most unusual farewell." "You are a most unusual enemy," the skipper replied. "Perhaps we will meet again."

Now, all this is, as we started to say, educational. Confronted

by the old *vs.* the new image of the Nazis and Japanese, we
conclude that they teach valuable lessons in history. Obviously, in
order to fight a war, you must persuade your people that the enemy
is subhuman. This the instruments of communication do well in
wartime. Then comes the victory, and the enemy quickly becomes
your ally. It is difficult, so soon, to love him, but an adjustment must
be made. So our entertainers, subtle antennae of our culture, play
the middle alternative. They deprecate, laugh at, romanticize, and
thereby neutralize the old hateful image.

The lesson may be carried further. The present enemy is the
Vietcong in Asia, who leaves us little room for subtle shades of good
or evil. But is this enemy destined, too, twenty years from now, to be
played for laughs? If so, are we, in a sense, laughing already at our
fighting men who are dying there? Exactly what are history's claims,
and how much are they worth in television's own terrible struggle
with its mortal enemies—silence and darkness and thought? Perhaps
little. Perhaps education itself, which searches for the truth of the
past so that we may more humanely shape the future, is only
a situation comedy.

NO EXIT   *August 7, 1965*

LIFE WITH THE MASS MEDIA in the privacy of the home, where you
can make choices, is difficult enough: the true test of character
comes when one is confronted by the media in public. I flunked
the test in recent weeks, in a plane over the Pacific, a restaurant in
Philadelphia, a home in Boston, a taxi in New York, and a motel
near the Canadian border. The last stop taught me a lesson and
I pass it on to all fellow-sufferers in this sermon for a hot summer
afternoon. Flying to Honolulu, there was a mix-up in my ticketing
and I couldn't get dinner aboard the plane. I offered to pay the
stewardess, but she said she couldn't sell me the dinner, and I
ruefully watched her throw the food away—but I got a free movie in
color. I didn't want the movie: I wanted to do some work; but the
lady in back of me cheerfully inquired if I would lower the back of
my chair so she could see Frank Sinatra. The sound track was
blissfully secreted in the plug-in earphones; but there loomed Sinatra
on the rectangular screen ahead; and fuming, I finally quit and

suffered the mob their taste. Back on the mainland a few weeks later, I dined at a small, pleasant restaurant in Philadelphia, enveloped by the *high-volume* signal of a local radio station. I knew it would be fruitless (and bad form) to ask the manager to switch off; but I couldn't resist asking him why he kept the station on.

The other diners would immediately complain, he said, if he tuned out. "People need it," he shrugged. "They really don't listen, but it makes a noise in the background and it permits them to talk. If there was silence, there wouldn't be any conversation. It would be dead in here."

The Boston experience came shortly after. I visited a home in the suburbs, where a woman was alone. She sat in a large room: the TV was on (it was early afternoon); but she was intent on a cross-word puzzle. Two rooms away, the radio was turned on, playing to nobody. In New York, another day, I got into a taxi at Penn Station. It was the evening rush hour; the hot city's garment center was clashing and raucous with west-side traffic: the cabbie had his dashboard radio belting above the din. I moaned inwardly but hid my frustration with another taxicab survey. "Do you have that radio on all the time?" I asked in a friendly fashion. "All the time. Never without it a minute," the driver answered.

"What do you usually listen to?" "Nothing," said the driver. "I don't hear a thing. No program. No commercial. I just have it on." "But why?" He turned the knob and shut off the radio. "See for yourself," he said. "I'd miss it. It's monotonous without it, driving all day." He turned the radio on again. "People get in the cab and start telling me their troubles. Like the guy who said he loved his wife but was going out with another dame. What should he do? he asks me. What do I care what he does? But I can't tell him that, so I turn up the radio real loud . . . like this . . . and they keep on jabbering away . . . and once in a while I throw them a yeah . . . yeah . . . yeah . . . but I don't hear a thing . . . not them . . . not the radio . . . nothing."

A few weeks after that, I was in Potsdam, New York, on a lecture engagement. I had breakfast at a motel's restaurant. The cheery waitress had her transistor radio atop the refrigerator the other side of the counter—and with my orange juice I had some bright and upbeat country music. The local newspaper couldn't assuage my resentment. "Is there no surcease anywhere from this ubiquitous, tribal, electronic collectivism?" I grumbled to my All-Bran.

Suddenly I stopped in the middle of a grumble. The announcer had spoken a familiar name—mine. Along with other items of local news, he was mentioning the talk I was scheduled to give at a nearby college that morning. The music came on again; I went back to the newspaper; but I had been hit—dead on target. All that horrible noise which other people listened to—had instantaneously been transformed into something clear and significant when the right index clue had come up—my own specific involvement. I recalled the taxi-driver who said: "The only time I listen is when they come on with traffic bulletins. Then I tune in—with my mind." At all other times the medium of radio was without message: its sound, to him, was shelter from the job's monotony, escape from the unwanted signals of his passengers. To the lady in the Boston home, the unattended tv and radio sets were barriers against loneliness: to the diners in the Philadelphia restaurant the radio's chatter and music were curtains for privacy. The transistor atop the refrigerator in the Potsdam motel met some felt need of the waitress, probably without verbal content. The excommunication of boredom —or fear: this was the meaning of the color film aboard the plane bound for Hawaii. There is no escape: the public media have interlocked us all. The only response is to learn tolerance—each to his own involvement.

IDIOT'S DELIGHT June 7, 1969

A RECENT, unusual Huntley-Brinkley NBC newscast raises the interesting question: What is the best way to beat the grotesquely absurd when we meet it on television? The answer is, to quote a Polish critic, "calling the absurd by its own name; *reductio ad absurdum* to its pure state." Only in this way can we see and be liberated.

Saturday, May 10, was a light news day perhaps. Or perhaps the production unit joined together odd pieces of unused film. Or perhaps they planned it just the way it happened. In any case, the thirty-minute program (Brinkley soloed; Huntley was off) was actually a unified documentary, even an editorial, devoted to the war in Vietnam.

Only one item (brief text without pictures) departed from the military theme—a light touch about the Irish providing an oversize bed for the extra-tall de Gaulle, while he vacationed in their country to escape the political campaign in France.

Dispersed throughout the entire program, however, were seven commercials, promoting the sale of Peter Pan peanut butter, S&H Green Stamps, Geritol tonic with iron in it, Sominex pills for sleep, Johnson's foot soap for tired, aching feet, Lanacane for any itching problem ("break that itch cycle!"), and Ocean Spray cranberry juice cocktail.

This was the show—a schizophrenic adventure in the bizarre, the cruelly ludicrous, and the fantastically incongruous. For on one track ran the tragedy and the solemnity, the heartbreak of the war, while on the other—darting in and out like a lunatic Toonerville trolley—chortled the monadic, machined happiness of the consumer in a paradise of food and drug products, and barbells for the paunchy man in the family, courtesy of S&H.

Mr. Brinkley and his colleagues, reporting in from remote locations, drew a somber, moving picture of the impact that the war has had in the last twelve months since the peace talks began in Paris. They covered the political front in Hanoi, Saigon, and Washington. They traced the uninterrupted coming and going of troops (500,000 leaving and the same number returning) through Travis Air Force base in California. They interviewed young GI's in Vietnam on patrol; one shy, candid youth said, "I don't care too much for killing. I'd rather walk all day and come back without finding anything."

There were the depressing figures about the war's continuing heavy cost in money—$2.3 billion a month. Soldiers in training in South Carolina were shown risking courts-martial as they encouraged an anti-war spirit in a coffeehouse near a camp. Wounded veterans in hospitals wondered wistfully why the talk goes on in Paris and no troops move out in American withdrawal.

The climactic story, done in two sections, was the case history of a young man, a sergeant, killed in action and returned home to California in a flag-draped coffin. The cameras showed his young widow at the funeral services, and his seven-month-old daughter whom he had never seen. An Army "escort officer" held the infant in his arms outside, while within the mother wept over the coffin. Then the interment—the minister's intoning, "a free nation spending for liberty, justice, and the rights of all"; the volley over the grave; the giving of the rolled-up flag into the hands of the seated widow; and the ceremonial depositing by officers of white flowers before her.

It was impossible not to be overwhelmed: the emotion had been cumulative, unlike that generated in fragments by discontinuous news shows of the standard pattern. The message was unmistakable —the war that almost nobody wanted, yet a year after the beginning of the peace talks, it went on still. And at four linkage points that joined the war to the commercials, the solemnity passed without a misstep into the rhythm of the peanut butter and the aching feet.

It was shocking, but Americans accept similar grotesqueries in newscasts every day. Why? Is a professional viewer aware of such subtleties, because he watches television searchingly? Do the average viewers mentally tune out the commercials and feel no dissonance? Or do they tune out the horrible news and hear only the happy messages, because that's the only way to keep one's sanity? Perhaps, if they were made aware, they, too, would feel outrage.

Ask any viewer: Suppose you stood near, in real life, to a young neighbor as she heard a messenger tell her that her husband had been killed in action in Vietnam. And suppose that as she wilted under the message, the messenger suddenly began to sing and dance to the tune of a jingle eulogizing itching powder. Would you not think that the messenger had gone mad? Why, then, is the very same action on television glossed over, as if the joining of death-in-war and Sominex pills for sleep to one another were perfectly appropriate, as though they were of equal or congruent value?

Only by awakening to perceive the grotesquely absurd on what, in this case, is truly the "idiot box," can we ever escape the price that we pay for suffering it—namely the truth that we ourselves are grotesquely absurd and do not know it.

TROBRIANDISH   *April 25, 1970*

WINS, New York, the first of three Group W (Westinghouse Broadcasting Company) radio stations to adopt an all-news format, recently passed its fifth anniversary. I would guess, however, that the event was not noted on the air by any of the station's announcers, reporters, or commentators. To have done so would have expressed an interest in historical causation and recognized that the present is the climax of some chronological, lineal order—a pattern of behavior distinctly un-Trobriand Islanderish.

The Trobrianders of New Guinea, as described by the late Bronislaw Malinowski, make no temporal connections between objects. There is a series of beings in their codification of reality, but no becoming. Value for the Trobriander lies not in change, but in sameness, in repeated pattern. His world is comprised of acts that lead nowhere; they are an aggregate of bumps that jerk along, like his speech, repeating the known, maintaining a point, incorporating all time in an undisturbed monotony.

All-news radio, as practiced by Group W stations in New York, Philadelphia, and Los Angeles (and by other conglomerates, including some CBS and some Time-Life radio stations), is very much Trobriander. The news is often billed as "stories in the making." They emerge from nowhere; they live briefly and blend indistinguishably into new emergences. One-sentence headlines, flecky details, weather, traffic, sports, stocks, compressed catastrophes, affairs of state, revolutions and coups, stabbings, shoot-outs, local fires, fender-benders, the jingle and sell of endlessly procreating commercials—they drone, they clip (fast, fast, no introspection, no navel) without emphasis, change of pace, or emotional tone in a sort of instant omnipresence, never *to* or *from*, only *at*, the re-creation of a mythical pattern of "nowness."

In a presciently non-Trobriand manner, the Group W people planned it that way. They are well aware that their listeners are not Trobrianders but lineal codifiers of reality in the Western tradition who have the line, the linkage, and the sequence bred into them from birth. As such, no one can stay in the all-news world for more than ten minutes at a time. For the lineal mind, instant omnipresence is dreaded nothingness; so people drop in and out (or vice versa), and this is fine for the all-news broadcasters. They operate on the principle of random tuning: Somebody is always tuning in, to decide whether to take an umbrella, to avoid a traffic jam, or to keep in touch; when they leave, someone else arrives.

In such random haphazardness, Group W listeners may miss

short bursts of some of the finest commentary that current radio offers. Rod MacLeish, Group W's chief correspondent, writes the best prose on TV or radio. Erwin Canham, Simeon Booker, Sid Davis, Bernard Redmont, and others comprise a staff of knowledgeable roving observers of the world scene; but they are uncharted points in a sea of anecdotes. Pitched into the schedule at irregular, unpredictable times, one never knows when they are imminent. To spot them predictably would make great lineal sense, of course, but would violate the principle of randomness and might scare some people away (commentary, after all, is a very lineal thing; it has a point of view, a sense of the past and future, an instinct for relationships and meaning). Joel Chaseman, president, Group W Radio, calls all-news radio "the ultimate refinement of McLuhan's 'global village.'"

The concept makes money for Group W and renders brief, small services; but our culture, unlike that of the Trobrianders, is presumably deliberately purposive—we have ends and means. All-news radio never asks why and it never says because. Its definition of news is antiquarian. A century ago, in a relatively stable world, it made sense to define news as the extraordinary, the violent, the sensational. Our world today is all three: News, in a global village, is paradoxically that which integrates, cements, and binds.

For listeners who get all their news from radio, the randomized violence and trivia of Group W's codification of reality provides false, undesirable models. It legitimizes the horror of an essentially irrational world. The Trobrianders are welcome to their codification of reality; we are stuck with ours. Would that Group W could conceive it so in the next five years. We would enjoy making the customary felicitations, but how can you say happy birthday to someone who has no sense of his own identity?

CHAPTER ELEVEN

The Making of a Killing

"You cannot step twice into the same rivers;" said Heraclitus,
"for fresh waters are ever flowing in upon you." The Mariner's
"strange power of speech," his dialectical criticism, is, like
all things, in flux. He clarifies his theory in practice, and his
clarified theory modifies his practice. He succeeds or fails in
harmonizing the two: he learns or does not learn from his
failures and successes; he meets every new Wedding Guest
with senses poised for collision and the hope for more novel
advances, more dialectical motion, more community.

CHAPTER V

BETWEEN WEDDING GUESTS, as the Mariner journeys, he thinks—of present conditions, of the future, and certainly of the past. He relives his own adventure of the voyage, as all of us often mull over the experiences of our own past, merely touching them again lightly or stopping to penetrate more deeply than before into a singular event. It may even happen that the Mariner is struck quite suddenly by a bi-sociation that he has never noticed before. Let us speculate upon one such combinatory perception that the Mariner might experience, en route from his most recent to his next citizen's arrest.

There are two crucial passages in the Mariner's recital that have to do with the notion of turning. One we have already commented on in the previous chapter: it is the final moment, at the end of the poem, when the Wedding Guest turns from the Bridegroom's door, symbolizing his turning away from the world of Callicles. The hedonistic world of instinct, consumption, power, pleasure, might—unredeemed by any sense of mutuality or consideration by the I, the ego, toward the Thou, the other. There is another point of turning, though, in the interior of the poem, which is worthy of attention. It occurs in Part VI: the Mariner has awakened from a trance to find the ship "sailing on as in a gentle weather." The Mariner is still held by the pang, the curse, the fixed stare of the eyes of the dead men of the crew; he cannot turn his own eyes away. Then the spell is snapped. He viewed the ocean green:

> And looked far forth, yet little saw
> Of what had else been seen—
>
> Like one, that on a lonesome road
> Doth walk in fear and dread,
> And having once turned round walks on,
> And turns no more his head;
> Because he knows a frightful fiend
> Doth close behind him tread.

Whatever Coleridge may have had in mind when he wrote the words "a frightful fiend," it is not implausible to assume, for our purposes, that the image could conceivably represent the apparently indifferent act of violence that precipitates the Mariner's misfortunes—namely, the killing of the friendly Albatross. The destruction of the great sea bird, as we have noted before, an apparently senseless, unjustified act, is, according to the evidence supplied by the narrative, entirely unpremeditated. Why should the Mariner suddenly, and without any recognizable motive, shoot the Albatross with his crossbow, when the bird had come to the ship out of the dangerous fog—a lucky omen? The crew "hailed it in God's name":

> It ate the food it ne'er had eat,
> And round and round it flew.

The ice did split with a thunder-fit;
The helmsman steered us through!

And a good south wind sprung up behind;
The Albatross did follow,
And every day, for food or play,
Came to the mariners' hollo!

In the literature of human violence, the act of killing is associated with fear or rage: it is seen in Freudian terms as an expression of the death-instinct. Another theoretical approach interprets it as the discharge of aggression as a response to frustration. Humans kill animals and birds for sport or coldly, for food—a calculated form of killing unaccompanied by instinct or blocked emotion; but we may doubt that Coleridge introduced the killing of the bird merely as a literal act. The poem, taken as a whole, strongly suggests the notion that the killing is symbolic of human violence which shatters community. Indeed, the Mariner's concluding moral to his tale provides the counterpoise of the separating action of the killing (estranging man from Nature) in the integrating message of love:

He prayeth well, who loveth well
Both man and bird and beast.

The Mariner, reliving the experience in his memory, could reasonably refuse to accept the testimony of his senses, which told him that it was an unmotivated action. Turning it over in his mind, as he journeys, he thinks about it critically, dialectically, trying out this assumption, experimenting with that possibility. Eventually he makes his discovery, by widening the range of his thought in order to regard the *context* of the act. Fredric Wertham, who has studied human violence clinically and from a variety of personal and social perspectives, asserts in *A Sign for Cain* that three phases or periods have to be distinguished in the phenomenon: 1) the action phase itself; 2) the previolence phase; and 3) the postviolence phase. "This is the pattern of violence," he writes. "All three phases are important and illuminate one another."

The Mariner finds his explanation in the previolence phase. There is a very acute pitch of anxiety in the Mariner's thought just before the shooting. The poem does not express it literally, overtly; but one can find it in the oppressive climatic and mental atmosphere. The Mariner remembers that the ship was driven by a storm toward the South Pole, shortly after the voyage had brightly begun. The STORM-BLAST arrived, "tyrannous and strong":

> He struck with his o'ertaking wings,
> And chased us south along.

Coleridge's verses are vigorous with power and force as he describes the ship's bending before the storm,

> With sloping masts and dipping prow,
> As who pursued with yell and blow
> Still treads the shadow of his foe
> And forward bends his head, . . .

Mist and snow appear: it grows "wondrous cold." Then ice comes floating by—mast-high, emerald green, with "dismal sheen":

> The ice was here, the ice was there,
> The ice was all around:
> It cracked and growled, and roared and howled,
> Like noises in a swound!

Into this ominous situation flies the welcome Albatross: the tension appears to be relieved, but suddenly, without warning or apparent cause, the Mariner is "triggered" to the killing. How reminiscent is the action, of so many contemporary murders that we often read about in the newspapers and hear about on television or over the radio! The murderer, up to that time, gave no hint of violent tendencies: he or she was an "exemplary person, a church-goer, quiet, well-behaved, conforming. Who would have expected, believed, etc.?" But the study of crime and criminals by professionals, and intuitive works of fiction by playwrights and novelists, all combine to teach us that underneath the unexpected murderer's calm exterior usually lies an explosive volcano, waiting to be "triggered" into eruption.

The Mariner has not solved the puzzle completely; to accomplish this, in clinical terms, would require an understanding, in depth, of the personal and social background of the killer. Coleridge uses the Mariner as an archetype; he gives no individualizing characteristics or details. We invent them here to serve our present purposes, which do not require an attempt to create an individual case history for the Mariner in full, human terms. Our intention is to proceed at least one step beyond the apparent lack of motivation for the killing of the sea bird: this we have done by postulating a pervading sense of continuous anxiety, a setting for the actual destructive moment.

The Mariner now carries the illumination a little further. He was struck, remember, by the problem of the two turning points in his narrative: the Bridegroom's turning away from the door of Callicles, and his own turning away, in the interior of the narrative, from the vision of "the frightful fiend." This, in Dr. Wertham's theory, constitutes the "postviolence phase." "If the past is minimized in the postviolence phase," he writes, "the seeds of future violence are sown." The Mariner does not minimize his past: that is why the turning away from the "frightful fiend," in the interior of the narrative, is of profound significance. The lesson has been learned; the curse is broken. Although the Mariner has yet to meet the Hermit, who will signify to him the full meaning of his experience, there is no doubt that he has suffered enough to make certain that, were he to be placed again in a similar situation, he would summon his anti-violent resources, his sense of mutuality, of respect for the worth of others, man, beast, or bird, and most assuredly not repeat his murderous action. There is lesson enough in the freedom that he won from the act of blessing the water snakes, as opposed to the bondage he earned when he shot the Albatross.

But the Mariner also, now, perceives the *coincidence* of the two turning points, and of their inherent values. The act of killing lies, in the poem, side by side with the contrasting harmony of the pleasure principle. Observe how the Albatross, happy omen, followed the ship accompanied by "a good south wind sprung up behind":

> And every day, for food or play,
> Came to the mariners' hollo!

Is this not an anticipation as well as an echo of the Wedding Feast itself, the value scheme of life, Dionysian in essence, from which all Wedding Guests will turn away, sadder and wiser? And ought they not also to turn away, to forsake, as the Mariner did in the interior of his narrative, the "frightful fiend"? Is the "fiend" the act of violence "triggered" by the context of pervasive anxiety in which it is inextricably set, or is it that web-like anxiety itself? The two are one: the capacity for violence in humans, psychology assures us, is not biologically autonomous. It is not, Dr. Wertham and other students of violence assert, an ineradicable instinct in man; man is not genetically fated always to be a killer. There is no single, total explanation for violence.

Each violent act is a complex of subtle, interrelated personal and social factors. The Mariner, connecting the two absolutely contradictory states of being in the tragic moment aboard ship—the mood of murder and the mood of pleasure—generates the electricity of the third beat, the anxiety level underlying the apparently disassociated experience, and fuses the fragments into a discovery which illuminates a wholeness—composed of the feast, the fiend, and the field!

Wertham writes:

> Reliance on the narrow frame of references of a basic inborn
> instinct of aggression in human nature deprives us of an
> understanding of some of the most outstanding manifestations
> of violence in our time.

He cites an example of the slave-labor death camps of the Nazis during World War II:

> The procedure has a prehistory in the colonies, where the
> same methods were used extensively—with the same cruelty

and the same profit. It was a collective rapacity . . . No instinct in an individual alone can explain it. In our time, it was free enterprise at its freest. The slave-labor-plus-killing methods were not just transitory eruptions of uninhibited instinct or hostility, but were fully integrated into the ordinary, successful, long-range industrial-commercial process. The shares of some of the firms which employed slave labor are internationally traded and are today higher than ever.

Wertham crowns this acute analysis of violence in human society with a brilliant etymological stroke: "The urge was not to kill but to *make a killing*" (italics RLS). "To make a killing," of course, is a colloquialism for achieving a sudden financial profit. Violence in television is a wedding of the feast and the fiend, the spirit of Callicles with residues of the darkest features of the human character, inherited from periods of struggle for survival—which periods could, perhaps, justify them—but which are useless and ominous in today's world, which is groping toward civility.

The triple concept of the feast, the fiend, and the field had not occurred to this critic prior to a close reading and comparison of the pieces that he has selected for this chapter. As he examined them collectively for the first time, to search for an "imagination" level, beyond the level of "fancy," of "fixities and definites," he found the shadow of "the fiend" in the violence that he described in the programs and in the value systems of the program producers. He also detected the paradigm of "the feast" in the sophistic behavior of the programers and of the senators who, for more than ten years of cumulative hypocrisy, "investigated" and "studied" crime and violence on television, in the context of its allegedly harmful effects on children. He even found a piece connecting the "feast" and "the fiend" which attempted to state for the reader the crucial, unbreakable relationship between both, under an advertiser-supported system of television, in which the "management of demand," in Galbraith's phrase, was the dominant motivation.

But "the field" in which the two forces were united had, it was clear, escaped him. Violence on television cannot be understood unless its overtly distant poles of fiend and feast are seen together. In all discussions of violence in programs and in newscasts, the juxtaposition of these programs to commercial messages is almost never commented upon. Yet they do exist together; and their *field* is the anxiety level, omnipresent and continuous in the concatenations of the hard sell and the cool kill. Commercials repeat the refrain of the mariners' happy hollo!—as "every day, for food and play," the Albatross circled the ship. They reiterate the good life which is the fortunate lot of the American consumer–television-viewer. On the other hand, cumulative exposure to violence in fantasy drama and in reports of war, crime, and disaster conspire to keep the viewers' anxiety level high.

Leo Bogart, past president of the American Association of Public Opinion Research, testified to this point, in 1968, before the National Commission on the Causes and Prevention of Violence. "The really great impact of media violence on our culture," witnessed Dr. Bogart, "may arise mainly from this diffuse raising of the general public level of anxiety, rather than from individual acts of behavior in response to individual media episodes or instances." It is a disproportionately hostile, violent world which television drama, films, and cartoons present to the viewer, where overt physical violence is unthinkingly and unfeelingly directed at victims who often cannot and do not resist. The perpetrators of violence are often members of outgroups, ethnically and politically "different." If, as television testifies, the world is hostile, the television viewer may reasonably conclude that one must be alert and ever ready to meet force with force.

The hostility of the world must be due to the good life which the viewer enjoys: the ethnic and political adversaries are the less fortunate (because less deserving) who threaten to take away what he enjoys. The threat validates the good life; and the good life validates the threat. It is a self-fulfilling prophetic cycle, a beautifully closed system. It reinforces the managing of consumer demand via television, in which the very programs themselves become symbols of a desirable type of life; it renders reasonable the maintenance of mighty and ever-mightier military establishments; and the interplay of the two concordant rhythms perpetually recharges the "field" of pervasive anxiety.

Another, non-physical form of violence, imbedded in the pattern of control, exercises its dominion over other disadvantaged groups in the consumer-abundant society, those who may be white but who are poor, ill, or elderly. The media generally ignore them; but when they are admitted to the pseudo-mirror-image of national life, they are usually portrayed in negative terms: the poor are lazy; the mentally ill are violent, unpredictable; and the elderly are burdens on the economy. Their conditions, therefore, are also self-inflicted, for if they deserved their proper share of the good life, they would undoubtedly possess it (Calvin, meet television!). That pattern of control which I have described, becomes in its totality, in Wertham's words, a "praetorian guard to preserve the status quo." In such a concept, research directed at establishing a causal relationship between physical violence on television and such violence in the real world becomes "reactionary." The pieces which follow take note of such ongoing research, which serves to direct attention away from the manipulative and centralized control purpose of the managers of the feast, the fiend, and the field.

The search for causal relationships still continues—like the bygone quests for the alchemy of gold, or the panacea, or the elixir of longevity. It may or may not be discovered in due course: certainly men once would not credit that there was a causal relationship between smoking and cancer. But the assumption of the existence of such a causal relationship encourages the fixed idea that human violence can be captured in the abstract, in a general formula, applicable to all humans alike, impersonally. Such a formulation is impossible even in the more precise field of medical pathology: its unlikelihood is far greater in the complexities of violent human behavior. But the complexities could be mastered by men, if they did not succumb to the temptation to believe that violence is an autonomous, biological instinct, ineradicable from the species. Violence is produced by men, by institutions, and by historical, economic, political, and social conditions. To change the fiend, attention must usefully be directed to the feast, and to the field which encompasses them both.

Wertham concludes his valuable exploration of human violence, with words that ring true to the dialectical Mariner-critic, in his journeys:

An intimate relationship exists between individualism, selfishness, and latent violence. When—and whenever—we can, we must oppose hyperindividualism and hypernationalism, both of which seek satisfaction for themselves at the cost of others. An equitable social-economic structure of societies must be the basis for bringing about a universal revulsion against violence. If the individual—all individuals—and society become the integrated entities which they truly are in a fully developed civilization, motives for killing will yield to habits of nonviolence, and nobody will have to be afraid any longer of violent interference with his life or that of his children.

The critic did not clearly understand this when he began this chapter. He at first planned to end it with the piece "Violence: TV's Crowd-Catcher." After consulting the Mariner on his journey, and sharing his unfolding discovery, he decided that the crowd-catching piece did not carry the dialectic far enough. As a consequence, he added the piece which now concludes the chapter, "The Lesson of Auschwitz." It suggests one small step with which the citizens of the United States of America could begin Dr. Wertham's realistic therapy for violence. The critic does not fault himself for the previous ignorance; he rather rejoices in the new illumination. After all, what's a Mariner's journey for—if not to make a killing in novel togetherness?

SPECIAL EFFECTS   *May 2, 1964*

EVER SINCE observers first realized that television and films have special effects on human behavior, experts have debated whether violence witnessed on the screen can stimulate viewers to aggression in real life. Probably a majority of psychologists, social workers, psychiatrists, and juvenile authorities have held that a causal relationship does exist. But some specialists have dissented. Both sides generally agree, however, that mentally troubled persons, unstable individuals already filled with hostilities, can be "triggered" by exposure to on-screen violence into criminal outbursts. Cases supporting this idea can be found in records on the subject. For example, a young man who committed a murder in New York told policemen that he had been watching TV when he was impelled to commit a brutal assault on a woman. A network representative, on the other hand, offered counterbalancing testimony at a 1961 Senate hearing on "Effects on Young People of Crime and Violence Portrayed on Television": "There is not even satisfactory proof that the emotionally disturbed child is harmed by television. Rather, it would appear that it is often the case with a disturbed child that that which he sees on television may help him drain off, vicariously, elements in his behavioral pattern which cause that disturbance."

In recent years the "catharsis" theory, which holds that observed aggression tends to release pent-up or aroused anger therapeutically, has been severely shaken by a number of psychologists in controlled experiments. Television at the same time has continued to produce filmed violence in vast quantities. A leading Hollywood producer told me this year how a top-level policy maker at a network received his proposal for a new romantic series. He said he would buy the series if every other program showed violence and someone getting "kicked in the groin," as well as other similar effects.

Recently, a causal relationship was said to exist between televised violence and the behavior of "normal" people. Dr. Ralph S. Banay, a prominent psychiatrist and president of the Medical Correction Association, referred at a New York symposium to "a confusion of fantasy with reality, fed by an endless stream of television violence."

"We underestimate the damage that these accumulated images do to the brain," said Dr. Banay. "The immediate effect can be delusional, equivalent to a sort of post-hypnotic suggestion." He partly blamed this special effect for the shocking murder in March of a woman in New York. Thirty-seven persons heard the victim's screams on a well-lighted sidewalk in front of an apartment building in the early hours of the morning. But not one of them responded to her calls for help.

Dr. Karl Menninger, director of the Menninger Foundation, also spoke at the symposium. "Public apathy to crime," he said, "is itself a manifestation of aggression." A point made by New York psychiatrists is that "persons with mature and well-integrated personalities would not have acted in this way." Here we are no longer confronted by the isolated, abnormal deviant, but by a representative group of thirty-seven apparently "normal" citizens. The complexity of such special effects is difficut to understand; and television cannot, of course, bear the exclusive burden of a violent age. Yet we seem to be witnessing a slow, cumulative crescendo of individual and group aggression, passive and overt. Many respected psychiatrists hold that television violence is significantly involved.

The important link between Hollywood and television where violence is concerned was dramatized recently at the nationwide televising of the annual awards of the Academy of Motion Picture Arts and Sciences. Among the nominees in the "Special Effects" category were *The Birds* and *Cleopatra*. From Alfred Hitchcock's film, an excerpt showed flocks of birds swooping to attack the heads and faces of terrified children. From *Cleopatra* was chosen the dagger assassination of Julius Caesar in the Roman Senate. A conspirator with a knife strode deliberately to Caesar's back and the camera caught the full impact of the blade's plunge. Other knives flashed swiftly and repeatedly. Splotches of blood appeared on Caesar. In this lengthy film spectacle, there must have been dozens of examples of the skill of the special effects creator warranting his Oscar. Out of all that footage, when millions of Americans in their homes were watching, why did the producers have to choose, unredeemed by context, such moments of gratuitous horror? What special effect will this "special effect" on television produce next?

TEN YEARS LATER   September 26, 1964

THE SENATE subcommittee to investigate juvenile delinquency had another talk in Washington recently with network chiefs about television's crime-and-violence programs. Senator Thomas J. Dodd, the committee chairman, wanted to know if the witnesses had taken into account in their programing practices a new body of scholarly research that points to "a significant relationship between violence shown in films and subsequent aggressive behavior committed by viewers of the films." The general tenor of the answers was: Yes, we are aware of the new data but we haven't changed our minds—no causal relationship has yet been demonstrated between crime and violence on television and violent action in real life.

The networks were concerned about the problem, they said: they would be glad to come to Washington at any time to discuss it further with the subcommittee. Senator Dodd pointed out that they had talked before. In fact, the discourse between Capitol Hill and Madison Avenue on this theme that went on during the 1961–1962 hearings of the subcommittee had been foreshadowed back in 1954. Senator Estes Kefauver was chairman then; and after three years of the hearings, he reported in 1957: "The industry, brought face to face with the problem of its influence on juvenile conduct, is already making efforts to improve its programs so that a more beneficent diet will be presented to the child turning to television for entertainment . . . it is certainly to be hoped that the industry will police itself and not force the federal government to intervene."

The Kefauver report recommended a presidential watchdog commission, a tougher FCC policy, minimum standards, and foundation-supported research. Four years later, in 1961, with Senator Dodd in the chair, the committee began yet another talk with the broadcasters. It found that "in spite of fears on the part of the public and the warnings of our behavioral scientists, network executives consciously fostered a trend toward violence by ordering more of it to be included in action-adventure shows, presumably to assure the maintenance of high ratings." The broadcasters were still glad to talk about it in 1961–1962, and again they predicted less violence in the future. Senator Dodd, still remonstrating in 1964, said to the networks: "Ten years later, we hear and observe that it is 100 per cent worse . . ." (He noted that CBS had made some improvement.) "Unjustifiable violence and brutality permeate new shows which center around college campuses, hospitals, psychiatrists' offices, and other unlikely locations." In addition, the senator went on, "The most violent shows of two years ago are today shown during earlier broadcasting hours than they were originally designed for. There has been little or no editing of objectionable content. This means that these programs, which we found so objectionable and which I felt that even the industry was embarrassed with, are being made available to a much larger and younger group of children than ever before."

To which the networks replied in essence: "No shows that we schedule ourselves or sell or lease to stations in syndication deals violate the NAB code; our continuity acceptance departments simply wouldn't permit that. As for the times at which our customers show these syndicated, adult-oriented shows, we, of course, have no control over that: it would be unwarranted." The dialogue between the continuity acceptance people and the Hollywood television studios, as reflected in the exhibits of the committee, makes diverting reading. What a pity that the transcripts of these hearings will, when finally released, probably not be read!

When the most recent talk ended, Senator Dodd said there would be more. At one point he said severely to the network executives: "I don't think you care. I am sorry to say that. But that is the way it looks to me. And I think unless you get to a point where you care, the American people are going to make you care. You keep feeding this stuff to their children, and I tell you they are not going to take it forever."

The senator said to the ABC executives, as he concluded his talk with them: "I hope you are not too unhappy about this hearing." To which one executive graciously responded: "Senator Dodd, we are not unhappy about the hearing. As I said before, we are of the belief that you are focusing the industry's attention upon a problem that exists by the very power of the medium that we are in. And we are aware of the efforts that you are making, and we are perfectly willing to come and talk to you on this subject at any time." Senator Dodd as graciously countered: "Well, I am glad you talked to me. But you talked to me before. And you talked to Senator Kefauver twelve years ago. You are awfully nice people to talk to, and I think you have good intentions. But we don't seem to be getting anywhere." No truer word was ever spoken more graciously. Whatever its faults, it's still our Congress. One hates to see it involved in an exercise in futility. Perhaps the subcommittee and the networks are both kidding the American people. How much exposition do you need before the action commences? Perhaps Congress doesn't want to act, perhaps it can't act; but if we're to keep the Dodd dance going, why can't we have equal time for all sides. The National Association for Better Radio and Television (NAFBRAT), a citizens' group that is gaining members and vigor, tried to get some of its own witnesses

heard at the recent hearings, without success. Senator Dodd said
it had testified before; he implied it had nothing new to offer.
Maybe so. But what did the networks have to offer that was new?
Or, for that matter, Senator Dodd?

THE TWO FACES OF VIOLENCE   *October 24, 1964*

THE LATENT VIOLENCE in the recent first program of "The Reporter,"
a new CBS hour-long television drama series on Friday nights, was
more significant than the manifest violence. The surface brutality
involved attempted rape and a near-fatal stabbing. The hidden
aggression lay in the advice of a city editor to a reporter who
inadvertently played a remote role in the stabbing.

Danny Taylor (Harry Guardino) had written a passionate
column in his newspaper about crimes committed before the eyes of
indifferent, passive witnesses. A nondescript, middle-aged bachelor
coming home from a late movie read the column. Shortly afterward,
when he saw four vicious young hoodlums attacking a woman, he
went to her rescue. Two of the attackers pinned his arms behind his
back while a third clicked open a switchblade and stabbed him twice
in the abdomen. When the four hoodlums ran after the fleeing
woman, he crawled to the basement of an office building, where,
with the aid of a telephone marked merely Extension 7, he called
the reporter at the newspaper to blame him for his impending death,
then collapsed. Taylor enlisted the telephone company in tracing the
location. He was overcome with guilt as he attempted to maintain
contact with the dazed and bleeding victim who was intermittently
unconscious at the other end of the phone.

At this point the city editor, Lou Sheldon (Gary Merrill),
absolved his mentally tormented reporter. "When you believe in
something," he told him, "you go after it with something like
passion. If you lose that good anger and start having second thoughts
about everything you write, this paper doesn't need you and
this city doesn't need your tears."

We were never told what Danny Taylor thought about this
advice. He was interrupted by the forward movement of the plot,
which led to the eventual, last-moment rescue of the victim and the
arrest of the hoodlums (the woman had escaped her attackers and

they had returned to look for the wounded intruder in order to finish him). The reporter walked alone into the night to think about his adventure—having second thoughts, no doubt, about second thoughts.

The advice of his city editor, unchallenged on the screen, seemed reasonable. Actually, however, it is, I submit, dangerous. This attitude violates human dignity in that it fails to take into account the rights of other people. The violent youths, for instance, believed in their passion when they attacked the woman; so did the man who attempted to rescue her. The very essence of a violent personality is just this lack of second thoughts—which are generally about other people.

The importance of noting the city editor's violence is that it gives us a clue to the violence of the perpetrators of this first story in the "Reporter" series. They had a passion for their values, too. A new dramatic series about a newspaperman must hit hard in its initial episode to bring viewers back next week. Public opinion has been shocked recently by a series of crimes committed before eyewitnesses who failed to help or call the police. These events have inspired horror and incredulity. Television could create helpful awareness of the conditions that contribute to both violent behavior and to public indifference to crime. The passion of those who prepared this program, unfortunately, was not for insight but for a gruesome experience.

The play, as an object lesson, possibly did more harm than good. Anyone watching it would surely think twice in the future before rushing to the aid of a person in distress on a dark street. The victim in this story was a straw man. He had been a loner all his adult life. Such a man would be least likely, in spite of a reporter's hot words, to depart from a life pattern and become involved in a stranger's fate. Unarmed and confronted by four physically superior toughs, he was merely an artificial setup for a calculated hour of premeditated horror. The television executive who sanctioned and encouraged talent to write and produce this program said in effect: "Get the audience, don't worry about the effects, you're no good to us if you have second thoughts." His is the more malignant violence.

COMMENTARY

The critic is guilty, in the piece above, in not taking second thoughts himself, at the time he wrote it, about the internal consistency of his logic. The flaw is small, and could conceivably have slipped by readers unobserved: the critic was tempted to leave the piece as originally written with no comment, or to edit out the inconsistencies. It is equally as important, he decided, to be faithful to one's values as it is to be consistent in one's logic.

The moral importance of second thoughts—that is the sermon the piece preaches. To believe in one's own passion, without taking into account the rights of others—this, the critic holds, is the evil. He accuses the violent youths of this error when they attack the woman. But then he adds that "the man who attempted to rescue her" also believed in his passion to play the Samaritan. This would seem to imply that the man should have himself thought twice before going to the woman's rescue. Maybe: but that introduces a new problem, which has subtle overtones involving the tricky question of when violence is justified in the cause of presumptive good. It is entirely too tricky for the brief touching upon the problem in the piece. The critic, whatever he may have chosen to do, had he recognized the problem at the time of the writing of the piece, certainly should not have hit and run.

Furthermore, in the last paragraph, the critic observes that anyone watching the play on television "would surely think twice . . . before rushing to the aid of a person in distress on a dark street." But thinking twice is precisely what the critic is so concerned about. If he faults the play for making people think twice in such a circumstance, he seems to violate the good neighbor principle.

The critic thus, in this piece, is twice confounded by his own passion. Whether or not this invalidates his sermon on gratuitous violence is another question. That would require second thoughts of another order—and a new third beat.

THE CASE OF THE MISSING TESTIMONY
February 27, 1965

A SENATE subcommittee on juvenile delinquency held hearings in 1961 and 1962 to investigate "Effects on Young People of Violence and Crime Portrayed on Television." A transcript of the hearings, running to 2,592 pages, was published in March 1963, but

Broadcasting magazine reported a few weeks later that "half a dozen executive sessions have not been made public." A group of network officials testified at one of these closed sessions; among them was David Levy, former vice president in charge of programs and talent for NBC Television. Mr. Levy left his network during the hearings in explosive circumstances that continue to mystify even the most knowledgeable observers of the broadcasting scene. Speculation has persisted that he was made a scapegoat by a higher executive officer for the latter's campaign to inject strong doses of sex and violence into NBC entertainment programs in order to bolster competitive ratings. Mr. Levy testified twice in open hearings before the Senate subcommittee. The first time he won company medals for adroitly defending his network's program policies. The second time, after he had resigned, he read a prepared statement in which he vigorously defended his own record as a program creator against the sex-and-violence charges, and he also spoke eloquently about the better job that television ought to be doing. He refrained from personal accusations against his former employers, however, and mentioned no names.

Mr. Levy, now an independent producer in Hollywood, developed "The Addams Family," a current situation comedy series on ABC Television. He is also the author of *The Chameleons,* a first novel published recently by Dodd, Mead that may well reflect to a significant degree the former NBC vice president's real-life adventures. Stephen Lane, the hero of the novel and president of a fictitious broadcasting network, reluctantly carries out an edict of his superior to inject sex and violence into programs. He is caught in a crossfire of sleazy corporate thuggery and the political opportunism of a senator who heads a committee investigating television programs. Victim of a bilateral double-cross, Lane is cast out of the broadcasting company's bosom. He resigns but, to protect his reputation, fights back in testimony at Washington. Finally, in a happy but implausible ending, he is brought back to his network as the Number One programing executive.

The novel's protagonist testifies twice before the Senate committee, just as the author did in real life. A climax of *The Chameleons,* however, is the fictional testimony of the network president at a third committee session. The hero is prepared, with the cooperation of the committee staff, to introduce evidence proving that his superior not only was responsible for the edict calling for more sex and violence but also had lied to the Senate committee in denying that he had ever issued such an edict. The headline-hunting senator in the novel outrages his own staff and the hero when he abruptly terminates the hearings, shutting off the explosive evidence. The inference is that the senator has been reached by powerful forces.

The Chameleons is fiction, of course, but it was written by a man who was a key decision-maker at a major network (there are only ten of these at all three networks, the author asserts). The events in the novel parallel in a striking manner those that took place in Washington during the actual investigation of the networks by a Senate subcommittee. Did the author write into that fictional third hearing any material that he testified to in his actual third appearance before Senator Dodd's committee in closed executive session—a transcript of which has never been made public? Did Mr. Levy invent it all—or is there a core of fact? Because a clear record is absent, one may reasonably raise such questions. The perennial investigations by Washington officials into network activities have always been characterized by contradictions unpursued and ambiguities countenanced if not encouraged. Transcripts of the hearings can never reveal all the subtleties of the power game played behind the scenes. It is important that Mr. Levy's novel be read—not for its unimpressive love story but for the detailed, authoritative glimpses it affords into the motives, hypocrisies, and ethically savage dealings of the television executives who inhabit the world of *The Chameleons*. The author infuses that world with values and aspirations of men within the industry who would like to command a change for the better. Stephen Lane may be marching on in the book's dream, but it is quite different with the real-life David Levy.

VIOLENCE: TV'S CROWD-CATCHER *January 11, 1969*

THE PRESIDENT'S COMMISSION on the Causes and Prevention of Violence continues to hold hearings and to conduct studies on the subject of violence in TV programs. The commission's activities have energized the press to make surveys of its own. The editors of

McCall's recently urged its readers to write letters to television executives to protest against the outpouring of TV violence. *The Christian Science Monitor* has reported the results of a six-week survey that show that video violence "still rides high on the airwaves, in spite of assurances by network chiefs that they are doing all they can to minimize the incidence of shootings, stabbings, killings, and beatings."

Social scientists discuss for the commission members the subtleties of defining violence, calculating its effects in terms of aggression, catharsis, and impact on social norms. Some witnesses have urged regulation and control even though research has as yet established no clear, causal relationship between violence in the media and in real life. Nobody, however, seems willing to talk about the true options that are available to the public, as it tries to decide what ought to be done about the problem of violence on TV. The implicit assumptions are that networks could cut down violence if they really wanted to do it; that corporations and advertising agencies have the power to reform the networks if they wished.

Thus, Dr. Leo Bogart, general manager of the Bureau of Advertising of the American Newspaper Publishers Association, told the Commission on Violence that "it must appeal to top managers of corporations . . . in order to induce change in TV programing, and other advertiser-supported media. There is still among them an overwhelming acceptance of the need to do what is right." Perhaps so, but the question is not one of regulation by the industry, government, or any other constituted authority of "them" (people in TV). The real question is whether we—all of us—wish to regulate the American way of life, which is inextricably interwoven with violence on TV.

To understand what the game is all about, one has to get rid of the notion that television is in the program business; nothing could be further from the truth. Television is in the crowd-catching business. The networks and stations are instant crowd-catchers who deliver their catch to the advertisers who inoculate them with consumer messages. Proof of this is at hand in any broadcasting or advertising trade journal, where broadcasters, addressing their real clients, boast of what great crowd-catchers they are at how cheap a cost.

The catching of instant crowds is necessary for the sale of

instant tea, coffee, headache relief, spot remover, and other assorted goods and services—not for profit maximization, as John Kenneth Galbraith has argued, but for the instant managing of demand. Planned growth, in his theory, is the driving rod of our industrial state; growth depends on assured flow of capital for long-term projections. Corporations cannot depend on the whims of the old "free market"—where the consumer was sovereign—for steady, reliable demand. Therefore, demand has to be "managed." Advertising is the manager, and broadcasting is the crowd-catcher.

Now, the essence of the art of catching crowds is conflict—the most contagious of all human experiences, the universal language. Of conflict there are many varieties, ranging from parliamentary debates and elections to strikes, games, and fights. Television could, and occasionally does, present conflicts of ideas, but you can't run a crowd-catching business at this level. Instant crowds require simple phenomena, quickly grasped. Furthermore, ideas are controversial, dangerous; people have convictions, they take sides, are easily offended. Crowd-catchers want only happy consumers.

The type of conflict that will deliver instant crowds most efficiently is physical violence. Consider what would happen if a crowd had three viewing choices on a street: watching a clown, a nude woman, or a no-holds-barred fight—which do you think would attract the biggest crowd? Physical violence grows in mesmeric power, while sex and humor diminish relatively. Violence, internal and external, is the young generation's hang-up, not sex. This is the way our world is; TV tells us so—TV is the true curriculum of our society. We fear violence and enjoy it with guilt, because it calls to our own deeply latent potential for violence in response to a violent world. With such a sure-fire, instant crowd-catcher providing the essential energy which runs our industries, our networks, our advertising agencies—in short, our style of life—to call for the voluntary or involuntary regulation of violence on TV is to call for instant self-destruction of the system. By "system," I mean TV based on advertiser support. Television can run on a different system, of course; it does so in other countries. Public funds can support TV directly; license-fees on sets, along with marginal income from controlled advertising, can provide another basis. But to choose another system is to opt for another style of life, one where corporate and consumer acquisitions are not the dominant values.

If the American citizen is to be addressed maturely on the subject of violence in TV, he ought, at least, to be accorded the dignity of being told what his real choices are. Anything less— any talk of regulating and minimizing physical violence on TV, while retaining the present advertiser-supported crowd-catching system—is to contribute to instant self-delusion.

THE LESSON OF AUSCHWITZ   *May 6, 1967*

AUSCHWITZ was in the news again recently. On an April Sunday, 200,000 Europeans gathered at the site of Hitler's Number One death camp in Poland to dedicate a granite monument to its 4,000,000 victims, most of whom were Jews. The same afternoon, in New York City, an estimated 600,000 television viewers watched "The Investigation," Peter Weiss's drama about the Auschwitz murders, on the local NBC station. A basketball game on ABC–TV had the highest share (15 per cent) of the local audience for the time period; but the NBC play was close behind with a 14 per cent share.

NBC's Sunday presentation of "The Investigation" was a repeat performance. Ulu Grosbard's adaptation of the play had been presented first on the NBC network on the preceding Friday night, in prime time. The repeat was scheduled when NBC realized that many Jews throughout the nation might be attending Friday night services and would miss the opportunity to see the play. The program's New York audience share that Friday night was 26 per cent, second only to a Dean Martin movie on CBS, which drew a 33 per cent audience share. NBC estimated that 18,000,000 viewers saw "The Investigation" nationally. Out of 207 stations which comprise the full network, 187 carried the play on Friday and 131 accepted the drama on Sunday.

The original stage version, which was constructed by the author in documentary fashion from court records of a trial of Nazi war criminals, had been edited for television audiences; yet the meticulous, unsparing realism of the accounts of tortures, medical experiments, and crematoria, proved too much even for tough-minded viewers who tuned out. Several Jewish organizations told NBC that they were affronted because the play never mentions the words Auschwitz or Jew. But the author meant to universalize his theme of the potential moral degradation inherent in human beings: in the play, Auschwitz became simply "The Camp," and the Jews and the Nazis were, respectively, "the prisoners" or "the prosecution witnesses," and "the accused." Of the 200 Jewish organizations advised of the telecast in advance, almost all endorsed it.

It was extraordinary that NBC bought the television rights to the play before it had appeared on Broadway, then put it on the network twice at times when large numbers of viewers were available. This is obviously not a presentation that attracts sponsors. Its basic theme is violence, but not the controllable kind that is presented in a context of reassurance and the final triumph of the good and the right. "The Investigation" has no hero, no villain, no suspense. It tells, directly and with little characterization, what people did to each other at Auschwitz and how they justified what they did.

The impact upon the viewer may be that of a confrontation with a cesspit in himself—his own fear, cowardice, and hidden impulses to strike back at authority figures. It is Peter Weiss's somber challenge that, given the accident of circumstance, the victims could have been the guards at Auschwitz. "The Camp" is, the author asserts, still here in the present world. Viewers sense this, and that fact would explain the rather surprising size of the audience.

The important question is: What will viewers do with the experience of watching "The Investigation" on television? Can the horror be transmuted into some meaningful action? The play itself offers hardly any hope. One or two witnesses in the drama, however, noted that some Nazi doctors in the camp did take stands against inhuman conditions. One doctor refused to help select victims. In these cases, the witnesses said, nothing happened to the rebellious doctors. If men can make tiny gestures of defiance in a totalitarian death camp, there is larger room for individual responsibility in a democracy.

I wonder how many viewers who watched "The Investigation" were aware of the fact that today, nineteen years after the United Nations General Assembly unanimously adopted the Genocide Convention, the United States Senate has still not ratified the agreement. The Genocide Convention makes it a crime to commit acts intended "to destroy, in whole or in part, a national, ethnical, racial or religious group, as such; killing members of the group; causing serious bodily or mental harm . . . deliberately inflicting on the group conditions of life calculated to bring about its physical destruction in whole or in part . . ." Viewers reminded of Auschwitz and "The Investigation" have the power to let their senators know how they feel about ratification.

COMMENTARY

The Senate Foreign Relations Committee, by a vote of 10–2, reported the Genocide Convention favorably, November 23, 1970. Final ratification by the Senate is still to be achieved; but the extrication of the Convention from the Foreign Relations Committee, where it had been bottled up for almost twenty-three years, was a giant step in the right direction.

CHAPTER TWELVE

The Citizen Critic

He holds him with his skinny hand,
"There was a ship," quoth he.
"Hold off! unhand me, graybeard loon!"
Eftsoons his hand dropped he.

He holds him with his glittering eye—
The Wedding Guest stood still,
And listens like a three years' child:
The Mariner hath his will.

LIKE AN APPARENTLY INEXHAUSTIBLE VEIN of precious metal under-ground, *The Rime of the Ancient Mariner* continues to yield new treasure. Consider the opposition of "the skinny hand" and "the glittering eye" in the two verses quoted above. How many times has one passed by them and bought their currency at its face value: the Mariner first touched the Wedding Guest, possibly put his hand on the latter's shoulder; and when this action was paid with a brusque rejection, the "eye" of the old seafaring man bound him with a spell. A flash of reflection, however, suggests that in "the skinny hand" and "the glittering eye" we are confronted by two significantly different levels of the power to command attention.

"The hand is quicker than the eye," the maxim runs; but it may be added that often the eye is more powerful than the hand. The hand can move at its owner's will quickly, here and there; but it touches merely the surface of things. Even when it moves from outer to inner surfaces or from higher to lower, it still collides merely with the molecular exteriors of phenomena. The eye, on the other level of power, penetrates and sees through surfaces; it detects relationships; it comprehends and surveys; the eye sees beyond appearances and it illuminates. I speak, of course, of the "insight" power of the eye, its capacity for mental discernment rather than its own atomistic bouncing, in the form of light rays, off billiard balls, particles of the armor of earth, sea, and air.

Having extended our Mariner in time and space, and having assumed that he visits himself upon a succession of Wedding Guests, we must not conclude that his sequence of hand first and eye next is a rigid, predetermined, automatic pattern of behavior. Sometimes he stops the man whom he must teach with his hand, sometimes with his eye: it all depends on the man and on the circumstances of the stopping, their geography and psychology. The hand, we may speculate, he employs when his communication problems are simple: it requires but a light touch, a flick of an attractive, readily understood subject to capture the attention of a Wedding Guest. Violence, politics, particular programs, well-known personalities from television and radio—these quickly involve a reader. He is already aware and interested; he shares a common fund of knowledge with the critic. The eye's gambit is offered when the subject at hand is difficult, obscure, superficially uninviting. The whole area of the institutional, corporate, legal, and judicial domains of broadcasting constitutes one such refractory category. The general citizen knows almost nothing of the legislative framework of broadcasting: neither the schools nor the media, certainly not the latter, take any great pains to inform him on the matter.

He lacks knowledge of the broad political philosophy that underlies the contract relationships in the United States between the licensees of the individual television or radio stations and the public as a whole. His ignorance may be due to lack of interest, true: or the reverse may also be correct. In any case, his blind spot in this regard is ubiquitous and largely impervious. The law, the regulatory agencies, the courts, the corporations great and small, which make the media decisions that influence the lives of very nearly all the millions who are citizens of the republic—these are jungles of complexity, comparable to fine print in leases and insurance policies. In a democracy, nevertheless, the most concentrated of juridical generalizations may have extraordinarily diffuse effects in the body politic; and the ignorance or indifference of individual citizens does not necessarily serve to shield them from the consequences of the generalizations. "Ought" is a charged moral term; but there are not many political philosophers who would quarrel with the notion that citizens ought to know, particularly in a democracy, more than they do about the legal framework upon which they weave the variegated fabrics of their personal and social lives.

Three main types of political justification have been prominent in Western thought—the religious, the organic, and the contractual. In the religious mode, the citizen obeys the state because it expresses a divine will: he asks no questions, makes no challenges, or criticisms. In the organic conception, the citizen submits to the state because he has a sense that he plays a vital part in its life, and that he gains, as a social being, by relating himself to others who play their parts. In the contractual mode, the citizen makes a contract with the state to keep peace and order, so that he may pursue his own selfish interests in an exchange relationship with others who also pursue their own selfish interests. Our contemporary society in the United States is a mix of the organic and contractual modes—of Aristotle and Hobbes and Adam Smith.

Ours is a business-oriented state, where people freely enter into contracts with each other, pursuing their own goals, and where, theoretically, that government is presumed to be the best which governs least. Though the reality is far removed from the myth, and pure laissez faire has long been a shibboleth without substance, free enterprise is still the popular assumption of a contract society. To an important extent, it has been tempered by the organic mode; but it is also true that the fundamental assumptions about the benefits of capitalism—larger output, lower prices, and better quality of products and services—have been modified negatively. It is often more profitable to advertise and to market inferior products than to improve their quality. Diminishing markets, giant mergers make the classical assumptions more and more dubious.

In this shrinking of the number of power centers, and the diminution in their capacity for control, affinities among lawmakers,

corporations, and courts, for the public good or ill, go largely unattended by the general run of the citizenry. The individual citizen
is not characterized by the presumptive participation in his government which marked the privileged freeman of Athens. He leads his
own rather narrow, provincial life of work and leisure. He may relish
the quadrennial political festivities of national elections, in which he
fulfills his duties of citizenship; but generally he walks his private
path and leaves the larger matters of law, justice, and public right
and wrong to the representatives and officers of the legal and political community. Yet it is an oft-repeated truism that democracy
depends for its health on the organic relationship of the citizens of
the state, when that state is a democracy. Alfred North Whitehead,
commenting on Plato's celebrated reflection that the ideal state
would never arrive till philosophers are kings, wrote:

> Today, in an age of democracy, the kings are the plain citizens
> pursuing their various avocations. There can be no successful
> democratic society till general education conveys a philosophic
> outlook.

Commenting on the domination of our society by the contractual, business mode of life, Whitehead also said:

> But the motive of success is not enough. It produces a short-
> sighted world which destroys the sources of its own prosperity
> . . . Also we must not fall into the fallacy of thinking of the
> business world in abstraction from the rest of the community
> . . . A great society is a society in which its men of business
> think greatly of their functions. Low thoughts mean low
> behavior, and after a brief orgy of exploitation low behavior
> means a descending standard of life.

Contractual freedom in the modern state is more than economic
freedom: it is human freedom, citizen freedom, a liberty defined by
Harold Laski as "the eager maintenance of that atmosphere in which
men have the best opportunity to be themselves." Whitehead, anent
the function of education to convey a general philosophic outlook to

democratic society, speaks of philosophy in terms that we may apply
to criticism:

> Philosophy [read criticism] is not a mere collection of noble
> sentiments . . . Philosophy is at once general and concrete,
> critical and appreciative of direct intuition . . . It is a survey of
> possibilities and their comparison with actualities. In
> philosophy, the fact, the theory, the alternatives, and the ideal
> are weighed together. Its gifts are insight and foresight, and a
> sense of the worth of life, in short that sense of importance
> which nerves all civilized effort. Mankind can flourish in
> the lower stages of life with merely barbaric flashes of thought.
> But when civilization culminates, the absence of a coordinating
> philosophy [read criticism] of life, spread throughout the
> community, spells decadence, boredom and the slackening
> of effort.

The critic, then, must educate; to educate, he must command
attention; to command attention in a world endemically marked by
"information overload," he must use the Mariner's "glittering eye,"
in its dual connotations of penetrating to the unseen, and its aspect
of showy splendor. When he must talk to his readers of justice, law,
and institutions in broadcasting, he must play the part of the dramatist. He must tell a tale, as the Mariner does; he must seek to wrap
his meanings and messages in contests, agons between personalities.
He must deal in heroes and villains, and men in tragic dilemmas.
Like Plato, he must choose the form of the dialogue to convey his
ideas: he must pit Socrates against the Sophists. He must, even as
he expresses scorn for them, indulge in theatrical eristics, debates
and arguments.

In his last dialogue, the *Laws,* Plato likens the building of a
community to the acting out of a play. "Our whole stage," a spokesman for the community says to a visiting poet, who wishes to stage
a play in the city, "is an imitation of the best and noblest life, which
we affirm to be indeed the very truth of tragedy." The critic, survey-
ing the real-life drama of the institution of broadcasting, has villains
aplenty but heroes few: when one such enters his field of vision, he
casts him readily for a fighting role. Such heroes may be men within

the institutions as well as citizens outside them. The critic knows that to call particular individuals either heroes or villains is largely a theatrical convenience.

The beauty of the critic's dialogue is that all men can play various parts; and he, himself, can enter empathically into the roles of the good and the bad alike. Even Socrates has some sophistry in him; and as for Callicles, his character—representative of even the extremists among the rhetoricians whom Socrates engages in "the great combat"—is ambiguous too. Speaks Socrates to that rhetorician as their own combat nears its end in the *Gorgias:*

> No, Callicles, the very bad men come from the class of those who have power. And yet in that very class there may arise good men, and worthy of all admiration they are, for where there is great power to do wrong, to live and to die justly is a hard thing, and greatly to be praised, and few there are who attain to this.

The essential quality of the critic's heroes is that they take their roles as citizens seriously, considering them paramount to, or at least on an equal level with, their roles as contractors in the business economy, or as officials of the republic or its subdivisions. They assume the responsibility of leadership, of coming out from the anonymity of the indifferent or cautious crowd; and they act on behalf of all the citizens, as they see the causes of justice affected by the actions of others.

They have a sense of conscience: in this respect they qualify as critics, for the Latin *con-sciens* means knowing something together, as a whole. This conscience in them may have religious origins or it may be grounded in humanistic convictions. The critic, recognizing a familiar spirit, identifies at once with his heroes. He amplifies the horn of warning that they sound to the community with the resonating power of his own critical horn. He commands attention for them; he follows and reports their trials and cheers them on. In their battles, they occasionally triumph, but they also suffer defeat. It is better, they reckon with Socrates, "to suffer evil than to do evil." To them we can apply the notion that Whitehead employs for "standards . . . which test the defects of human society" when he writes:

> . . . they must spread the infection of an uneasy spirit . . .
> [they are] at once gadflies irritating and beacons luring,
> the victims among whom they dwell.

In the pieces that follow in this chapter, we will see the critic's eye at work, illuminating with his dramaturgy broadcasting's backwaters—its institutional arrangements. These comprise the Communications Act of 1934, the Federal Communications Commission (FCC), the National Association of Broadcasters (NAB), the sponsors, the courts, and a modest multiplicity of individuals who are cast as heroes, villains, or men in honest dilemmas of citizenship. The reader may wonder, as the critic did, if there is some pattern which explains just why the heroes sometimes win and more often lose. A clue exists; it lies in the degree of awareness that the general public has of the issues encountered, and in the public's corresponding levels of conscience concerning the issues. Where threats are widely understood and when their impact on the individual citizen is plain, awareness and conscience are relatively high. In such cases, the Congress, the FCC, the broadcasters, and the sponsors tend to be more responsive to restraints upon corporate freedom. The relationship between cigarette advertising on television and radio and health hazards is one such issue; the question of children's programing is another; a third is the right of reply, under the FCC's Fairness Doctrine, for individuals who are attacked over the air.

Health is a universal issue, in a society where millions smoke cigarettes; children have progressively been afforded the wider protection of special laws; and fair play is a strong strain in the American tradition. But in the single issue where public awareness and conscience are markedly low—the question of the conditions under which broadcast licenses should be granted to contractors, or renewed or revoked—there, the men of power in the Congress, the corporations, and in the government agencies, tend to work their will, regardless of the courts or of the play of valid, rational debate within the public. The Mariner-critic's task, then, when the Wedding Guest rebukes his "hand," is to stop him with the "eye," to have his will until the Wedding Guest's conscience is aroused, so that the latter, as a single citizen, may, by ever more active participation (as his circumstances permit) enrich his own role in the democratic drama. Indeed, it may be the critic's role, as he progresses, to employ the eye more often than the hand, to confront the difficult rather than the simple.

But if, as a dramatist, he stages "the great combat," relishing his heroes and his villains, and often speaking his own thoughts through them, he would do well to bear in mind a prescription of Paul Tillich's for the drama of the dialogue: "Listening love is the first step to justice in the person-to-person encounter." The critic's dramaturgy may be only a compensatory fantasy for his own lack of control of the real world. Social theorists become dramatists, A. W. Gouldner remarked, "when men lack or lose their historical moorings . . . when experience is losing its continuity and is dissolving into episodic shreds . . ."

On the other hand, the dramatist-critic's eye can have another function, which Whitehead described:

> It is our business—philosophers, students, and practical men—
> to re-create and reenact a vision of the world, including those
> elements of reverence and order without which society lapses
> into riot, and penetrated through and through, with unflinching
> rationality. Such a vision is the knowledge which Plato
> identified with virtue. Epochs for which, within the limits of
> their development, this vision has been widespread are the
> epochs unfading in the memory of mankind.

THE LITTLE STATION THAT WON'T   *February 8, 1964*

CONCORD, CALIFORNIA

VICTOR IVES, vice president of KWUN, a small, independent radio station thirty miles northeast of San Francisco, recently received a complaint from the Associated Press. The Bay Area's AP representative said he never got any news from KWUN.

A few days later, Ives, a minority stockholder, telephoned the AP in San Francisco to announce that his station, located in Concord, would henceforth accept no cigarette commercials, as a result of the recent Surgeon General's report on smoking and public health. The news service immediately put the story on the wire, and papers across the country picked it up. While networks, tobacco companies, and advertising agencies were shifting gears ponderously to "reexamine" their policies on cigarette commercials, one local independent station had acted.

To look into the situation, I visited KWUN's office, where I met Ives and Ken Blasé, his news director. Ives told me that R. A. King, a Santa Barbara dentist "fascinated by investment in a radio station," is KWUN's majority stockholder; the wives of the two partners are the only other owners. KWUN went on the air in November 1961, and King and Ives later bought it from the original licensees. The previous owners had carried campaigns for Kent and Newport cigarettes.

KWUN had no tobacco accounts at the time the station announced its ban on cigarette commercials. "We're a suburban station, and we don't get much national spot business," Ives said. "Most of our accounts are local merchants." Since the FCC licenses radio stations to operate in the public interest, Ives said, "I don't see how broadcasting cigarette advertising can be consistent with the public interest in view of the government report." Ives and Blasé (both nonsmokers) estimated that KWUN had earned about $2,200 on cigarette advertising last year—a small portion of the station's annual $100,000 gross.

KWUN may have closed the door on a minor source of potential income by announcing its ban on cigarette commercials. Ives said that a salesman for a rival radio station in Contra Costa County had told clients that KWUN was "owned by a church." "That's not true," Ives said. "There's no hidden ownership here. I'm not against people smoking. I don't want to alienate tobacco companies. They will probably diversify and make other products. But we're operating an adult, family-type music, news, and sports station. We editorialize lightly and we're trying to follow the FCC recommendation that we encourage discussion of controversial public issues. We're the only station in town and we want the community to rely on us as authoritative. The big advertisers use the San Francisco stations. We must compete with those stations for the local housewife's ear.

"If the public understands what it read in the Surgeon General's report," Ives continued, "what can it think of a radio station that tells people on the hour every hour to go out and buy poison? It would be hypocritical to stress the pleasures and joys of smoking and not say that it contributes to cancer."

Ives said that he also plans to broadcast thirty-second spot announcements discouraging smoking. He does not think networks and large stations will take drastic measures but will tone down cigarette commercials and place them later in their schedules. "There's too much money involved," he said. "Here it was one man's decision. In a network, many men must decide—but if I were there, I think I would try to swing my weight." He hopes local stations can follow his example; he thinks that many suburban stations could ban cigarette commercials without being hurt too much financially. "Anyway, we don't get our licenses just to make money," he said. "A station can't be all take and no give."

Later I checked with the other two radio stations in Contra Costa County. One said it had no tobacco accounts but would definitely not ban cigarette advertising. The other had no tobacco commercials, either, but didn't know what its policy would be. "It's an interesting question," said the pleasant-voiced lady at the other end of the telephone.

It is indeed—the profound economic interests of the great tobacco-growing states, big companies, and large numbers of citizens confronted with dilemmas of liberty, laissez faire, and ethics. The decision apparently comes easier to Victor Ives in Concord than to the directors of a more impersonal network with vast responsibilities. But does the greater magnitude of the dilemma release one from the obligation of trying to solve it?

WHERE THERE'S SMOKE   *September 25, 1965*

SIX MAJOR CIGARETTE COMPANIES were among the top twenty television advertisers in 1964. Together they invested almost $190,000,000 in sponsoring their brands on the small screen. In one case (Philip Morris) the television share of the manufacturer's total budget was 89 per cent; R. J. Reynolds had the lowest TV share of total budget (62.7 per cent), although its investment in TV was the highest ($46,450,000). So many millions would not be spent unless the retail sales of cigarettes justified their television

advertising cost. A host of smokers are still "lighting up" in the
belief that they are "getting a good thing going," despite
the Surgeon General's report. Others would like to quit smoking
but seem unable to overcome the habit. No one knows how much
of their compulsion is nurtured by the blandishments of television's
cigarette advertising. A third group, intricately trapped in the
dilemma of the tobacco industry, share an economic ambivalence.
These are the people who earn all or part of their income from
the manufacture or sale of cigarettes.

The following account is about a television actor who recently
made a cigarette commercial. Even the occasional viewer cannot fail
to have seen it at least once. The sponsor is giving it an intensive
run, and before its first cycle is through it will probably have earned
several thousand dollars for the actor. The monetary gain, however,
is offset by a tiny tragedy.

The actor who epitomizes the classic flaw is a tall, handsome
man, as virile as Marlboro country. I met him a few months ago
during the production of the first program of a new television series
that may eventually be shown in schools. For this reason, the actors
do not smoke. Since the schools are actively participating in
anti-smoking education, it is feared that smoking on the programs
may endanger their acceptance in the classroom. As a matter of policy,
also, broadcasters these days are sensitive to the need for barriers
between youth and cigarette advertising. Our hero, I observed
during breaks in the rehearsals, was a nonsmoker in real life. He
explained that he had once been a chain smoker (three packs a day);
had been frightened by the Surgeon General's report; had quit with
great effort; now he had gained weight, he felt better, and never
would go back. About a month later, when the company
reassembled to shoot the second program, I noticed very quickly
that the actor was smoking.

With a wry grin, he unfolded the cause. A successful actor, he
had always kept busy playing roles and had never done a television
commercial. Recently East Coast production had fallen off; so had
his income from acting. His agent suggested that he swallow his
artist's pride and do some on-camera selling. Cigarette commercials
were the best place to begin. Since the scare, the cigarette
companies were asking the networks to keep them out of the 7:30 to

8:30 P.M. hour, which is heavily viewed by children and teenagers. The tobacco advertisers had also adopted a self-regulating code that forbade the use of models in cigarette commercials who were under twenty-five years of age.

Our actor fitted the requirements perfectly, so he finally hit the advertising-agency trail. The producers who interviewed and auditioned him would ask him to sit down and pass him one of their cigarettes to light up. Part of the audition was to see how he held a cigarette, puffed it. He had steeled himself to get the jobs without being caught up again in the cigarette habit, so at first he tried to fudge inhaling—but the steelier eyes of the producers put an end to that very quickly. Deep, satisfying inhalations were what they wanted; you had to look as if you were enjoying it. He made the rounds of all the agencies that handled cigarette accounts, smoking his way through the ordeal.

At last he landed a job and spent two days on location filming his first cigarette commercial. The director made many takes for each shot—and a fresh cigarette was handed to him for each take. When it was all over, our actor realized that he was "hooked." He doesn't enjoy smoking; he knows it involves a health hazard; but since he took the first audition cigarette that the producer handed him in his first agency interview, he has been unable to stop. Cigarettes will cost him about $200 a year, he figures: it will take ten years before he eats up the minimum amount of residuals he will earn from the commercial. At that point he will have to count up the real pleasure and the real profit. A second actor in the company, who stood by while the first told his tale, declared that he, too, was about to do his first cigarette commercial. A nonsmoker, he was sure he could resist. Next time the acting company meets to shoot another show, I'll find out. Did he make it, or was he another who switched rather than fight, and is now "smoking more and enjoying it less"?

HISTORIC REVERSAL FOR THE FCC   *May 7, 1966*

THREE JUDGES of the U. S. Court of Appeals in the District of Columbia, in a lucid, historic opinion, have literally changed the rules of broadcasting regulation—opening the way for the public to have a voice in determining whether a station has operated in the

public interest. They held, on March 25, 1966, that the Federal
Communications Commission erred in renewing the license of
WLBT, a television station in Jackson, Mississippi, and they directed
the commission to hold hearings on the station's renewal application.

The case, under FCC scrutiny since 1955, would never have
come to so unexpected and stunning a denouement, had it not been
for the Office of Communication of the United Church of Christ,
directed by the Reverend Everett C. Parker. In 1964 the church
petitioned the commission to deny WLBT's application for renewal.
It asked for hearings to present evidence that the station was guilty
of racial and religious discrimination and of excessive commercialism.
The FCC, by a four to two vote, dismissed the petition and granted
the Jackson station a restricted, conditional license renewal for
one year instead of the customary three.

The commission, in effect, thus accepted the charges of the
church's Office of Communication, but ruled that the city "needed"
a second TV station, and put WLBT on probation. Chairman
E. William Henry and Commissioner Kenneth A. Cox dissented
vigorously from the majority view, arguing that a renewal could not
properly be granted until hearings resolved factual issues raised by
the church petition. Ordinarily that would have ended the matter;
the FCC had "ducked" another tough case, shown leniency to a
licensee, and refused to give a public group, the United Church of
Christ, "standing" which would have made hearings mandatory
under the provisions of the Communications Act.

The right to intervene officially in a license renewal had been
granted only on grounds of "economic injury" or "electrical
interference." Standing, thus, traditionally had been granted to
competing stations but not to the listening public. Presumably the
audience did not suffer any "injury," and allowing it standing
"would pose great administrative burdens" on the commission.
Mr. Parker, backed by his church, deemed the matter too important
to drop. Ignoring the gloomy predictions of top communications
lawyers, he appealed the FCC decision to the federal court.

The Court of Appeals judges—Burger, McGowan, and Tamm—
had probably never attended a convention of the National Association
of Broadcasters. More interested in theoretical law than in industry
practices, they looked at the record and stood the FCC on its head

at every point of the argument. They emphasized that "standing is accorded to persons not for the protection of their private interests but only to vindicate the public interest."

"We cannot believe," the judges added, "that the congressional mandate of public participation . . . was meant to be limited to writing letters to the commission, to inspection of records, to the commission's grace in considering listener claims, or to mere non-participating appearance at hearings . . . Consumers are generally among the best vindicators of the public interest. In order to safeguard the public interest in broadcasting, therefore, we hold that some 'audience participation' must be allowed in license renewal proceedings."

As for WLBT's license, it is not long for this world if the FCC takes seriously one sentence in the court's opinion: "We agree that a history of programing misconduct of the kind alleged would preclude, as a matter of law, the required finding that renewal of the license would serve the public interest." The key phrase is "as a matter of law." It suggests the irrelevance of any reforms WLBT may adopt during its probationary period. "When past performance is in conflict with public interest," the judges said, "a very heavy burden rests on the renewal applicant to show how a renewal can be reconciled with the public interest."

The judges squelched the FCC's argument that Jackson "needed" the WLBT renewal, even though the station had been unfair to its Negro community (50 per cent of the area population). The area, said the court, might better be served "with one TV outlet acutely conscious that adherence to the fairness doctrine is a *sine qua non* of every licensee." The commission, thoroughly spanked, has decided not to appeal to the Supreme Court; and it has ordered a hearing. WLBT could appeal, but it would be foolish to go to the high court with a case so apparently blemished with racial discrimination. The church's Office of Communication, preparing for the hearing, reports that the station even now is still discriminating against the Jackson Negro community.

Mr. Parker deserves an award for courageous public service. His church has shown the way not only to other churches concerned with the impact of the media on their congregations, but also to civic associations, professional societies, unions, and educational institutions. Captious or purely obstructive protests are not in order. But informed, organized monitoring and evaluating of performance versus promise, as the court stated, can provide "a means for reflection of listener appraisal" of a licensee's statutory obligation to operate in the public interest.

Perhaps the FCC in the future will hesitate to renew a license without a hearing when serious issues of fact are involved, and stations will hesitate before politely brushing off complaints from articulate public groups.

COMMENTARY

Everett Parker received the first Alfred I. Du Pont–Columbia University Award, 1968–1969, "for his long and devoted advocacy of the public interest in broadcasting."

As this is written, August 1970, the FCC has still to make a final disposition of the WLBT license renewal matter. The old licensee is still operating the station pending the selection of a new licensee. The decision of the Court of Appeals, in vindicating the rights of individual listeners and viewers, and groups of them, to intervene in license renewals, opened the way for an ever increasing activity of citizens in matters before the FCC. The critic wrote seven pieces on the WLBT case, commenting on its progress through the commission and the courts. "Historic Reversal for the FCC," and "Burger *vs.* FCC," the next piece in this chapter, are two among the seven. For readers who may be interested in closer attention to the history of this important case as reflected in the critic's comments, he appends the titles and dates of the other five SR pieces: "A Church Looks at Television," May 16, 1964; "Rating the Broadcaster," July 11, 1964; "The Public May Be Heard," June 26, 1965; "FCC on the Carpet," August 24, 1968; "Mephisto and the FCC," May 14, 1970.

BURGER VS. FCC   *July 26, 1969*

WHEN WARREN BURGER, the new Chief Justice of the United States, was a Court of Appeals Circuit Judge for the District of Columbia, he wrote two decisions in the celebrated case *United Church of Christ vs. FCC and Lamar Broadcasting.*

The first decision, in 1966, was a landmark opinion that gave interested citizens the right to participate in FCC hearings involving license renewals for TV and radio stations. This opinion, carefully reasoned and lucidly written, has been widely quoted in law journals. That Mr. Burger was justly proud of it is indicated by the fact that he included it in his biography submitted in support of his Supreme Court appointment. The second decision, recently handed down, was his last upon the appeals bench; it may have been written in haste, for it does not compare in stature with the 1966 decision. Affirmative in general, with important consequences for the public interest in the long run, it is nevertheless ambiguous in some respects.

On the positive side, it follows up Justice Burger's 1966 decision in which he ordered the FCC to permit the United Church of Christ to intervene in the license-renewal hearing that involved WLBT, a television station in Jackson, Mississippi. The station was charged with violating the Fairness Doctrine, discriminating against its black community, and over-commercializing. The FCC, obeying the court's order, had held a hearing, but had treated the church as an "interloper" and "opponent," and not as an "ally," and had acted with "hostility" and "impatience." This was wrong, the Circuit Court judge wrote in a unanimous three-man opinion.

The commission further erred, said the court, in making the citizen group prove that the license should not be renewed; the burden of proof that a renewal would be in the public interest should always be upon the licensee.

The second decision nails down the full operative meaning of the first; it is hard to conceive that any FCC majority, however hostile to a citizen intervener, could ignore it again.

The note of ambiguity was struck by Judge Burger in his curious disposition of WLBT's license renewal. One might venture that it was the court's best solution to a dilemma. Judge Burger found that WLBT clearly had failed to prove that it would be in the public interest to have the FCC renew its license for a full three-year period. He also found, unambiguously, that the commission had used the wrong standard in allocating the burden of proof in the hearing. Having thus found, the court could have

remanded the case to the FCC, with instructions to do it over again
—this time right.

But a new hearing would have meant that the United Church
of Christ would be required to spend another small fortune pursuing
the case; the church had done more than its share fighting in behalf
of the public interest. Even if the court did remand the case, it
apparently could not trust the FCC majority, for Judge Burger
wrote: "The administrative conduct reflected in this record is
beyond repair." Never, in fact, in the history of administrative law,
has a regulatory agency been so firmly rebuked by a court.

Judge Burger's solution to the court's dilemma was to "vacate"
the license and to instruct the FCC to "invite applications to be filed
for the license." In vacating the license, however, he did not
disqualify WLBT from being one of the new applicants.

This failure to disqualify WLBT seems to contradict his
unequivocal finding that WLBT hadn't convinced the FCC that the
station should have a full license renewal. What, according to the
court's own prescription, constitutes disqualification if not failure to
prove that the public interest would be served by a renewal?

Courts have been generally sensitive in respecting the powers
of regulatory agencies; perhaps Judge Burger refrained from going
too far in doing the FCC's job. His reluctance to burden the United
Church of Christ with a new hearing was correct; his reluctance to
disqualify WLBT was questionable.

Meanwhile Civic Communications Corporation, a local racially
integrated group, has applied for the disputed Jackson license. The
corporation includes Charles Evers, the new mayor of Fayette,
Mississippi, and Hodding Carter III, publisher. The applicants
propose a program philosophy and schedule that sparkle with
authentic public service promise.

Whatever the fate of Channel 3 in Jackson, the two opinions of
Judge Burger in *United Church of Christ vs. FCC and Lamar Life
Broadcasting* will have important effects in broadcasting's future.

COMMENTARY

After the publication of the last piece, the WLBT license case continued its protracted journey through the FCC's adjudicatory ma-

chinery. In addition to Civic Communications Corporation, the local racially integrated group which the critic mentioned in the piece, four other business venture groups (including Lamar Life, the dispossessed operator) applied for the "vacated" franchise.

Then a sixth group applied for permission to operate the station on an interim basis, while the commission was making up its mind as to which of the five applicants for the permanent license should be chosen. The new group was a nonprofit organization, Communications Improvement, Inc., financed by the Office of Communication of the United Church of Christ. The critic commented on the complicated situation in "Mephisto and the FCC," March 14, 1970, in which he wrote:

> Now comes the . . . church offering the commission an attractive chance to redeem itself and to bring some good out of the six-year mess for both black and white citizens in the WLBT area . . . The [new] group wants to improve race relations in the South and to demonstrate that a station can program imaginatively in the public interest and still make money. It includes among the black and white incorporators noted figures in journalism and broadcasting, educators, churchmen, a hotel operator, and other businessmen in the Jackson area. They plan to turn over all profits from the temporary operation of WLBT to other "nonprofit organizations engaged in activities relating to broadcasting primarily in Mississippi."
>
> One-half would go to the development of educational TV in the state, and one-half to "a predominantly Negro college in Mississippi to train blacks in communications techniques."

The critic weighed the pros and cons of awarding the interim grant to the nonprofit group, as opposed to the commission's other alternatives, which included awarding the grant to one or more of the business-venture applicants or to a consortium of all of them. Of the United Church of Christ offer, he wrote:

> The offer . . . has poetic justice and a Christian spirit. It breathes of reconciliation and the public interest.
> Goethe's Mephistopheles, when he presented himself to

Faust, described himself as "a part of that force which always wills the bad, yet always achieves the good." Any resemblance between Mephisto and the FCC is purely coincidental, but there is an aptness to the role in this particular instance which invites the playing of it.

On September 4, 1970, the FCC, in a 4–2 decision, ordered that the nonprofit, church-sponsored group be assigned the interim operation of WLBT, pending the final selection of a permanent licensee. Chairman Dean Burch voted for the grant, as did Commissioners Nicholas Johnson, Robert E. Lee, and Kenneth A. Cox. It was one of the latter's final decisions before leaving the commission, after serving a full seven-year term as a Democrat appointee, during which he compiled an admirable record as a regulator seriously concerned with protecting and extending the public's stake in broadcasting.

THE FAIRNESS DOCTRINE   *July 15, 1967*

WRITE A LETTER, if you want to complain about something in television or radio; it may actually bring results, contrary to dim views of the practice taken by professional observers of the media. Two men wrote letters recently, in separate cases, to broadcast stations and to the Federal Communications Commission, and triggered thunderstorms in the industry.

Fred J. Cook and John F. Banzhaf III are the activating letter-writers. The first is a well-known author-journalist; the second is a twenty-six-year-old graduate of Columbia University Law School and of the Massachusetts Institute of Technology. The stations to which they wrote rebuffed both men, but they carried their cases to the FCC, and the commission supported them.

In Mr. Cook's case, the United States Court of Appeals for the District of Columbia has upheld the FCC's action in a landmark decision. In the case of Mr. Banzhaf, some two dozen stations have filed a challenge to the commission's ruling, and undoubtedly it will be tested in the courts. Both actions involved the commission's Fairness Doctrine, promulgated, ironically, in 1949 at the behest of the broadcasters.

The doctrine requires that stations devote a reasonable percentage of their broadcasting time to public issues of controversial importance, affording the public an opportunity to hear opposing sides of issues. Cook was verbally attacked by Billy James Hargis, a radical right broadcaster, on WGCB, an ultra-conservative station in York, Pennsylvania. The program was commercially sponsored. When Cook asked for free time to reply, he was told by the station that he would either have to pay for it or stipulate that he was financially unable to "sponsor" a reply. The FCC then ordered WGCB to give him free time.

The station, in district court, challenged the constitutionality of the Fairness Doctrine. The court, however, affirmed the commission's action and asserted that the doctrine is "a vehicle completely legal in its origin which implements by the use of modern technology the 'free and general discussion of public matters [which] seems absolutely essential for an intelligent exercise of their rights as citizens.' "

Banzhaf wrote CBS last December asking its New York-owned station to give him roughly proportionate time to counter cigarette commercials with his own anti-smoking messages. The FCC, after CBS had rejected Banzhaf's request, wrote a public letter to all broadcasters noting that they were responsible for making available "significant" amounts of time for presentations of the anti-cigarette viewpoint. "The commission would be content with stations' 'good faith and reasonableness'—and a 3-to-1 ratio of cigarette ads to anti-smoking messages," said Henry Geller, the commission's general counsel.

Both cases have aroused the industry spokesmen to a renewed vigorous attack on the constitutionality of the Fairness Doctrine. The WGCB case (Red Lion Broadcasting) is considered a dubious one on which to go to the Supreme Court. The right-wing record of the station (it is currently involved in other quarrels with the FCC involving "hate" broadcasts) could taint the case. In effect, the station is asking for the right to run its programs as it pleases, and, in the words of the FCC, "making radio unavailable as a medium of free speech."

The commission's cigarette ruling, however, has produced more pragmatic jitters in the trade. Networks and agencies see $200 million worth of tobacco advertising in danger. They say the extension of the doctrine from political controversy to advertising is "absurd." They worry about its application to other "potentially controversial" products—beer, wine, fluorides, etc.

The FCC, however, has no intention of unlimited application. The Fairness Doctrine, in its estimate, is too important to be extended to ridiculous limits. Congress has ruled that cigarettes are a health hazard, and the FCC, in its cigarette ad ruling, is merely following congressional cues. It won't apply the doctrine to products that do not involve significant health hazards. It wants more balanced presentation, not a knockout of all cigarette commercials.

Thank Banzhaf, then, if in the months ahead, you begin to see and hear more warnings on television and radio about the hazards of smoking. And thank Cook for inspiring Circuit Judge Tamm, in the *Red Lion* case, to remind us—as was stated in *U. S. vs. Associated Press*—that "right conclusions are more likely to be gathered out of a multitude of tongues than through any kind of authoritative selection. To many this is, and always will be, folly; but we have staked upon it our all."

THE CIGARETTE ISSUE *October 21, 1967*

VOLUNTARY HEALTH AGENCIES (the American Cancer Society, American Heart Association, et al.), which have carried on aggressive research and public education campaigns against cigarette smoking for years, have suddenly found themselves in a novel, complex situation vis-a-vis broadcast licensees in television and radio. The agencies have been charged with being more concerned with maintaining friendly relations with the broadcasters (on whom they depend for free time in fund-raising activities) than with a vigorous, no-holds-barred drive to compel licensees to carry anti-smoking messages.

The charges arose after John F. Banzhaf III, a young New York attorney, complained to the Federal Communications Commission that WCBS–TV, the CBS station in his city, refused to grant him time to broadcast anti-smoking messages as counter propaganda to the cigarette commercials that the station regularly carried. The FCC subsequently advised licensees that they would be expected to grant free time to public health agencies for anti-smoking messages, in the ratio of one such message to every three cigarette commercials broadcast. The ruling was based on the commission's Fairness Doctrine, which governs station policy in public issues of a controversial nature.

The broadcasters, who are fighting the Fairness Doctrine generally, argued before the FCC that the commission has no authority to extend the doctrine to product commercials. Mr. Banzhaf, in the posture of a lone defender of the public interest, supported the FCC during a challenge period, relying entirely on his own meager funds and dedicated effort. The National Interagency Council on Smoking and Health (a confederation of voluntary and governmental health agencies) entered no petitions during the proceedings to support the FCC rule, although it did send the commission a letter of nonlegal support.

The National Association of Broadcasters, after the FCC had reaffirmed its original decision, asked a circuit court in Richmond, Virginia (tobacco country), to overrule. Banzhaf, in a quick legal maneuver, filed an appeal in a District of Columbia court, presumably to challenge the FCC decision (which be backs), but really to get the matter into what he considered a more favorable court. In addition, at the recent World Conference on Smoking and Health, the young attorney accused the health agencies of timidity for not entering the legal fight. I can't buck the mighty broadcasters alone, he said. Why don't you support me with funds and legal counsel, or hire independent counsel, or enter the case yourselves? The health agencies said their lawyers told them to stay out of the legalities, to offer only expert testimony on the link between cigarettes and health, and that the FCC did not need any assistance in fighting its case.

The health agencies, which have been in this fight a long time, are irritated by the driving young attorney who stole all the thunder with his forthright attack at the world conference. They commend him for his original appeal to the FCC, but they assert that he obscures the formidable record of the agencies. The conference, for instance, adopted recommendations for intensifying anti-smoking education via the mass media. One recommendation urged that the agencies "must exercise every means at their disposal to sustain the FCC decision."

If the broadcasters lose and the FCC wins, the public gets $50,000,000 worth of free time on TV—and the same amount on radio—to educate the people, especially teenagers, on the mounting scientific evidence linking death and disability to smoking cigarettes. Effective use of the time by the research and health agencies would no doubt persuade the cigarette companies to stop advertising on TV and radio, for they would actually be subsidizing the opposition. The eventual impact on the Congress could be important. The legislators have temporized with the Cigarette Labeling Act of 1965, putting their money on the broadcast industry's self-regulation, plus general education. Both phases have failed. Smoking is up, deaths are higher—and the tobacco companies have launched their "longer" smokes, which can be deadlier than the shorter. It is difficult to understand why the health agencies persist in staying out of the courts in this fight when they say they must use "every means" in the struggle. They may be following their legal advisers in good faith; but to the public, their behavior is contradictory.

The only true wealth this nation has is our children. An overly cautious posture by the health agencies is irresponsible. The public gives them funds to use in the public interest. Joining the fight in the courts would be impressive education for all concerned. To hesitate is public disservice.

COMMENTARY

The nation's voluntary health agencies elected not to join John F. Banzhaf III in his campaign to secure time on television and radio for anti-smoking messages; but other organizations and individual citizens rallied to his support. The young attorney wrote the critic that, had it not been for the SR piece above, and the consequent attention which it drew to his work, his early, lone effort would have expired. The critic remembers this—and other instances where his pieces have had some salutary impact—whenever he is afflicted by Mad Hatteritis, by idle ships upon painted oceans, and by *déjà vu*.

As for Banzhaf, his organization, Action for Smoking and

Health (ASH) successfully prosecuted his fight against cigarette advertising on the air to the threshold of the Supreme Court. Congress legislated; and at midnight, January 1, 1971, tobacco advertising on television and radio in the United States ceased (the legislators accommodated the broadcasters by setting the ban for the end of the first day of the new year, instead of for the last day of the old year, so that the networks would not lose their customary revenues derived from tobacco advertisers who buy commercial time on the sportscasts of the annual New Year's Day football games played around the nation).

ASH then turned its attention to other areas where consumers need protection—misleading advertising, provision for no smoking sections on airlines, and the banning of smoking on interstate buses.

THE QUIET MERGER   *February 4, 1967*

THE RECENT APPROVAL by a majority of the Federal Communications Commission of the merger of American Broadcasting Companies, Inc. (ABC), into the International Telephone and Telegraph Corporation (ITT) is a sobering reminder of the portentous need in this country for a national organization that will ably represent the public by continually scrutinizing the actions of the FCC. People will stir up storms over a single dubious program. Yet the largest transfer of broadcasting properties in history was made without the slightest whisper of public understanding or protest.

Several members of the Congress raised questions during the proceedings, and small-business committees of the House and Senate have suggested studies of the FCC's action—but the motions are of moot value. If the Congress should hold hearings on the FCC decision and find it unsatisfactory, it couldn't do anything about it anyway, unless it rewrote the statutes governing the FCC. The transfer of seventeen radio and television stations and the ABC network and its affiliated stations, has been officially approved, placing one of the three largest purveyors of news and opinion in America under the control of one of the largest conglomerate corporations in the world, a company that derives 60 per cent of its

earnings from foreign sources, and 40 per cent of its domestic
income from defense and space contracts.

The four commissioners who approved the merger said that it
would serve the public interest by strengthening ABC's capacity
to compete effectively with the other two networks. They said
that ITT's financial help would enable ABC to enhance its
programing services to the public, and that ITT, which now wholly
owns ABC, would give support to the advancement of UHF
broadcasting. Commissioners Bartley, Johnson, and Cox dissented.

Nicholas Johnson, the newest member of the FCC, wrote in an
eighty-four page dissent: "The majority's treatment of this case . . .
makes a mockery of the public responsibility of a regulatory
commission that is perhaps unparalleled in the history of
American administrative process." Robert T. Bartley, in his
opinion, asserted: "The commission has rushed into an approval of
the merger without more than superficial attention to a study from
the U. S. Department of Justice in which it states that the merger
raises substantial anti-competitive questions." He warned of
"the inherent danger of the broadcast operations' becoming a tool
and image-builder for the corporate conglomerate . . ." Johnson
asserted that the ITT take-over would tend to reduce competition
in broadcasting and that "the public interest will be significantly
harmed by the merger."

At first no hearing at all was to be held. When Commissioner
Bartley insisted on "a full evidentiary hearing," a compromise
oral hearing was set; it lasted two days. "The most notable
peculiarity of the 'oral hearing,' " Johnson said,

> was the total absence of any party whatsoever representing
> the public . . . There was no cross-examination of a single
> spokesman for the applicants. There were no witnesses
> whatsoever presented by the staff. The applicants came with
> able lawyers, economists, businessmen, and distinguished
> citizens. The commission had none . . . To say that the
> individual commissioners were there to represent the public is
> to totally miscomprehend the administrative process at this
> commission. A commissioner has but one legal and one

engineering assistant . . . Between them, ITT and ABC combine financial resources represented by total gross revenues well in excess of $2 billion annually. It is questionable whether the entire staff of the FCC (with an annual budget of $17,000,000) would be adequate match for such corporations . . .

There is not the space here to begin to report adequately the complex issues involved. The whole point is that not even professional observers of broadcasting could begin to study the transfer until after the FCC order was a *fait accompli*. The merits of the case cannot be debated here, nor can the efforts of ABC and ITT to effect the merger be questioned; their executives pursued personal and corporate goals that may or may not be in the public interest.

The majority of the commission relied on the promises of the applicants never to let conflict of interests prejudice ABC's handling of news and public affairs programs. Broadcast journalism, said the majority, demands "eternal vigilance" and it "will receive our continuing scrutiny." Countered Commissioner Johnson: "The kinds of decisions which this merger will encourage are not susceptible to scrutiny even by the most vigilant agency. And the Federal Communications Commission has the well-earned reputation of being less than a thoroughly vigilant agency."

On the matter of ABC's alleged need for financial strengthening by ITT, the two dissenting commissioners noted that the broadcasting company was doing very handsomely indeed. Actually, the financial assistance could flow the other way. Donald F. Turner, assistant attorney general, Antitrust Division, Department of Justice, in a letter to Chairman Rosel H. Hyde commenting on the proposed merger, said: "It was anticipated that after capital expenditures and debt repayment, and assuming ABC continues in third place, it would yield a cash flow approaching $100 million between 1966 and 1970, almost all of which was thought by ITT to be available for reinvestment *outside* the television business." A month later Mr. Turner asked the FCC to stay the merger, reconsider its approval, and reopen the proceedings. ABC and ITT agreed to delay the merger until February 2, but the commission gave no indication that it meant to take any action to reopen the case.

Two of our three national networks are now subsidiaries of conglomerate corporations wth important foreign investments and military contracts. It seems inevitable that CBS will eventually seek to make the act a threesome, giving it corporate advantages comparable to those now enjoyed by NBC and ABC. The FCC has got itself into a mind set in which transfers of broadcast licenses are made as a matter of routine: Anyone who raises questions is somehow flying in the face of free enterprise.

It is not a question of the integrity of the applicants; it is a question of risking so much on the assumption of that integrity, at a time when America is deeply involved in the affairs of foreign countries, not to speak of domestic conflicts of interest. Surely the public has the right and the need to be better informed, *in advance,* about a situation where, in Commissioner Johnson's words, "ITT as the owner of ABC constantly will be faced with the conflict between the profit-maximizing goals which characterize all business corporations and the duty to serve the public with free and unprejudiced news and public affairs programing."

Perhaps the dissenting commissioners should have sent up a signal—but even if they had, where are the public organizations with staff, with funds, with energies to keep on top of intricate dealings of corporate giants? Perhaps a foundation could provide the answer. Meanwhile, the public's interest lies in Commissioner Bartley's appeal to the Congress to "study the matter of licensing broadcast stations to corporate conglomerates and enact legislation definitive of national policy with respect thereto."

COMMENTARY

On January 1, 1968, ITT canceled its agreement with ABC and aborted the merger. Prior to that action, the FCC had granted the reconsideration sought by the Justice Department, but had reapproved the merger. The Justice Department took the matter to the U.S. Court of Appeals, District of Columbia; but while the court was deliberating, the merger was terminated.

FCC'S "TEENYBOPPER" UNDER FIRE   *April 12, 1969*

IN JUNE 1966, President Lyndon Johnson appointed Nicholas Johnson (no relation) to the seven-man Federal Communications Commission for a seven-year term. Commissioner Johnson's tenure to date has been marked by an activist regulatory philosophy. The main thrust of the work by this former professor of law at the University of California (he was also national maritime administrator, and prior to that a law clerk serving Associate Justice of the Supreme Court Hugo L. Black) has been directed at the achievement of a healthier level of competition in the communications industry, particularly broadcasting. He has been a vigorous dissenter, often alone, against majority FCC decisions that sustained multiple-ownership media practices, and he has objected to conglomerates that merge broadcasting structures with other corporate interests.

It was Commissioner Johnson who wrote the majority opinion in the Carterfone case, as a result of which independent companies have been permitted to attach their gear to the AT&T switching network. With other commissioners, he has helped to stimulate the development of public broadcasting as another option for viewers and listeners. The promotion of diversity through the greater use of UHF channels has been among his objectives. He has supported the general principle that citizen groups ought to know of their rights to compete, at license renewal time, for franchises that are granted to station owners—privileges heretofore renewed largely *pro forma* by the rubber-stamp Broadcast Bureau of the FCC.

Currently, he is at the center of a pattern of intense regulatory activity at the commission, along with his colleagues, particularly Kenneth A. Cox, and Robert T. Bartley, but the FCC has known activist phases before. Other so-called rebel commissioners, such as Fly, Durr, Hennock, Minow, and Henry, have come and gone. Nicholas Johnson may not have helped to achieve significant competition in broadcasting by 1973, when his term expires, but he will have contributed to the general recognition among broadcasters and communications lawyers that the industry badly needs a new trade journal to compete with *Broadcasting,* the magazine that now dominates the press of this important field. Published since

1931, *Broadcasting* provides the most complete coverage available of the FCC. Vital industry statistics may be more quickly found in *Broadcasting*'s annual review issues than in the commission's files, but in a deeper sense, the magazine is out of touch with the complex realities of today's rapidly changing communications world. It feeds its subscribers, especially in its editorials, a mix of images compounded of fantasy and propaganda. Its highly selective packages of information may support the biases and self-fulfilling prophecies of its readers, but these serve more to gratify the readers' emotions than to render them real service by independent, tough-minded analysis.

Such a performance is generally the rule in any trade press, and this fact is not overlooked in evaluating *Broadcasting*. Successful trade media mute the obvious nature of their role with acceptable rhetorical manners that are temperate in tone and accent. Generally speaking, this has been true in the past even of *Broadcasting,* but the magazine, in its treatment of Commissioner Johnson, has dropped its mask of good manners and revealed an *ad hominem* stridency that grows ever more shrill, to the uneasiness of more thoughtful broadcasters. This situation has come about because Johnson has refused to quit the agency despite the barrage of attacks leveled at him by the magazine. He hasn't been bought off by a better job. *Broadcasting* suggested this in an editorial in its March 17, 1969, issue: "To remove a commissioner appointed for a specific term without substantial cause . . . is a sticky business. Perhaps an offer of another position in government or on the bench, paying as well, would do it, and that prospect, it's hoped, will be pursued."

A look at the record is instructive—thirty pieces of news and editorials (the two are often hard to separate), beginning December 5, 1966, and ending March 17, 1969. They reveal a pattern that emphasizes slogan and invective rather than the serious debate of issues on their merits. The pattern begins with scorn and disdain, and escalates to almost preemptory commands to President Nixon to fulfill his campaign promises to rein in the government's regulatory agencies. In 1966, the magazine took early editorial notice of Commissioner Johnson in connection with his objections to the aborted ABC–ITT merger. Although the

editorial answered briefly a point about conflict of interests between
the conglomerate and the network, it made three irrelevant
thrusts. It said that both Johnson and Commissioner Cox "seem to
dote on" publicity; it noted that Johnson was Mr. Cox's "thirty-two-
year-old disciple"; and it warned them that "the Administration
wouldn't relish action that would frustrate more aggressive
competition among the three major networks." The magazine
generally kept its cool in future editorials and news briefs when
dealing with Johnson, but its tone grew increasingly sharp, as the
commissioner, often with Cox and Bartley, challenged routine
license renewals, fought against concentration of media control,
and wrote and spoke out publicly about program surveillance by the
commission.

Broadcasting warned the commissioner that he was "not
winning friends"; it called him a "teenybopper" and "the shrill and
frequent critic of the actions of his elders." It rebuked the National
Association of Broadcasters, the major trade group, for providing
"a platform for an FCC member who makes a practice of beating
his captive audiences over the head." It charged unethical conduct
by Johnson in several situations, and printed replies by him and
others that countercharged misinformation and inaccurate quotation.
In the summer of 1968, *Broadcasting* abandoned any efforts to
deal with the merits of the positions taken by Commissioners
Johnson and Cox. An editorial in the June 10 issue looked with
favor on "various proposals for ripper legislation [which] would
enable the President to appoint a new commission, eliminating
those who want only to attack and destroy." Commissioner Cox was
accused of "espousing rigid control of program and business
affairs, in defiance of the law—a sort of socialism." It said of Mr.
Johnson, "his number should be up."

In its issue of February 17, 1969, the magazine asserted that
"an erstwhile reasonably safe majority [at the FCC] has lost control
to a makeshift radical minority." The article continued:

> It is shameful that at the root of most of the trouble-making is
> Nick Johnson, who, in his two-and-one-half years as a
> commissioner, has made a fetish of throwing sand in the FCC
> machinery . . . This brash, thirty-four-year-old self-anointed

savior, who was removed from his last job as maritime administrator, jams the FCC processing lines with his dissents, automatically opposes routine renewals, personally woos reporters, editors, and pundit-columnists with his double-spaced documents (SOP is single-spacing to save paper and money), maintains a private mailing list at government expense, and stands accused of brow-beating FCC personnel.

Interest in *Broadcasting*'s treatment of Johnson is heightened when one considers the credibility of the magazine's past cantankerousness. The trade journal said in its first editorial (1931): "Broadcasting in the U. S. today stands in grave jeopardy. Politically powerful and efficiently organized groups, actuated by selfishness and with a mania for power, are now busily at work plotting the complete destruction of the industry we have pioneered and developed." Somehow the plotters were foiled, and the AM-FM-television broadcasting industry went on to achieve an annual revenue of $3.2 billion in 1967. Nevertheless, in the June 10, 1968, editorial cited earlier, the apocalyptic strain surfaced again: "The nation is witnessing the most audacious and unethical assault upon broadcasters ever contrived. It could spell the end of American-Plan 'free' broadcasting."

As of March 17, 1969, the situation was still at emergency level. "The regulation of communications—particularly broadcasting —has reached a critical point, and is threatened with a breakdown. When the FCC takes actions that encourage reckless applications for occupied facilities worth millions, anarchy lies ahead unless remedial measures are invoked."

The truth or falsity of pictures in our heads may be tested against reality; we must ask whether or not they correspond with the pictures in other peoples' heads. *Television Age,* an advertising trade journal, commenting on Johnson in its January 2, 1967, issue, wrote: "He has kept out of the public glare, spending his time instead devouring information on communications, talking to industry leaders, and observing his FCC colleagues in action. Even his detractors agree that he has strong assets: he's intellectually curious and he is intellectually honest."

Newsweek, on April 20, 1967, reported: "He professes to

prefer the role of a youngish communications don, working
monkishly over his long opinions, and returning each evening to
his wife and three children in quiet suburban Maryland." *The
Christian Science Monitor* noted in an interview on June 12, 1967:
"Nearly 95 per cent of the time he has voted with the commission
majority, for whose chairman he has 'great respect and affection.' "
The National Association of Television and Radio Announcers in
August, 1968, gave Johnson an award with this citation: "A bold,
fearless, and humane man who has made the industry aware of its
legal and moral obligation to serve the communities of America,
making them cognizant that broadcasting is a privilege and not a
right." The U. S. Junior Chamber of Commerce voted him one of
its Ten Outstanding Young Men for 1967, noting that he had
"consistently worked to achieve a more coherent communications
policy in the best interests of the general public. Within a short
time, he has injected life and imagination into the workings of a
crucial government agency."

    Broadcasting has responded by harking back to the good old
days when the magazine's editors, linked importantly with major
corporate interests in broadcasting, gave marching orders to a
complacent commission that knew its place. Participatory democracy
is in the air; the people want in, even in broadcasting, and the
magazine cannot grasp the change.

    In the context of a democracy, there is nothing wrong with
the phenomenon of strong views in real conflict—even views that
cannot be reconciled in agreement or consensus. It is entirely in
order for a trade journal to present the views of its constituents as
vigorously as it can, and to attack the views of its opponents, but
the times demand reason in the trade press. Broadcasters help shape
our images of the world with the pictures and words they package
on TV and radio, but the images of the world that the broadcasters
have in their minds are shaped in large measure by their sources
of information. The purity of their wells of information is of grave
import to the public at large.

    Station owners who have read *Broadcasting*'s attacks on
Johnson are surprised to find, when they meet him at conferences
and discuss industry problems with him, that he is as reasonable as
the next fellow, intent on seeking out, with them, rational

policies for an astonishingly complex communications world.

The dissonance gives them pause, and has set some to doubting whether their major trade journal adequately meets their needs. Even prophets are necessary in our society to proclaim their passionately held private truths, but we desperately need ground rules for the process of opposition as we confront change. *Broadcasting* seems unable to tolerate opposing views without hostility; it demands that its truth alone must prevail.

A responsible trade press should maintain a creative sense of confrontation, channeling opposition rather than allowing it to engulf all other values and all other parties. Should *Broadcasting* succeed in "dumping" Commissioners Johnson, Cox, and Bartley, the issues will not disappear. Even President Nixon cannot exorcise the very real challenges that beset the industry. Total control is an obsession: it can destroy not only the opposition but the would-be controller. What the broadcasters and the public need is not "an enemy," but better data about the issues at stake, about the estimated costs and possible effects of alternative courses of action. Conscience ought to be persuaded, not manipulated nor coerced. If *Broadcasting*'s treatment of Nicholas Johnson of the FCC has brought about even a glimpse of this truth, and if a competitive, responsible trade journal is the result, then whatever else he may accomplish before 1973, an enduring contribution will have been left behind to the broadcasting industry by the embattled young "teenybopper" commissioner.

THE CASE OF THE RED LION   *July 12, 1969*

THE UNITED STATES SUPREME COURT'S DECISION on *Red Lion Broadcasting Company vs. FCC* has handed down one of the most important opinions of the century by telling the public what broadcasting is really about in this country. Broadcasting, according to the land's highest court, is not a message system serving the right of viewers and listeners to receive entertainment and information. Further, it is not an industry serving the right of entrepreneurs to cultivate, package, and sell audiences to sponsors for a profit. What broadcasting is, fundamentally, is the most powerful tool in our democratic society whereby the electorate may make informed choices involving its destiny—through the presentation and consideration of vital, controversial public issues.

Controversy is the heart of the First Amendment, said the justices in a unanimous (7–0) holding; Justice Byron White delivered the opinion of the court. The Constitution's guarantee against congressional abridgment of speech or press does not essentially protect your right to say what you please without interference from the government. It does not essentially protect your right to hear what I have to say or vice versa. The message that passes between us—to qualify for First Amendment protection in the broadcast area—must illuminate matters of great public concern.

"It is the purpose of the First Amendment," the court said, "to preserve an unhibited market place of ideas in which truth will ultimately prevail, rather than to countenance monopolization of that market, whether it be by the government itself or a private licensee."

The court also stated, "Speech concerning public affairs is more than self-expression; it is the essence of self-government . . . It is the right of the public to receive suitable access to social, political, esthetic, moral, and other ideas and experiences which is crucial here. That right may not be constitutionally abridged either by Congress or by the FCC." In adding the words "social," "esthetic," and "moral" to the conventional "political," and in further adding the phrase "other ideas and experiences," the court ventured far beyond hitherto limited interpretations of what constitutes "controversy." It is conceivable that, under these dicta, a viewer could assert constitutional support for his complaint against a network for canceling "The Smothers Brothers" television program. The broadcaster, under this ruling, has the duty, in exchange for his franchise, to seek out matters of public concern, to find and present citizens with clashing views on the subjects; and to see that the debates are presented vigorously and fairly.

If, during the course of a controversy, a person is verbally attacked on the air, or if a station broadcasts an editorial against a political candidate, it is not unreasonable, the court said, for the FCC to require that the victim or the candidate be permitted to make a response personally, rather than allowing only a proxy or the broadcaster himself to handle the reply. The FCC has

statutory and constitutional authority for promulgating specific
rules, Justice White wrote, to implement the Fairness Doctrine
which serves the ends and purposes of the First Amendment.
As for the licensee, he may be required "to share his frequency
with others and to conduct himself as a proxy or fiduciary with
obligations to present those views and voices which are
representative of his community and which would otherwise, by
necessity, be barred from the airwaves." The licensee must do this at
his own initiative and "at the broadcaster's own expense if
sponsorship is unavailable." His franchise, which is a temporary
privilege, may be taken from him when he applies for renewal
every three years, if he fails thus to serve the public interest.

The court brushed aside arguments by broadcasters that radio
and television frequencies are no longer scarce and that, therefore,
continued regulatory control is unnecessary. It rejected also the
assertion by the broadcasters that the Fairness Doctrine and personal
attack rules, at issue in the *Red Lion* case, would inhibit rather
than encourage controversy on the air. The threat is speculative,
the court replied; it will be dealt with should it arise. Observers
have been holding their breath for months while the Supreme
Court deliberated. Had it ruled against the FCC's Fairness
Doctrine in *Red Lion,* the results would have been momentous.
Licensees, under a narrower interpretation of the First Amendment
as applied to broadcasting, might have had unconditional control
over the manner in which public issues were presented on their
stations—if they elected to present any such issues at all. Section
315 of the Communications Act—the equal time requirement during
political campaigns—could easily have gone down next, for a
licensee could argue that, if it is unconstitutional to require him
to present both sides of a controversy, it is equally unconstitutional
to require him to present opposing candidates during an election.

Elections are inextricably tied to the presentation of issues
between elections. The Fairness Doctrine, between campaigns,
determines the context from which candidates and issues emerge.
The Fairness Doctrine and equal time are either equally valid or
monolithically vulnerable. If both had fallen, the whole principle of
regulation of the airwaves in the public interest would have lost
its meaning.

Broadcasters generally were aggrieved and surprised by the sweeping nature of the *Red Lion* decision. They had pressed the assault on the Fairness Doctrine with deliberate power and at great expense in legal fees. The Warren court, they reasoned, had broadened First Amendment protection recently in press and films. The *Red Lion* case—an action arising out of refusal by a Pennsylvania radio station to give reply time to Fred J. Cook, a reporter who had been attacked on its air—was considered by the industry as not the best case upon which to make a Supreme Court test of the Fairness Doctrine's constitutionality.

The organized broadcasters, through the Radio-Television News Directors Association, therefore, brought an independent action generally attacking the doctrine, which was joined to the *Red Lion* case by the Supreme Court. The broadcasters, anticipating a victory over regulatory powers that they have sought for forty years, have been stunned by what they consider the court's "overkill." Not only was the opinion unanimous, it was delivered by Justice White, who is labeled a conservative. It was as if the Supreme Court had decided once and for all to put the debate over the FCC's regulatory powers unequivocally at rest. Supporters of government control over broadcasters have been rejoicing in the court's decision and in its breadth.

It is well understood, nevertheless, that implementation of the court's decision depends on the majority of the FCC. As Robert M. Lowe showed in his exhaustive Senate subcommitte report on the Fairness Doctrine, almost 27 per cent of 3,000 stations replying to a questionnaire said that they never broadcast any programs dealing with controversial issues of public importance, while just under 70 per cent said that they "sometimes" carry such programs.

Yet, the FCC majority has continued imperturbably to renew the licenses of all stations thus reporting. Networks have generally been careful about possibly violating the Fairness Doctrine; they are constrained by commercial necessity to appeal favorably to all.

Operators of larger stations may be a bit more cautious in the wake of the Supreme Court's *Red Lion* decision. Some may feel irritated at having to grant time more widely than before, but the price is cheap for protecting a multimillion-dollar property in a top market. The *Red Lion* opinion is most significant for small, local

stations that are owned by strong-minded men, often of a
conservative political persuasion. In such cases, the court's ruling
provides a fulcrum upon which community forces may exert
influence to secure a larger voice for the public in broadcasting. Two
strategies are available, but at the moment the Congress is acting to
blunt both of them.

The first tactic involves competing applications for broadcast
licenses, filed at renewal time by well-financed commercial groups
who assert that they can make money operating the station but
serve the public better than the incumbent. The Pastore bill
in the Senate, and identical versions in the House would prohibit
the FCC from considering such "strike applications."

The second method comprises actions by citizen groups that
petition the FCC to deny renewals of stations for allegedly not
operating in the public interest. A tentative decision on tax-reform
reached by the House Ways and Means Committee would forbid
private foundations from granting funds to such groups which
seek "to influence the decision of any governmental body." Since
citizen groups depend on foundations for the funds required to
plan and carry out monitoring studies and legal actions before the
commission and the courts, the tax-reform measure, if passed, would
effectively cut the ground from under citizen groups that wish to
scrutinize the behavior, in their communities, of station licensees.
Ironically, broadcasters maintain very expensive lobbies in
Washington to influence government agencies, and are permitted
by law to deduct the cost in tax returns.

As a possible consequence of the *Red Lion* case, a group
representing the public interest by this time may have already
petitioned the FCC to institute a rule that would require all
stations to maintain, for public inspection and use, audio logs and
tapes of all broadcast controversial program material, as well as
records of network programs not cleared by local stations. At present,
groups challenging licensees at renewal time find it difficult to
build cases that support charges of inadequacies in station
performance because vital records and tape exhibits either have
never been kept or have been withheld or destroyed.

The *Red Lion* case is a historic assertion of the public's stake
in the effective use of the broadcast media for the ends of

self-government. But the court can only pronounce; it cannot legislate or implement. The power to make *Red Lion* practical rests with the public. The Congress—elected representatives of the people—seems dedicated to the proposition that the people shall remain unorganized, unfinanced, and powerless to secure the use of the airwaves in the public interest. One wonders if any message system can be devised that will get through to the politicians.

THOSE SUBSTANTIAL LICENSES   *February 7, 1970*

IN A RECENT modification of the statutory framework that governs broadcast licensing, the FCC played an intriguing game with semantics in which it pitted the word "better" against such substitutes as "substantial," "solid," "strong," "ample"—all to the detriment of the public interest.

In *Policy Statement on Comparative Hearings Involving Regular Renewal Applicants,* the commission said that it will renew the license of an incumbent broadcaster who can show that his program service has been "substantially attuned to meeting the needs and interests" of his area, instead of taking the contested channel from him and awarding it to a new applicant who would be willing to do a "better" job of program service. The concept of "better" service is what the Congress intended in the 1934 Communications Act. The idea was to promote competition and get the best service possible. No one should have a permanent right to a license; a new entrant who proposes to exceed the incumbent's level of performance should win the license no matter how excellent the past record has been.

The commission, in replacing "better" with "substantial" (the latter undefined, not even quantitatively), reasons that it is unfair to the incumbent who has rendered substantial service to have his license captured by an applicant who merely *promises* something better. Fly-by-night entrants can promise the stars and not deliver, or give the property a quick milking and run. If the "solid" broadcaster can't be protected, the FCC's reasoning runs, chaos will reign; the industry's financial underpinnings will erode; the public interest will suffer. Predictability and stability of operation, the FCC decided, win against the benefits of the unadulterated statutory spur. Even Commissioner Nicholas Johnson (the lone dissenter in a 6–1 decision) says that there may be small gains under the new policy: Given "harsh political reality," it is a "negotiated compromise of sorts." He dissents "with no feelings save understanding, frustration, and sorrow . . ."

What it all means is that—in an admittedly tangled web of complexities—the FCC has taken the position that the money stakes in licenses have grown too high, never mind what the Congress intended in 1934. The operators are entitled to reasonable protection; therefore, keep the better licensees in business permanently and try to bring the poor performers up to that "substantial" level. It would have been more accurate to say that there really are no fly-by-nights. Even the FCC policy statement notes that it requires a lot of money to qualify for a license; furthermore, the commission can detect and knock out fly-by-nights very quickly.

But suppose an incumbent who is doing a substantial job is challenged by a new applicant who says he can do a better one. There could still be a comparative hearing (as the statutory scheme provides) in which all the relevant issues are weighed. The FCC, after considering the full spectrum of issues, performances, promises, cross-ownership, diversification, minority representation, could then determine whether incumbent or applicant would better serve the public interest. If the new entrant wins the license, the FCC might require him to purchase from the loser the necessary properties involved in the operation—at reasonable cost— thus protecting the incumbent from unwarranted financial loss in the transfer. This requirement would preserve the sharpness of the competitive spur.

As it is, that spur is dulled. Under the new policy, as with the old, a hearing is set when a challenge is filed, but the new hearing, unlike the old, is divided into two parts. In the first, the challenger cannot propose his better service; he can only try to show that the incumbent's service has not been substantially attuned to the needs and interests of his community. The hearing is restricted. If the FCC examiner quickly decides that the incumbent has performed solidly (again, standards are vaguely defined), the hearing is summarily terminated and the license is renewed.

The hearing enters phase two only if the examiner finds less than substantial service or if the case is close. Only then are all the relevant issues examined and the better service question considered. It is difficult to see how any objective judgment can be made within the restricted confines of the present hearing procedure. Adequate determination can be made only if the challenger is permitted to point out unmet needs and to say precisely how he will meet them.

Even the commission concedes that its formula lacks "mathematical precision." It asserts that the details can be hammered out in future cases, given the good faith of all parties, including the interested public. Perhaps—but in dulling the competitive spur in favor of protecting the industry, the FCC leaned in the wrong direction. It gave the broadcast lobby the better and left the public with the substandard. The commission acted to bail out the Congress, after Senator John O. Pastore's bill, aimed at killing license challenges and comparative hearings altogether, ran into stiff and unexpected opposition from citizen groups, including representatives of the black community, who dubbed it a racist measure. Leading the fight against the Pastore bill (now quietly dead) were Black Efforts for Soul in Television (BEST), the National Citizens' Committee for Broadcasting, the United Church of Christ, the newly formed Citizens' Communications Center in Washington, D. C., and Action for Children's Television (ACT), a Boston mothers' group.

BEST and the Citizens' Communications Center have challenged in the courts the legality of the FCC policy statement as a device to make substantive law. The Center's director, Albert H. Kramer, has asked why the commission did not elect to hold open hearings so that the public could be heard on this controversial matter of great importance. The FCC might reply that it did not make new policy. The organizations that successfully opposed the Pastore bill might now consider joining in the new court fight, to see that the public interest is more widely represented. The new FCC policy at least provides for restricted hearings in license challenges. But in creating or clarifying the new procedures, the commission acted without any hearings. In that

sense it went as much against the public interest as the Pastore
bill sought unsuccessfully to do.

ACT WITH ACT   *March 7, 1970*

THE FCC made quiet history recently when the commissioners
published a notice which they had accepted for filing. The notice
asked for comments on a succinct proposal by Action for
Children's Television (ACT), a Boston-based group of mothers
that is rapidly acquiring national prominence. ACT asked the FCC
to rule that each station, as part of its public service requirements,
carry at least fourteen hours of children's programing, on a weekly
basis, in specified time periods, for preschool, primary, and
elementary school groups. ACT also asked the commission to make
a rule that would bar sponsorship of, and commercials, on children's
programs, and to prohibit performers on such programs from using
or mentioning products, services, or brand names.

The FCC's action came rather quickly after ACT committee
members Lillian Ambrosino, Judith Chalfen, Peggy Charren,
Evelyn Sarson, and Joann Spiro had met with the commissioners in
Washington, D. C., and submitted their proposal. Interested
observers should understand that a request for comments (within
thirty days, but extensions can be arranged) indicates that the
commission is neutral on the proposal. Actually, no one believes
that the FCC seriously contemplates any such revolutionary step.
The commission may wish to prod the networks into more
children's programing; or Dean Burch, the new chairman, may be
setting a precedent that will be useful in an expected move on the
"indecency" front.

Viewed in historical context, however, the request for comments
bristles with speculative possibilities. Only twice before has the
FCC approached the sensitive areas of program categories and
content—domains left entirely to the discretion of licensees. In 1947,
the commission's famous Blue Book study proposed minimum hours
of public service broadcasting, but the idea was shelved after stormy
protests from the industry and the Congress. In 1960, the FCC set
forth certain categories of programs that all stations were expected

to carry. A licensee's record in this area is still part of application and renewal procedures, but it is a notorious fact that stations that carry no news and public affairs programs (two of the categories) have had their licenses routinely renewed. In justifying its failure to act, the FCC has traditionally cited the Communications Act of 1934, which bars the commission from censorship and excludes stations from common carrier law.

Over this background now falls the shadow of the commission's request for comments on the ACT proposal. If the FCC can request comments on children's programing, why not on other types of broadcasting? The commission could reason that the law traditionally recognizes children as a special case, and that action taken in that area cannot serve as precedent for action in others. It may be agreed that the proposed prohibition in the content area of commercials on children's programs falls in the special case area and may not be transferred to other content areas. But it also may be reasoned that a requirement to carry fourteen hours a week of children's programing in specific time periods is a category request, and that the FCC, in the past, has asserted its legal power to regulate categories. If the commission is willing to discuss rule-making for categories in children's programs, why not discuss rules for categories in news and public affairs?

Stations need not be required to carry such programs without advertising (an unwarranted extension of the children's special case), but they could be required to carry news and public affairs on a sustaining basis. For concerned television viewers, the immediate opportunity lies in accepting the FCC's invitation to comment on the ACT proposal. The Boston mothers have shown one way to effective reform. They have harnessed a sense of outrage at the commercialization of children's programs and taken legal steps.

Parents who suffer silently can now act with ACT by filing comments with the FCC, pro or con. The procedure is simple but must be technically correct. The Citizens' Communications Center will supply free legal and administrative assistance and duplication of documents at cost. The address is 1816 Jefferson Place, N. W., Washington, D. C. 20036. (Telephone: 202-296-4238. Ask for Albert H. Kramer.)

COMMENTARY

Following the publication of this piece, the Citizens' Communications Center, in Washington, D. C., received several hundred requests for assistance from individuals who wanted to support the ACT petition before the FCC. The response imposed a severe strain on the limited staff of the center; but the work was done; and the FCC's file on ACT's petition (as of this writing it is still in the commission's procedural machinery) contains the greatest number of citizen filings on one case in the history of the regulatory agency. Time will tell how much real action will be the final result: but if citizen participation truly has the power to effect change in broadcasting, this action was a beginning.

CHAPTER THIRTEEN

A Noble Discontent
and Glimpses of Perfection

The Mariner, whose eye is bright,
Whose beard with age is hoar,
Is gone . . .

THE CONTACT is broken: as suddenly as he appeared to the Wedding
Guest, so now does the Mariner vanish. The Wedding Guest,
"stunned," turns from the Bridegroom's door "a sadder and a wiser
man," but the final line carries the ultimate thrust of the poem:
He rose the morrow morn.

The rising, and "the morrow" and "morn" are fresh reaffir-
mations of the principle of the dialectical third beat—a sense of a
new beginning, an ingression of reinvigorating energy. Presumably,
in our exegesis, the Wedding Guest is now prepared to enter upon
his own career of cell-firing, to join the critical fraternity at a higher
level of power. What of the reader, selectively stopped in Chapter I,
whose motor started revving, when critical contact between him and
the Mariner-critic was first established? If he has successfully been
held by "skinny hand" or "glittering eye" or by varying combinations,
at different times, of both arresting forces—then, by all the ground
rules of our self-serving game, his own motors should now be revving
at a somewhat higher speed. He has suffered an exposition of the
prescribed dialectical method of criticism, a delineation of its alleged
theories of being and of value, and a long pursuit of the critic's
intellectual history, as the latter retraced his steps in his dialectical

collisions with the brute facts of broadcasting among a variety of arbitrary categories of subject matter.

From all this, hopefully, the reader has gained a few insights, has been stimulated to challenge, reject, accept, ponder, or be perplexed at the critic's suggestions or conclusions. If the critic is to fulfill his contract with the reader satisfactorily, he must make an attempt, even now at the moment of his own leave-taking, to answer the final question, "So what?" to the long arpeggio that he has been developing. He must provide "the chordal collapse." Let me attempt to do so now by touching again the cool, lucid intellectualisms of Whitehead, who has, through the growing years, fired my own cells with so great an amount of valuable, lasting critical energy. Whitehead writes, in *Adventures of Ideas:*

> In all stages of civilization the popular gods represent the more primitive brutalities of the tribal life. The progress of religion is defined by the denunciation of gods. The keynote of idolatry is contentment with the prevalent gods.
>
> The factor in human life provocative of a noble discontent is the gradual emergence into prominence of a sense of criticism, founded upon appreciations of beauty, and of intellectual distinction, and of duty . . .
>
> For European thought, the effective expression of critical discontent, which is the gadfly of civilization, has been provided by Hebrew and Greek thought . . . Between them, the Hebrews and the Greeks provided a program for discontent. But the value of their discontent lies in the hope which never deserted their glimpses of perfection.

The "gradual emergence into prominence of a sense of criticism" is the factor that provokes "a noble discontent," whose value lies in hope that never deserts "glimpses of perfection." If the emergence or sharpening, in the reader's mind, of a sense of criticism has been encouraged by his collisions with the rime of the modern critic, then he will have for his future use a pattern, a paradigm, a number seven central organizing notion of a method of criticism, a way of life, promised him fitfully in small doses as the critic developed his concept of the three. A dialectical critic, as I have defined him, is continually pushing and pulling, somewhere along the equatorial middle, between the contrary poles of "noble discontent" and "glimpses of perfection."

This is the highest mountain top at which he may operate, the Everest of the critical perspective. Coleridge, as we have noted before, was keenly aware of the equatorial equation, and built it into *The Rime of the Ancient Mariner* at many points. One such crucial point occurs in Part V of the poem, when the Mariner's destiny is the object of a tug-of-war between the troop of angelic spirits that seek to carry him safely home, and the vengeful Polar Spirit that seeks to hold him in its grip, for the murder of the Albatross. The sun, "right up above the mast," had fixed the ship to the ocean:

But in a minute she 'gan stir,
With a short uneasy motion—
Backwards and forwards half her length
With a short uneasy motion.

Then like a pawing horse let go,
She made a sudden bound: . . .

The "sudden bound" breaks the grip of the detaining Polar Spirit; and the ship, carrying the penitent Mariner, is set on the course that will finally carry him home. For the critic, the "sudden bound" can never be a final resolution: it can only be another third beat for another small discovery in the unending circuitry of novel togetherness. But for the critic, the "short uneasy motion" (Coleridge repeats the phrase in order to emphasize its rhythm) "backwards and forwards" is the inescapable pulsation of the ever-recurring pattern of noble discontent and glimpses of perfection.

The pieces which the critic selected for this final chapter were chosen to illustrate this pulsation. A critic is entitled to discontent; that is his business: but his discontent is at its best when it is "noble," that is, when it strives to be "lofty and exalted in character, showing greatness and magnanimity." There ought to be nothing mean or petty in dialectical discontent. Indeed, there are revealing connotations, in Germanic, Greek, Latin, and Old English offshoots of the proto-Indo-European root of the word "noble," which is *gnō,* denoting "to know." The Greek form gives "thinking, judging, inter-preting." The Old English gives "friendship, kinfolk"; and the Latin suggests "connoisseur." Thus, when I speak of noble discontent, I mean to signify not only expert and thoughtful judgment but also friendly, human criticism which seeks to bind and cement rather than to antagonize. And when I speak of glimpses of perfection, I mean to imply a sense of excellence, wholeness, and the propensity for setting extremely high standards and for refusing to be content with anything less. But this refusal, again, is not a narrow perfection-ism, but a call to the slumbering quality of excellence which, it is the critic's faith, waits to be awakened in every individual.

The reader may find, in the pieces that follow, a discontent with parochialism and a reaching for universals in human experience. He may find an elegy over the decay of high principles in the neutrality of ethically value-free professionalism. He may find a hymn to the stubbornness and contagion of innocence, "honest people interacting with each other in an honest way." He may find disdain for exploi-tation of the human personality, and enunciations of a moral im-perative to men of one culture to value the dignity of the individuals of another culture. He may find appeals for the expansion of human consciousness to build bridges between the past and the present for the instruction of mankind. He may find idealism, a sense of the brotherhood of man, a wish for individual tranquility and peace, as well as a sense of defeat and of the shattering of the family of man, at global, personal, and national levels. But the affirmations and the negations—at a high level of mutuality and benevolence among men and nations—are indispensable, one to another, in the critic's armament. They are dialectical necessities, entropy and negentropy, life and death.

When, in *The Rime of the Ancient Mariner,* a spectral ship approaches the becalmed vessel with its thirst-tortured sailors, it carries two nightmare figures, Life and Life-in-Death. They dice for the Mariner, and it is Life-in-Death that shouts: "The game is done! I've won! I've won!" If Coleridge had constituted the gambling duo as Life and Death, and if either had won, such an outcome would have been a renunciation of the critical process. The essence of a living system is process, relationships, transaction. We refer again to the Second Law of Thermodynamics and Carnot's Principle: it holds that physical energy can be effective only where there is resistance formed by two levels of differing potential. There is a gap, and energy flows to close it; when equilibrium is established, there are only "frozen assets" and no "work." In the critical universe, as in the physical, when the gap is eliminated—when either noble discontent or the glimpse of perfection triumphs completely in transaction—then there is entropy. The dialectical necessity renders such an event impossible. Heaven or Hell, triumphant and exclusive, is entropy, nothingness. They both require Earth as their dialectical field of exchange.

The critic, moving backward and forward with his short uneasy motions, calls for the victory of perfection over discontent, but he neither expects it nor actually wishes it. The true critic is not in the business of liquidating criticism: a non-dialectical universe is to him an unthinkable third beat; a discovery which cannot be transcended is death. Does the critic then want no improvement, no betterment, either in broadcasting, in the world, or in the practice of criticism? Not at all: it is a question of distances. Mankind moves but slowly, and the severest changes, the greatest steps that it might take in the foreseeable future, would be giant enough to bring about a sense of progress. Many contemporary philosophers have renounced the idea of progress—at least, at its literal level. They either fear change as change for the worse not the better, or they conceive change to be organic, a cycle of birth, growth, maturity, and decay. To the Greeks, progress had little meaning: their Golden Age was behind them in the past, a myth. To the modern mind, which holds man to be a Promethean partner in the shaping of his destiny, change is both a desirable and a realistic possibility—somewhere on the equator between despair and optimism. The critic, in human or meta-human terms, using gross or fine measures of time and space, can reconcile progress and dialectic.

As the Mariner departs, so exits the critic, leaving his reader with a prescription—to rise the morrow morn. Join, he perorates, the ship of critics who make sudden bounds between noble discontent and glimpses of perfection. Begin the cell-firing, the *trampin'* (a word which the reader will find in the Marian Anderson piece), and the dialectical play of the skinny hand and the glittering eye. Have you filled your quota of Wedding Guests this week? They are all around you, waiting for fresh ingressions of critical energy, just as you yourself wait for your Mariner. It is not really true that the Wedding Guest in Coleridge's poem was stopped *unexpectedly* by the Mariner. Each Wedding Guest *knows* that the Mariner is coming and expects his arrival. Like the five wise virgins in the New Testament (Matthew 25) who kept their lamps trimmed with oil, so that they would be ready for the bridegroom when he suddenly appeared—each Wedding Guest is alert for the midnight hour, an equatorial point.

It is the moment when his own critical energy has run down, gone stale, flat, and needs that invasion, that critical aggression from without. The expected cell-firing, when it comes, will inaugurate a new dialectical struggle, with its ambivalences, its frustrations and delights, and its miraculous rising the morrow morn. The "sudden bound," the exhilarating sense of going home will come to each individual critic, and perhaps, eventually, to the great critical mass. The exact time, place, and circumstance are all in the hands of the great Meta-Critic, who is an old hand at the dialectical game. Whitehead, to suggest critical fission, makes use of the number seven, which may be characterized as the millennial integer:

> . . . a great idea in the background of dim consciousness is like
> a phantom ocean beating upon the shores of human life in
> successive waves of specialization. A whole succession of such
> waves are as dreams slowly doing their work of sapping the base
> of some cliff of habit: but the seventh wave is a revolution—
> "And the nations echo round."

It is an old game which the revved-up Wedding Guest, Hermit-Mariner-Critic, joins. He is neither the first nor the last to enlist. It is a continuing conversation. Each critic enters the room, listens a while until he picks up the gist of the buzzing, booming confusion; then he joins the transactions, makes his meager contribution, and passes out of the room, rubbing elbows with another critic who is entering. Edmund Burke, the great conservative, wrote (in *Reflections* [1790]):

> Society is, indeed, a contract . . . It is to be looked on . . . with
> reverence; because it is not a partnership in things subservient

only to the gross animal existence of a temporary and perishable nature. It is a partnership in all science, a partnership in all art, a partnership in every virtue and in all perfection. As the ends of such a partnership cannot be obtained in many generations, it becomes a partnership not only between those who are living, but between those who are living, those who are dead, and those who are to be born. Each contract of each particular state is but a clause in the great primeval contract of eternal society, linking the lower with the higher natures, connecting the visible and invisible world, according to a fixed compact sanctioned by the inviolable oath which holds all physical and all moral natures each in their appointed place.

Burke was a man of the eighteenth century, a period when cosmologists rested contentedly on Newtonian cushions of a steady-state, clockwork, infinite universe, untroubled by the paradox inherent in a concept of finite matter distributed throughout infinite space and time. His notion of society's contract reflects the major scientific paradigm of his era, and is contaminated somewhat by its rather rigid monistic spirit. But aside from that cavil, in its sense of partnerships, of linkages, chains, and of metaphysical whispers, Burke's contract is the contract of Coleridge's fancy and imagination, of fixities and definites, and of Whitehead's creative advance into novelty.

It is the critic's contract.

COMMENTARY

It is altogether fitting that the selection of pieces which illustrate the theme of noble discontent and glimpses of perfection should begin with a column on the occasion of the passing of Edward R. Murrow. To his colleagues in broadcasting, and to many in the public, for whom he represented a popular and widely admired exponent of the art of broadcast journalism, no other figure, perhaps, contributed so much constructive discontent to the industry and so many examples of its finest product.

The critic knew him personally, having worked with him at CBS from 1945 to 1949. The first CBS Documentary Unit, mentioned in the piece, was headed by the critic, who remembers a telephone call he received from Ed Murrow backstage at the Library of Congress in 1945. Under Murrow's administrative leadership, the critic, then a writer-producer for CBS, had just concluded "Operation Crossroads," a special, one-hour radio documentary on the threat and the promise of atomic energy in the world. The broadcast featured, among other participants, Albert Einstein, Justice William O. Douglas, Archibald MacLeish, Henry A. Wallace, Dr. Harold Urey, Harold L. Ickes, Harold Stassen, and Mrs. Wendell L. Willkie. Murrow, calling to express his approval, said over the telephone to the critic: "Tonight broadcasting came of age."

MURROW'S LOST FIGHT   *May 22, 1965*

FRIDAY EVENING of the week Edward R. Murrow died, CBS Television presented a special one-hour program of excerpts from his radio and TV broadcasts. It was odd, and perhaps not without some significance, that "An Hour with Ed Murrow" was preceded by a cancellation announcement for a program called "The Great Adventure" and followed by a next-week-we-will-present announcement for a regularly scheduled entertainment show. Mr. Murrow's passing symbolized the end of a great adventure in broadcasting. His colleagues, who put together their deeply felt obituaries of Murrow at CBS radio and television, knew it. Newsmen at rival networks and local stations who paid their tributes were aware of it too. Actually, however, the broadcasting idealism that Murrow represented died many years ago, even before he left CBS to become the director of the U. S. Information Agency. But as long as he was alive, the illusion, if not the substance, survived. It was not Murrow alone that the newsmen saluted, but their own hopes, their own past. Most of them were his contemporaries; they were in Europe at the birth of broadcast journalism, shortly before and during World War II. Their professional baptism coincided with the war's high drama.

Amid the V-2 rockets in London, aboard a bomber over Berlin, with the parachute drop at Antwerp, Murrow and his fellow reporters were on the same ideological and emotional wavelength as their audience. It was a time of unity and expectation of a better world after the victory. The broadcasters came home after the peace, determined to maintain and extend the level of wartime aspiration and performance they had created. In London, shortly before the war's end, Murrow knew he would be returning to the States to become a program executive at CBS in news and public affairs. There was a general hope among newsmen that radio, which had helped defeat external enemies, would now be useful in fighting subtler battles against injustice and ignorance. In September 1946, Murrow established the first CBS Documentary Unit, "devoted exclusively to the production of programs dealing with major and international issues and involving extraordinary research and preparation." But after a few years the climate of idealism dissolved. The industry turned full stride to its market orientation.

Murrow left his administrative post and took up his work as a reporter, presumably because he felt more comfortable in that role. There is evidence to suggest that he had already seen the true outlines of the opposing forces in broadcasting. Television enhanced his prestige greatly; he was the prototype of the photogenic reporter on camera. Teamed productively with Fred W. Friendly, he was always imaginative and responsible, but his thrust into areas of political, social, and economic significance grew weaker. Occasionally the old Murrow bite was hard, as in his attack on Senator McCarthy; in "Harvest of Shame," a program about migrant farm laborers; and in some of the "CBS Reports" programs dealing with the integration struggle in the South. But shows like "Person to Person" and "Small World," however popular or engaging, hardly represented Murrow's real conception of the role of broadcast journalism. In 1958 he stated his fears about the trend in American broadcasting in a speech to the Radio and Television News Directors' Association.

In that speech, three years before Newton Minow's "vast wasteland" comments, Murrow found evidence, in one week's programing of the three networks, of "decadence, escapism, and insulation from the realities of the world we live in." He challenged television to "produce some itching pills rather than this endless outpouring of tranquilizers." He believed strongly in the potential of commercial television to "exalt the importance of ideas and information."

"The trouble with television," Murrow told his fellow broadcasters, "is that it is rusting in the scabbard during a battle for survival." It was really his final, most deeply felt word on broadcasting. "An Hour with Ed Murrow" failed to mention that 1958 speech. The sword was still in the scabbard.

AND AFTER TELEVISION   *June 2, 1962*

MOSCOW

A FIVE-MAN television documentary crew has recently finished shooting film here for an hour-long program which will give American viewers their first glimpse of elementary and secondary education in the Soviet Union. The program will be presented in the fall on the ABC–TV Bell and Howell series *Close-up,* which is produced by the network's Special Projects Unit headed by John Secondari. I was the writer member of the team.

One of the Soviet cameramen who participated in part of the project was introduced to us by our hosts, the Soviet Radio-TV Committee, as Vladimir. Tall, lean, and sandy-haired, with sharply outlined features, he could almost always be spotted by his gray cap and navy blue trench coat. Very early in the operation, Vladimir was seized with a passion to emulate Bill Hartigan, a genial ABC cameraman who handles his battery 16 mm. cameras with unorthodox flexibility, imagination, and intuitive skill. Vladimir was so impressed with the novelty of Hartigan's style, that when asked by our Soviet colleagues to cover a scene himself, he would strive constantly for the American cameraman's mobility. He knew the American could move the way he did only because his camera was equipped with a special wide-angle lens yielding constant focus —but Vladimir would often forget and have to be reminded of this in his enthusiasm for the American's style.

The Soviet Radio-TV Committee acknowledged that they were all stimulated by the operational procedure of the ABC team. They will probably experiment with and perhaps introduce some of these techniques in their own future documentary work. The experience recalls Toynbee's theory of the psychology of encounters among civilizations. The English historian has suggested that, in the past, nations faced with cultural "aggression" by their neighbors have

often permitted the intrusion of trivial strands (usually
technological) of the aggressor culture into their spiritual bodies
on the assumption that these could do no serious damage to the
defending culture. Toynbee says, however, that the flaked-off
splinter of the aggressor's technology, when absorbed, inevitably
draws after it the other "component elements of the social system
in which this splinter is at home . . ."

Thus, India, Japan, and even Russia have been unable to
"decontaminate" Western technology, once they have absorbed it.
Moreover, other strands of Western culture have invariably followed
after the technological Pied Piper. It may be that, on a modest but
nonetheless important scale, something like this may have happened
in the recent encounter between the ABC–TV documentary team
and their Soviet hosts.

The Russians—fulfilling an agreement made with James C.
Hagerty, vice president, ABC News and Public Affairs—had
selected a Moscow school as the scene for the filming. The plan
was to show, for half of a sixty-minute program, what Ivan's
education is like and then compare it, in the second half, with a film
to be shot on the crew's return to the United States, showing an
American Johnny's schooling. The Russians had set a ten-day
time limit for their end of the operation—time enough to photograph
the school life of a typical Soviet boy. Both the ABC crew and the
Russians, however, soon realized that the angle of observation was
too narrow, and that the two educational systems could not really
be compared usefully in this manner, differing as they do in their
ultimate objectives. So by common consent the scope of inquiry was
widened to show vocational-technical secondary schools in Moscow,
as well as a basic school which placed heavy emphasis on academic
training, and also to glimpse Pioneer Palaces and Houses of Culture
for Labor Reserves, which are important centers of extracurricular
activity for communist youth. The Russians granted Nick Webster,
the ABC producer, a four-day extension to accomplish the expanded
schedule. Since usually Soviet government bureaus are severely
compartmentalized and protocol complex, the step seemed
significant. Perhaps American attitudes were beginning to tell.

It had become quickly apparent to the Russians that the ABC
team was there to get the story and to transmit it as honestly as it

was able—against the grain of inescapable cultural prejudices. This assessment by the Russians of the crew's motives may have been the most important factor in their decision to expand the original agreement. Toynbee's notion of the penetrating power of a strand of cultural radiation worked even deeper in this encounter. Photographing Nikita Garanine, the sixth-grader chosen by the Russians, led to an interest in Alyosha, his ninth-grade brother. This in turn led to a request by the Americans to film the boys at home, so as to show the connection between family and school. After due consideration, this further penetration was permitted, and in the several days' shooting at home, mutually friendly relations were established with the boys' family.

Toward the end of the extended time period, crew and cameras were permitted into both Moscow University and an *Internat*, or boarding school, the prototype of all future institutions of basic communist education. Finally the Russians agreed that the network might scrap, if it chose, the original premise of the show, which was to compare Soviet and American schools, and utilize its full Bell and Howell hour in the fall for a view of Soviet schools in Moscow.

The evidence permits an obvious inference—namely, that the Russians are the gainers in this new design, winning as they do a broader platform for the material they chose to show us. The enlargement of scope creates, however, a stronger tension among the producers to counterbalance the Russian gain. Whatever the opposite pull in this interesting encounter, the interpenetration of attitudes cannot help but be civilizing. The ABC team (which included Mike Campus, Russian-speaking researcher, and Dudley Plummer, English sound recordist) came with Western curiosity to inquire into Soviet education. The Russian teachers responded, in their turn, with many questions about American pedagogy. The Radio-TV Committee has, furthermore, invited the ABC crew to return and to travel throughout the Soviet Union to film other documentaries. Hopefully, the adventure will bear fruit by way of a visit by a Soviet TV team to the U. S.

This was an exchange between one major American network and the Soviet government—something of a semi-official innovation. Sooner or later other networks should follow. The zeal of Vladimir, the Russian photographer, for the galloping camera of the

American Hartigan could well turn out to be a peaceful symbol and a hopeful portent. The wide-angle lens of television's cultural "aggression" operating at fundamental settings of human relationships, may contribute more to world peace than many a more formal diplomatic or political interaction.

GENERALS OR MUSICIANS? *July 1, 1967*

THREE PERIODS of history—ancient, the ninteenth century, and contemporary—meeting briefly on television during the Arab-Israeli war, produced a strange, moving commentary on man's quest for peace. On Monday evening, June 5, the networks were reporting heavy clashes between Egyptian and Israeli forces in the Negev and Sinai. CBS–TV was carrying a special report on the Mideast crisis, gathering together late news bulletins, old films of former Arab-Israeli fighting, and commentary by a military expert on the progress of the desert battles.

Channel 12 in Philadelphia (WHYY), the noncommercial station, coincidentally with the CBS report, had scheduled (in advance and quite by accident) a film of the Israel Philharmonic Orchestra, led by Joseph Krips, in a special performance in Tel Aviv of Beethoven's Symphony No. 9 (the "Choral"). This viewer kept switching from the local CBS channel 10 (WCAU–TV) to the educational station, unwilling to forego the pleasure of a full-scale television performance of Beethoven's work, yet impelled to seek the latest news and evaluation of the military engagements and the U. N.'s cease-fire efforts. The double exposure achieved an ironic climax in the dramatic finale, "The Hymn to Joy."

The baritone proclaimed the theme in the words: "Men throughout the world are brothers . . . In the haven of thy wings." Musicians and singers in an idealistic hymn to brotherhood—at the very moment that many men and women of the orchestra and chorus, possibly, had lain down their instruments, taken up guns, and were killing or being killed in defense of a homeland in which, if the choice were theirs, the citizenry would infinitely rather make music than war. As the CBS reporter told of the early Israeli victories, the image of the small nation was far from warlike. Conductor Krips bounced imperceptibly with smiling joy as he beamed at his players and singers. Indeed, of all the vivid cast on TV during the ongoing crisis, the most unwarlike appeared to be the Israeli Minister of Defense, General Moshe Dayan.

The outstanding quality projected by this incredibly successful military strategist and one-eyed warrior is an ebullient, childlike charisma of happiness. The contemporary image on television of peace-loving men fighting wars in the Holy Land is a mirror of biblical times. Nehemiah (Old Testament), the scholars assert, was endowed with unusual energy and, presumably, with exceptional charm. Like General Dayan, he served Israel with "rare single-mindedness." This cup-bearer to Artaxerxes Longimanus (465–424 B.C.) was permitted by Persian authorities to return to Jerusalem and rebuild its walls.

Geshem, an Arabian, was among the local enemies of the rebuilders of Zion. He mocked, scorned, despised, and tried to slay Nehemiah, his royal bodyguard, and Judean enlisted men. "Every one with one of his hands wrought in the work, and with the other hand held a weapon," reports Nehemiah in his first-person, on-the-spot account of the successful repairing of the wall.

The uncanny bridges that history builds between past and present were evident also in the debates in the Security Council of the U. N. Nehemiah's enemies, in seeking to abort the wall reconstruction in Palestine, sent messages and letters to him accusing him of trying to be king. If the walls were left unbuilt, Arab, Edomite, or Ammonite raiders could attack the Holy City at will. "Come now therefore, and let us take counsel together," they urged. To which Nehemiah, like Israeli representatives in the United Nations, replied: "There are no such things done as thou sayest, but thou feignest them out of thine own heart." He told his enemies, "I cannot come down . . . I am doing a great work . . . why should the work cease?"

The contemporary parallel departs here from the ancient. Israel talked in the halls of the United Nations, but it also fought; and it is prepared, apparently, to continue doing both, if necessary, in its struggle to pursue the works of peace. As for the nineteenth-century Beethoven, the schools were closed on the day of his funeral, March 26, 1827, and 20,000 people turned out. A stranger asked an old woman at a fruit store what the commotion was all about.

"Don't you know?" she said. "They are burying the General of the musicians." Between the ancient and the modern Zion stand men of all nations and races, struggling with the dichotomy that divides them, one from another and each from himself. Which would we all rather be—generals or musicians?

FOR ALL TO SEE *July 8, 1967*

A REAL HERO of the Middle East war and its aftermath, it became apparent after the recent convening of the United Nations General Assembly, is television. The medium has won another victory for reality over fantasy. The small screen, David-fashion, has slain with its smooth stone of truth the Goliath of bombast, rhetoric, and deception in international diplomacy. Domestic political conventions and election campaigns have had to accommodate themselves to the electronic mode, and now it is the turn of men who speak in the court of world opinion.

Why now and not before? We have had television coverage of sessions of the U. N. General Assembly and of the Security Council, and the confrontation was not apparent, the victory not plain. The crucial difference in television's image of the Middle East struggle was the collapsing of the time dimension that historically has separated fantasy and reality in wars. This was the sixty-hour war, and the explosion and implosion of information were almost simultaneous. The effect was to illuminate the whole context of the experience in so blinding a blaze of immediacy that propaganda could not survive. Statesmen must take notice—not only the Russians and the Arabs but the Israelis and the Americans. The medium, per se, is capable of sublime indifference to parochialisms.

The big drama on television when the General Assembly convened was the arrival of Premier Aleksei N. Kosygin to present the Soviet resolution condemning Israel as the aggressor in the swift war. Television's stage was set for him by President Johnson's morning address to educators in Washington and by Ambassador Goldberg's stepping aside to let the Russian delegate make the first speech to the United Nations. Mr. Kosygin's case, it quickly became clear, was hard line and familiar. It had all been said during the Security Council sessions.

The Premier spoke of Israeli arrogance and atrocities that brought to mind "the heinous crimes perpetrated by the Fascists during World War II." Viewers who had followed the Council meetings had been confused when they heard similar charges hurled back and forth across the table by representatives of both sides of the debate. How could you know which delegates were telling the truth? All nations fighting modern wars have lied during the actual conflict: but here, in the General Assembly, as the impassive Russian chief intoned the ritual of diplomatic obfuscation, an entirely novel element was present in the great Assembly chamber and in the minds of viewers striving for objectivity.

They had seen the war's images with their own eyes. The tragic conflict had unrolled like film on a projector in their living rooms, a great cinemascope classic. Slowly at first the scenes came, then more swiftly as Israeli censorship was lifted and the correspondents and their camera crews got around, until the scenario literally gushed forth from the fount of history like an *Iliad* cut to a ninety-minute special.

Viewers had seen the Egyptians in the streets of Cairo leaping exultantly for the holy war. They had heard the Arab chieftains calling for the liquidation of Israel. They had witnessed the Israeli troops going efficiently about their campaign with sadness and no lust for killing. In one of the most memorable television scenes, a young Israeli soldier, a musician, wounded and burned in his first day's fighting, wept more over the unwanted cruelty of the war than over his own pain. All communications are selective, and all are selectively perceived; but if objectivity can be approximated, the evidence that television had amassed in the battles, of who was out to get whom, was extremely persuasive.

Yet here was the Soviet Premier, followed by delegates from Czechoslovakia and Syria, rehearsing the old script of diplomacy, ignoring television's evidence, and building a case for future back-room bargaining. It was a traumatic experience for patient viewers whose hopes for peace are heavily invested in the U. N. One knew this was a mere holding operation with endless *pro forma* reiteration for the record by all sides. The real story had gone on behind the scenes. The medium has its message for the great and small powers, comfortable in their ritualistic verbalizing: Cut the script, speak to the point—and to people. When statesmen learn this lesson, as they must, perhaps television will have made a contribution to the search for peace.

The irony of it is that the fantasy of the diplomats should have been so ruthlessly exposed by a medium founded in this country so heavily on fantasy itself. If television can reshape diplomacy, there is hope that someday it may even reshape itself—if it turns its truth lenses inward.

THE LIGHT GOES OUT   *August 3, 1968*

TEN DAYS spent observing the local television scene has been a sobering experience: conversations with program executives of the BBC and ITV (commercial TV), with producers, media critics, research experts, and a member of the governing board of the Independent Television Authority, have produced the impression that a light has gone out in British broadcasting, an institution so long held up as a model of socially responsible and superior mass communication.

Rhetoric abounds among the BBC staff, talk of "serving the great audience," competing, giving "insight and delight," not "elevating the masses but taking programs seriously." Money problems loom large: so do the challenges of expanding facilities. There is an air of show biz in the mental processes of the creative people, but when one raises the questions of aims, purposes, and directions—the "whys" of broadcasting—responses are evasive, non-committal, or derogatory of "paternalism and missionary zeal."

The BBC's Royal Charter speaks simply of "disseminating information, education, and entertainment," but the corporation's reputation down the years came essentially from the manner in which Lord Reith, its first director general, interpreted that elusive triptych. The BBC, in the minds of observers overseas, is still riding the knightly Reith legend: the man of high moral and ethical principles who stamped the BBC with his own peculiarly Christian version of public service in the 1920's. When he walked out on the job in 1937, Lord Reith thought that the character he had given the BBC was fixed forever.

Lord Reith had fashioned a corps of nonprofessionals who came to him from the arts, sciences, and universities. They were hand picked; he indoctrinated them; and they shared his passion for putting out programs of high moral and intellectual standards. The World War II period was a sort of broadcasting interregnum, in which the corporation earned its reputation for truth in news, fighting to maintain its independence from the war government's Ministry of Information. When, in 1954, government authorization made commercial television competitive with the BBC, Reith's "old pros" were gone or on their way out. The fact of life for the "new pros" was competition, not a paternalistic monopoly. High principles receded before the wave of "share-of-audience."

The same creative people played musical chairs, moving from Aunty BBC to the more "gutsy" and popular domains of the commercial program companies. The BBC grew (one old pro describes it now as "a mastodon with a small brain"); policy making became a pluralistic sprawl. As guidance from above diminished, program executives gathered power. The government also asked the BBC to undertake new projects (color, local radio, a second channel), but deferred raising the license fee which Britons must pay for TV and radio. The Wilson Labor government at present is beset by too many headaches, foreign and domestic, to slap a tax rise on the restive, critical voters. Neither Conservatives nor Labor are eager to "mess with television."

In those nations where broadcasting has been controlled by governments or by an economy based on advertising, it has often been asserted that the solution for the ills of TV-radio lay in giving control of the media to the professionals. In the BBC the creative producers have the control, and the effect grows curiouser and curiouser. Programers are not immune to the urge for self-aggrandizement: they tend like others to build empires, and empire building is expensive. The way to justify more funds is to give evidence of public popularity. Thus, pleasing the great audience becomes an important priority. It is expedient also to be harmless to the Establishment. However, along the broader spectrum of information, education, and entertainment, BBC television maintains the appearance of autonomy in politics and of occasional seriousness in programing.

The asserted drive is to enjoy the best of both worlds—ratings and quality. Critics assert, for example, that BBC 2 was created especially to accommodate "cultural" programing, leaving BBC 1 free to slug it out with the commercial lads on ITV for audience numbers. The criterion for a successful BBC 2 program is how fast it can be moved over to BBC 1, thus demonstrating its catholic appeal. The ultimate result of BBC television programing (and the same must be said for the commercial schedules) is not essentially different from what may be seen today in Europe and the United States—generally speaking, an endless flow of pop, pap, and pomposity destined to be unmemorably consumed, which may superficially modify attitudes but which seems to change the world not one jot or tittle.

It is certain that the world needs changing, and if television is to be judged, the criterion ought to be the degree to which it stimulates scrutinizing and analysis of social institutions, including its own behavior. But this requires thought, and thinking has never enjoyed high ratings. Perhaps, commented an Englishman, if the light has gone out in the BBC, it is because it has also failed in British society where there is a malaise, a drift, and a perplexity not peculiar to the Isles. The BBC's highest accomplishment in television has probably been its probing of social pathology in programs that have dealt candidly with such matters as abortion, homosexuality, and the troubles of youth. This has been socially useful; but the lack of a clear philosophy of broadcasting is painfully apparent.

All this has a lesson for public television now experiencing the thrust for popular emergence in American broadcasting. The struggle here is also for autonomy and independence of the creative people. The danger on one hand is "nannying and patronizing the less well educated," and on the other, the scramble for large audiences that insist on being pleased. The hard middle road is beset by the temptations of self-aggrandizement: we, too, may wind up like the BBC, with a broadcasting model possibly the best in the world but not good enough. Programers without a philosophy are merely professional politicians or professional advertisers.

Lord Reith, in an address, commented on the Roman Empire: "On that hard pagan world, disgust and secret loathing fell, deep weariness and sated lust made human life a hell"; and he added later, in another context, the plea, "For God's sake prevent it happening here." The paradox is that we must save ourselves not only from true believers but also from those who believe in nothing but themselves.

FAIR FARE   *September 12, 1970*

IT BEGINS TO LOOK as if the FCC's Fairness Doctrine is unfair to the principle of fairness itself—in the absence of specific rules which say precisely who gets what time on the air for what purposes and how much and at what price. Such specific rules today exist only in cases that involve the right to reply to personal attacks and when a station endorses one political candidate in preference to others. A one-time declaratory ruling by the commission which allowed anti-smoking commercial spot announcements, is the only other case where specificity was involved. Otherwise the general principle, enunciated by the Supreme Court, that the right of the public to be informed by TV-radio on controversial public issues is paramount to the rights of all to individual or group access to the air, is put into the hands of the individual station licensee, to be interpreted at his personal "fiduciary" discretion.

If, in the licensee's judgment, he is presenting on the whole a balanced treatment of controversial issues, he may turn down a request for air time from someone who wishes to make a political, social, or esthetic communication to the public. Only the President appears to be exempt from this power: the Congress, according to a recent FCC decision, is not exempt, nor are pro- or anti-Vietnam-war groups, anti-pollution groups, or people who wish to balance controversial army, navy, or marine corps recruiting commercials with spot announcements of their own, explaining the disadvantages of enlistment in these military service organizations. The curious aspect of the licensee's turning down of such requests, is that he does so even if the makers are willing to buy time at market rates. The broadcasters are quite content to huckster sponsors' goods at a profit, but they are unwilling to huckster political ideas (presumably vital to the survival of the republic) at a comparable profit.

The commercial huckstering is preferable to the political because it involves less headaches and is less calculated to diminish audiences that are allergic to the realities of vigorous debate over issues that affect their lives and not their fantasies. There is no question but that the broadcasters—if they were a bit less greedy, not too much so—could master the admitted complexities of public conflict of ideas and still make a handsome profit. The fact is that they are not willing.

It is also true that the FCC will avoid, as long as it can, the unpopular task of making specific rules. Especially in any conflict between the White House and members of the Congress, it will be reluctant to judge between the rights of the President (who appoints its members) and the Congress (which gives it its money to operate).

Certain senators and congressmen have recently grasped the lesson they have for so long ignored—that unless you do make specific rules, the broadcasters and the FCC will play the discretionary game to the sacrifice of public debate over important issues. But the Congress is many men, of clashing views, and the free play of partisan party advantage and the general philosophy of the least regulation the better, seems always to result in leaving things as they are, to the clear advantage only of the broadcasters themselves and the man who happens to be in the White House during a particular administration. As for the courts, they can proclaim bold principles, as they did in the *Red Lion* case (loud cheers), but they can't focus them in specific rules unless they are willing to risk the usurpation of legislative prerogatives as in the messy one-man, one-vote case.

The upshot is that anybody can step up to a broadcaster's window and buy time, first-come, first-served, cash on the barrelhead for the sale of any gidgit or gadget, no questions asked: but your money is simply no good if you wish to talk about death of our young men on the battlefield or poison in the air that we breathe.

The Supreme Court has repeatedly held that the First Amendment protects political or social speech, and that it does not protect commercial speech to a comparable degree. Yet when people including United States senators come to the broadcasters and the FCC, they are told that political or social speech definitely plays an inferior role. The role that it plays, it would seem, is directly a function of the rule that governs access to the people's air. At the moment there is no such rule, merely hot air. Until there is a rule, the Fairness Doctrine will remain unfair to fairness.

COMMENTARY

"A Child Again," the radio program which is the subject of the following piece, passed unnoticed by the press when it was first broadcast. Brought to the critic's attention, it made a profound impression on him, and prompted him to write a column, concluding with the suggestion to WNEW, the New York station that presented the program, that it could discharge an important public responsibility by making it widely available.

The managers of the station acted on the suggestion quickly. They took a full two-page ad in *Broadcasting*, the industry trade weekly, in which they reprinted the SR column in full, and announced that tapes and records of the program would be distributed without cost to individuals who wrote for them, and to stations that would rebroadcast the program. The offer was widely picked up and the unforgettable Marcy, the protagonist of the program, left her imprint on the minds and hearts of thousands of hearers that she might never have reached.

FROM A HIPPIE'S SOUL   *December 16, 1967*

IT WOULD BE DIFFICULT to put a price on the twenty-minute interview that Marcy recently gave WNEW, the Metromedia station in New York, without price. How does one evaluate by cost accounting the intimate, ingenuously revealing, shatteringly poignant testament of a nineteen-year-old-girl—a self-styled hippie— to the troubled empathy that bewilders so many parents and children today? The station that unwittingly came across the gemlike piece of broadcasting can cancel its debt by making tapes of the Sunday News Closeup program, "A Child Again," available as widely as possible without cost.

The program, rebroadcast once, has already evoked requests

from many listeners. A taxi driver who heard it while in his cab was "so moved" that he wants to "present it to my family and friends on my own tape recorder." A teenager would like to "play it to my high school sociology class." A mother, after visiting her daughter at an upstate New York college, heard the program while driving home, and found it devastating: "I am certain everyone listening must have felt as we did—'there but for the grace of God . . .' No playwright could have conveyed what you did by allowing us to listen to Marcy's telephone conversation. I don't know whether to say thank you for the experience, or please, no more."

Steve Young, who produced and narrated the program and wrote brief notes surrounding Marcy's interview, made the tape in his apartment, where he had offered a night's haven to the girl and her five friends. They had been evicted from an East Village "commune" and were leaving the next morning for another "flower people" rendezvous in Missouri and thence to California. "Marcy wanted money in return for an interview," Young said. "I did not give her any because I wanted to hear what she thought and not what I had bought." The girl spoke in a husky, velvet voice. She was amazingly uninhibited, articulate, even eloquent.

"I'm the White Rabbit. I can characterize everybody with *Alice in Wonderland* . . . I dig that book so much! . . . Children have beautiful lives, and I wish I could be that for the rest of my life. Sure, I'm a child. I'm playing dolls. These dolls are beautiful people and they love me. They really love me! But not in the sense that they are going to try to own me. I won't be owned; I'm not a slave." Marcy was captivating—and lost. She had run away from her home in a Midwestern state, had had an abortion, and was "high" on "speed"—methadrine. "Ooh, beautiful, I dig that . . . I'm caught up on drugs. I just can't come down. I've tried. I think I just went too high and never came down."

Marcy had been tempted to steal to get "bread" for her commune "family." "I bitch—I really bitch, but they like me. I'm a mama. Some day I want a baby, but I really don't want a father. I just want the baby for me." She was sad, happy—and disillusioned. "We're not all love anymore. That's gone. That flower power was great stuff—I mean, it's beautiful, but you can't be kind and gentle all the time; it doesn't work. Because like people get raped and mugged; and I knew those people that died down in the Village, Groovy and his chick . . . He never hurt anybody, and he died; they bashed his head in."

Steve Young offered to let Marcy call her parents long distance. She dialed and kept on talking. "It's ringing. It's not ringing; it's just doing the switching still. I dig that. When you dial long distance you get these little clicks. It's wild." You heard only Marcy's voice, but by intuition you knew the feelings at the other end of the wire. Marcy loved them, but she couldn't come home— not yet, maybe in the spring. She was unhappy at home with her sister Jeannie—they fought all the time. "I'm different there; people don't take me as I am. You two want me to be things I'm not."

Marcy reassured her mother: She was not an addict; she had lied about working at Macy's, but "everybody is getting a job this week, you know, regular jobs . . . Mother listen, I'm happy. I'm having a good life." After the call, Marcy said: "Oh man, they're not mad. I love them, wow! My father never would talk to me, and he loves me. He says, why don't you come home? I can't cut it all. I love them, but I can't cut it."

The precarious balance between love and alienation that characterizes the relationships of parents and children probably explains the profoundly moving impact of Marcy's telephone call. It affords a glimpse of the abyss on the other side of the broken communication thread. The experience compels an empathic review of one's own family life, a determination to examine and rebuild broken bridges, to clear barriers to rapport. In this vivid fragment of one child's life, a listener senses, is the key to so many felt, yet unarticulated, mysteries of family ambivalence. A teenage boy to whom I played the tape of "A Child Again" protested: "It's beautiful, but why don't they explain the causes of what went wrong with Marcy! My father belongs to the Depression generation. He suffered so much from lack of material things that he's spent all his life making sure we have the things that warm us outside, but he's never had time to give us the things that warm us inside."

Marcy, the narrator said, had had a nervous breakdown before she ran away and joined an East Village commune. Behind her words probably lie subtleties unique to her own family that cannot be generalized; but her testament bears the mark of universality in our culture. It symbolizes much that has gone awry with most of us. Marcy lost her true family. She is trying to find a substitute family in the commune of the flower people. Though it can afford her scant comfort, she will continue to create, in a categorical sense, a much larger family of parents and children who will hear this remarkable tape. The widest possible enlargement of the communication kinship is now the responsibility of WNEW.

ORCHESTRATION OF CULTURES   *April 26, 1969*

A RECENT "reality adventure" color special, "Adventures at the Jade Sea" (CBS), filmed on location in the Republic of Kenya, was an object lesson in the importance of the drawing of parallels when comparative cultures are examined by the mass media. Parallels, when they are present, make a contribution to what Margaret Mead once described as "the hope of the orchestration of cultures, efforts to envision a growing world culture to the building of which each culture could make a unique contribution." When parallels are absent no contribution is made; indeed, there is an intensification of the noise of cultural discord.

The hour-long program about Lake Rudolf—billed by Metromedia Producers Corporation as "the legendary Jade Sea, a remote and hostile area"—broke even in the contribution department: about 50 per cent harmony and the same per cent discord. Written, produced, and directed by David Seltzer, the program was structured in a "tease," four sequences, and an epilogue. William Holden, who lives most of the time in Kenya and prefers to be called a conservationist rather than an actor, narrated and played himself as the on-camera host in what appeared to be a "laid-on" conservation-anthropology adventure "with both capture vehicle and camera car." The essential message observed that the modern world of "fishing camps, big game safaris, and accommodations for tourists from all parts of the world" was an arrow aimed at the heart of "this primitive shore . . . surrounded by dormant volcanoes where mammoth crocodiles sleep."

Mr. Holden acted as a sort of advance scout, penetrating "Kenya's last holdout of primitive life" and discovering, while engaged in animal census-taking, exotic native tribes—"primitive, proud, and aloof, small and impoverished." In one segment, the invaders recorded a traditional "rite of passage," an adolescent circumcision ritual; in another they gained the cooperation of a tribe in the restoration of the ostrich in their area. The natives had exterminated the bird for its feathers, which they consider to be symbols of manhood. Along the trail they touched on the problem of poaching, which "has depleted Africa's wildlife by 70 per cent in the last 100 years." Finally, among the El Molo, the poorest tribe, the adventurers found an Italian missionary who symbolized the region's best hope for non-exploitative treatment in the inevitable modernization that lies ahead. The cross-cultural parallels were present in the sequences that featured the Turkana tribe, which had exterminated the ostrich, and the El Molo, suffering "a conspiracy of hardship: protein starvation, calcium deficiency, a high infant mortality rate, and an average life span of just thirty-five years."

The Holden expeditionaries, in persuading the Turkanas to refrain from slaughtering newly transplanted ostrich offspring, showed the tribesmen Polaroid pictures of themselves; they also projected film on a screen exhibiting shots of lions, elephants, rhinos, and chimpanzees—animals these people had never seen. The TV film cameras recorded the astounded, delighted reactions of the adults and children to the images of themselves and the unfamiliar animals. Similarly, among the El Molo, the Westerners distributed bubble gum, kites, and balloons to the children. The shots of the boys and girls chasing the flying balloons and pulling on the kites provided an exhilarating exposure to universal, childlike joy. Here the parallel of the gleeful, wonder-filled faces and outbursts of emotion leaped across geographic and ethnic frontiers, and captured viewers in a common humanity. No such parallels were present in the other sequences of "Adventures at the Jade Sea." Their absence reinforced conventional stereotypes of Africa as a land of darkness, peopled by ignorant primitives being swept away by progress.

Who was responsible, in this production, for the presence of the parallels, and for their absence? Were event and non-event due to fortuitous accident, calculated strategy, or to unconscious cultural blinders? Some students of comparative cultures would assert that "the system" operates to control negative images of Africa for manipulative purposes. A more sympathetic view would ascribe the negative images to "our peculiarly American tendency to believe ourselves able to think for the whole of mankind." Had the notion of cross-cultural parallels been consciously pursued by the producers, it would have been simple to note that we Americans have our own manhood and warrior rituals, which make sense to us. Just think of a football game at half time or of a political convention at the moment of nomination.

Such parallels would have balanced the cultural prejudices inevitably set in motion by images of the exotic and alien, and would have reminded us of the relative and tentative nature of our own cultural imperatives—a usefully humbling experience.

"Reality adventure" specials on television may no longer be classified simply as entertainment. They selectively focus our attention and help shape our beliefs and behavior. Television must watch its parallels in projecting cross-cultural images. In the orchestration of the cultures, it has a moral imperative to phrase statements about other cultures so that they are acceptable to all men everywhere who value the dignity of the individual.

COMMENTARY

The next piece, "Senatorial Goose Bumps," comments on a significant incident that occurred at a congressional hearing in 1969, on a Senate bill which authorized federal funds for the establishment of the Corporation for Public Broadcasting. The critic was present in his professional capacity at a double level: one, he had been invited by National Educational Television (which reported on the hearings over a period of two days) to do on-camera commentaries on them; and two, he covered the hearings for SR. A critic's job ought, occasionally at least, to carry him into the world which lies on the other side of the screen and the loudspeaker, so that, as an active participant in the production of programs, he may refresh at first hand his awareness of the problems faced by the professionals whom he is called upon to criticize.

SENATORIAL GOOSE BUMPS   *May 24, 1969*

A "MR. SMITH" went to Washington recently and gave "goose bumps" to Senator John O. Pastore, chairman of the Senate Committee on Communications. The senator may even pass those goose bumps along to his colleagues in the Congress, and the ultimate result could be a giant step forward in the building of a viable, independent system of public television in the United States.

Fred M. Rogers was the Mr. Smith in this encounter: he is the producer-talent of "Misterogers' Neighborhood," a very popular NET daily children's television program which recently won a Peabody award. Testifying toward the close of the subcommittee hearings on the Magnuson bill (S. 1242), which would authorize $20 million for 1970 for the Corporation for Public Broadcasting, Mr. Rogers had to exhibit the stubbornness of innocence in order to be granted ten minutes in which to touch the senator from Rhode Island with his gentle spirit. It was getting near lunch in the fifth floor hearing room of the Senate Office Building: the senator was unambiguously in a hurry to wind up the day-and-a-half session. By this time it had become clear to observers that a rather transparent game was being played.

The purpose of the hearings was not to invite serious debate on alternative proposals for crucial long-range financing of public TV or even to examine whether or not it was to be a bland, supportive reporting of "the good things about our country," or an independent prober into social problems. The purpose was to build up "a record" of public TV's achievements, needs, and promises, so that Senator Pastore could use that record to persuade all those busy colleagues of his, who rarely showed up at the hearings, that they ought to vote "yes" on the money authorization. This, apparently, is how many congressional committees function—in a sort of operational, often benevolent paternalism; its frustration costs are high. Witnesses at these hearings earnestly wanted to talk about the serious issues with the senators, but most of the time only the chairman was present. Most witnesses, old hands at the game, knew the score, and obediently went along with the chairman's suggestions that they get it in the record, "syncopate" their testimony, and "just give us the highlights—you can be sure we'll read it."

When Mr. Rogers' turn to testify came, Senator Pastore was galloping along like Majestic Prince to the wire, but public television's new star believes in "honest people interacting with each other in an honest way," and he refused to take the whip. The chairman coolly gave him his head; the senator didn't know it at that moment but he was on his way down the track to his "goose bumps." Mr. Rogers talked simply and without hesitancy about such un-congressional matters as a child's need for acceptance and care; about human potentials for constructive living; about a network of communications with the public that would "treat viewers with the dignity they deserve." He told of the success of his own program, and of the chance each station should have "to develop its own unique expressions rather than being forced to spend the greatest percentage of its energies meeting its monthly payroll." He even recited the lyrics of a song he had written, in which he encourages children to discover feelings about themselves and others that can be mentioned and managed, producing "the good feeling of control." The senator from Rhode Island melted, evidently quite moved.

"I'm supposed to be a tough guy," he said, "but this is the first time I've had goose bumps in two days." He concluded with, "I think it's wonderful. Looks like you just earned the $20 million." At which remark all the other tough guys in the room applauded.

The record and the syncopation might have been all, had it not been for Mr. Rogers' enchantment. One may hope that the spell will linger long enough on the chairman so that he may rub some off on his associates in the Congress, particularly the economy-minded representatives in the House. From the Hill the magic might even work its way to the White House and conceivably open the coffers of our GNP to that $270 million that the Carnegie Commission dreamed of, as the sum required for a vigorous public broadcasting system. Possibly the nation could catch some of the contagion—on the campus, in the ghetto, at the corporate height. Then there's Vietnam . . . and the Russians. Maybe there's a yellow brick road that leads from "Misterogers' Neighborhood" to the world—and its name is public broadcasting.

COMMENTARY

Following the appearance, in sr, of the following piece, J. M. Mathes, Incorporated, an advertising agency which had as its client at the time the International Telephone and Telegraph Corporation, the sponsors of the Marian Anderson program, bought the back page of *The New York Times* for an ad reprinting the column in its entirety, as "one of the thousands of editorial and personal tributes to 'The Lady from Philadelphia.'" The agency noted: "We find it stimulating to work with clients like IT&T, who have the vision and the will to communicate so much that is so worthwhile."

The reader may remember the piece (see p. 266) in which, eight years after the Anderson program, the critic raised serious question about the proposed merger between IT&T and the stations owned and operated by the American Broadcasting Company. Between noble discontent and glimpses of perfection should lie the solid equator of a critic's integrity, impervious alike to flattery or frown.

THE LADY FROM PHILADELPHIA   *January 18, 1958*

I SINCERELY HOPE that our State Department does not cut the commercials out of "The Lady from Philadelphia," the recent CBS–TV "See It Now" broadcast featuring Marian Anderson, the singer, when they show prints of the program in Asia. The comments of Mr. Edmond H. Leavey, president of the International Telephone and Telegraph Corporation, which sponsored the broadcast, and those of Edward R. Murrow, the narrator, speaking for IT&T, are essential to the propaganda aims of Miss Anderson's 35,000-mile, twelve-nation concert tour. Their remarks create a most favorable impression of American business. "Communication is our business," said the sponsor; then he defined the main problem of international communication today in terms of the question: "Can man get along with man?" Miss Anderson's tour was an act of affirmative communication. Mr. Murrow, noting that IT&T had waived the final commercial, said: "They know that their communication can never be substituted for human communication. Miss Anderson's communication is something with which they—and we—would like to be identified."

This was television in the highest altitudes. What the "See It Now"–State Department–American National Theater and Academy (ANTA) trio of organizers of the tour were saying through Miss Anderson to the people of Korea, the Philippines, Vietnam, Burma, Thailand, Malaya, and India, was this: "You have been slaves to the white masters from the West. Now you are your own masters, free to choose between the communists and us. Both are prepared to radiate to you the West's industry, literacy, and material betterment. But the communists will make you pay a price for that—a second slavery and a poverty of spiritual values. Choose the West and you will gain your freedom and dignity as well as science and technology. Marian Anderson is the image of your own future— if you follow us."

The singer never spoke this argument, of course. Her only instructions from the State Department were: "Be yourself." She gave her own message—in her inspired artistry, her joy, enthusiasm, compassion, humility, and religious faith. Her music was, in turn, a deep yearning, an adoration, a cry for freedom, a national anthem, a morality lesson, and a Christian hymn.

Her doctrine was a sense of journey, a "trampin', a tryin' to make heaven my home." It was, "Now we will do the thing in a new way ... There is no particular thing that you can do alone ... The 'I' in it is very small, after all ... All have a right to enter the gates ... One will give his all if he feels that he belongs ... Yes, I would sing for Governor Faubus if he were in a frame of mind to accept it for what it is ... Do not let hate or fear restrict you from being a big person ... All people seek to be great ... If all is right on the inside there is a divine pattern ... I will go, I shall go to see what the end will be, because I believe in what I shall find at the end." This is the poetry of feeling, and I know of only one poet in America who sings this way: Carl Sandburg. The ethos of Abraham Lincoln is in his rhythms and Miss Anderson's.

The Asian response to her character and artistry was a complete propaganda triumph, to judge by the pictures and sound track of "See It Now." The King of Thailand had never before risen from his throne-chair to greet a distinguished visitor. In India, no visitor had ever been invited to speak at Gandhi's memorial in Old Delhi. The Prime Minister of Burma complimented her on her "good voice, technique, and acting ability," and on her "beauty and charm of mind." At Ewha University in Seoul, Korea, she was awarded an honorary degree for her "Christian service to mankind." In Bombay the tour dramatically illustrated the interpenetration of cultures when, for the first time, "a visiting artist [Miss Anderson] sang with the only Western symphony orchestra between Tel Aviv and Tokyo."

Less formal, but nevertheless expressing an undeniable sympathy for Miss Anderson as she greeted them and sang for them "in close fashion," were the faces in her audiences—impassive, rapt children; old men and women; Eastern cosmopolites; peasants; clerks; lawyers. These faces of Asia, photographed and edited with perception and taste, burst with startling, vivid reality upon our parochial TV consciousness, smogged and sodden with the gunsmoke and mayas of Madison Avenue and Hollywood. The United States can be proud to have had such a great lady as Miss Anderson to send forth on this tour.

There were other rewards for the "See It Now" audience here in the United States. We saw and heard a native orchestra in Bombay playing Indian music, which Miss Anderson told us "has resisted all foreign influences." We shared the thrill of an item of raw material for history when, in Kuala Lumpur, in the Federation of Malaya, citizens of the newest nation on earth heard the first singing of their national anthem by a visiting artist. Miss Anderson's journey was not that of an individual—she was a symbol of individuality as it is conceived and given historical meaning by contemporary Americans. The broadcast derived its very moving impact from some degree of awareness in the viewers' minds that they were watching not only a propaganda tour but a veritable collision of many cultures—religious, political, esthetic, ethical. At each moment there were overtones of the diffusion, challenge, and potentials of unique civilizations.

We must recognize that "The Lady from Philadelphia," as an act of high creative imagination in television, marshalling the resources of our technology for great human purposes, is uncommonly rare. There is only one Marian Anderson, not many Ed Murrows and Fred Friendlys, and less than a multitude of sponsors like International Telephone and Telegraph whose institutional character permits them to spend shareholders' money on a TV broadcast like this one. Yet we must never cease to hope, with Miss Anderson, that the gates are there for all to enter. What we peddle to Asia we may well use at home; and we are indebted to "See It Now" for this grand reminder of what TV sometimes is and can more often be.

Index